The Post–9/11
City in Novels

The Post–9/11 City in Novels

Literary Remappings of New York and London

KAROLINA GOLIMOWSKA

McFarland & Company, Inc., Publishers

Jefferson, North Carolina

LIBRARY OF CONGRESS CATALOGUING-IN-PUBLICATION DATA

Names: Golimowska, Karolina, 1985– author.
Title: The Post–9/11 city in novels : literary remappings of New York
    and London / Karolina Golimowska.
Description: Jefferson, North Carolina : McFarland & Company, Inc.,
    Publishers, 2016. | Includes bibliographical references and index.
Identifiers: LCCN 2016004832 | ISBN 9780786499373
    (softcover : alk. paper) ⊗
Subjects: LCSH: American fiction—21st century—History and
    criticism. | English fiction—21st century—History and
    criticism. | Cities and towns in literature. | New York (N.Y.)—In
    literature. | London (England)—In literature. | September 11 Ter-
    rorist Attacks, 2001—Influence.
Classification: LCC PS374.C5 G66 2016 | DDC 823/.9209358421—
    dc23
LC record available at https://lccn.loc.gov/2016004832

BRITISH LIBRARY CATALOGUING DATA ARE AVAILABLE

ISBN (print) 978-0-7864-9937-3
ISBN (ebook) 978-1-4766-2454-9

Front cover photograph of One World Trade Center and memorial
fountain, New York City © 2016 Vladone/iStock

Printed in the United States of America

McFarland & Company, Inc., Publishers
    Box 611, Jefferson, North Carolina 28640
    www.mcfarlandpub.com

Acknowledgments

I would like to thank the Department of English and American Studies at Humboldt-Universität zu Berlin, the Department of Social and Cultural Analysis at New York University and the English Department at the University of Richmond, Virginia, for their institutional support. My thanks go to the Konrad-Adenauer Foundation for supporting my PhD research that this book derives from. I would also like to thank the Caroline von Humboldt Program of the Excellence Initiative of the German Federal Ministry of Education and Research for the International Research Award I received in 2014. I am also indebted to *The Journal of American Culture* for its permission to reprint part of an article on Joseph O'Neill's *Netherland*.

I would like to thank several scholars who have inspired me during my work on this book and took their time to discuss it with me at its different stages: Bertram Ashe, Eva Boesenberg, Antje Dallmann, Reinhard Isensee, Kathy Merlock Jackson, Martin Klepper, Sukhdev Sandhu and Monika Siebert.

My thanks go also to Alexander Gumz, Elizabeth Maneli and Melvin Singer for their kind help and support in collecting documents and compiling the bibliography. Finally, I would like to thank my parents for their continuous and unconditional support of all my ideas and moves related to this project.

Table of Contents

Acknowledgments   v

Preface   1

Introduction: Reactions to 9/11 in American and British City Novels   5

Part One: New York

I. Remapping New York City in Jonathan Safran Foer's
Extremely Loud and Incredibly Close   39

II. Metropolis as Source of Literary Energy: Teju Cole's
Open City   55

III. The Ambiguity of the Other in Mohsin Hamid's
The Reluctant Fundamentalist and H.M. Naqvi's *Home Boy*   70

IV. The Plurality of Voices and Urban Paths in Amy Waldman's
The Submission: The Metaphors of Submission   98

Part Two: London

V. Unpredictable and Insane: London as a Body, London as Brain   117

VI. Hemisphere 1: London East End   122

VII. Hemisphere 2: London West End in Ian McEwan's *Saturday*   153

VIII. New York versus London: Joseph O'Neill's *Netherland*   165

Conclusion   182

Chapter Notes   189

Bibliography   193

Index   199

Preface

When I think of 2001, I recall a hot summer in Canada and a mild concern about the first few months of George W. Bush's presidency that sometimes came up in after-dinner discussions at the peaceful lake house north of Algonquin Park where I was spending my vacation visiting family.

A few weeks later in Warsaw, on my way to school on September 12, getting on the subway in the early morning I bought *Gazeta Wyborcza*, a daily newspaper. On the front page black letters announced "A War with the U.S." beneath a photo of the north tower of the World Trade Center collapsing. For some reason I recall seeing the front page as an experience as frightening as joining my father in front of the TV a day earlier and watching my mother keep trying to reach her friend in Queens. Eventually the friend returned her call.

The next months and years were marked in Europe by an internal political conflict regarding the issue of supporting the U.S. in the Iraq war and in what came to be known as "the war on terror." Poland's president at that time, Aleksander Kwaśniewski, declared its full support for the country's beloved big sister, America, the attacked paradise and home to many Polish immigrants. Polish troops were sent to Iraq—in Europe this action has been highly criticized and was seen as a symbolic statement not only for the U.S. but also against France and Germany. Many Poles became concerned about their safety and the safety of their relatives—a concern that grew rapidly after the 7/7 attacks in London, the capital of the United States' main European ally in the war on terror. This concern was particularly shared by people living in cities, especially in the capital Warsaw, where I grew up.

In the summer semester of 2005, immediately after the 7/7 attacks, I started studying English literature in London. Riding the subway, I saw "London Stands United" posters everywhere and inhaled the fear floating in the air.

I lived in the east, in Tower Hamlets, a borough with the largest Muslim population in the city. I was surrounded by women with covered faces and by restaurants serving Bangladeshi curries. In one of my seminars at UCL I read Monica Ali's *Brick Lane*, named after a street in "my" east London neighborhood where I bought bagels and met friends on weekends. The life of the protagonists

1

of that novel changes drastically after 9/11; it becomes covered with what Ali calls "New York dust." I decided to write my MA thesis on post-colonial London and began to search for other novels that addressed the September 11 attacks. My interest in the subject derives from outside of the U.S. It begins with looking at the U.S. from abroad, from other places covered with the dust that was blown over the Atlantic.

Later, when working on my PhD, New York revealed itself gradually to me through the novels I read. When I moved to New York, I explored the city by following their paths, always on foot, often until exhausted. I felt close to the characters and also felt their city was slowly becoming my city as well.

Quite early in my research it became apparent that fiction reacting to September 11 can be seen as a key to understanding social processes in metropolitan settings. It provides unique possibilities of approaching and addressing cities and generates knowledge about life in the metropolis. It became the main focus of my studies and a lens through which I consider the fiction in this book.

When teaching post–9/11 literature to undergraduates it is clear to me that the attacks are becoming more and more remote in the collective memory. Already it is often the case that the young people in my classes have no memories of that day at all. This requires a new approach toward the literature in question but also a new way of seeing New York. When looking at the city from above, standing in the observatory on the top floor of One World Trade Center, it strikes me how unreal and remote the city becomes. Through windows marked by the fingerprints of thousands of people taking photos, one can see the 9/11 memorial marking the "feet" of the absent Twin Towers. This whole area in Lower Manhattan has redefined itself and is now a new place. The "new" World Trade Center with its Freedom Tower offers new views over the city, new perspectives which accommodate the new approach of my young students and the next generations. The slogan used to advertise the observatory, "See forever," where "forever" is a registered trademark, is to me a clear proclamation of eternity, indestructability and power. It shouts its message to the world: "The world saw it rise. The world saw it take shape. Now the world can see forever." I am waiting for literary characters to enter the elevators of One World Trade Center and go up to the 102nd floor and look at the city and their lives from above.

Throughout different stages of my work, the writing of Birgit Däwes and especially her monograph *Ground Zero Fiction* has been a great inspiration and reference point. I used it as a concise and thorough systematic overview of post–9/11 fiction up to 2011. When writing about the importance of imagining disasters for the development of cities, I often referred to Max Page's *The City's End*, which explores that relationship thoroughly through the centuries. I also frequently refer to Richard Gray's *After the Fall* and Kristiaan Versluys's *Out of the Blue*, both important voices in the debate on post–9/11 fiction. I also felt inspired by Arin Keeble's *The 9/11 Novel: Trauma, Politics and Identity*, which worked closely with the primary texts and brought the attention back to them. I hope that my book distinguishes itself from the aforementioned scholarly work by its focus on cities in the context of 9/11 and by its city-centered readings of the discussed novels. This book positions itself at the intersection of literature and metropolitan studies and is thereby an interdisciplinary project that chooses fiction as a guide to post–9/11 cities. It draws new maps of the post–9/11 metropolis and provides a comparative transatlantic perspective that will reveal new insights to the texts and new reading possibilities from outside.

Introduction: Reactions to 9/11 in American and British City Novels

Even in New York—I long for New York (DeLillo *Falling Man* 34)

London is a smiling liar his front teeth are very nice but you can smell his back teeth rotten and stinking (Cleave *Incendiary* 5)

Standing here, as immune to the cold as a marble statue, gazing toward Charlotte Street, towards a foreshortened jumble of facades, scaffolding and pitched roofs, Henry thinks the city is a success, a brilliant invention, a biological masterpiece—millions teeming around the accumulated and layered achievements of the centuries, as though around a coral reef, sleeping, working, entertaining themselves, harmonious for the most part, nearly everyone wanting it to work (McEwan *Saturday* 5)

The Post–9/11 City Novel

In the multidimensional and constantly developing field of studying, researching and examining post–9/11 fiction, the question and specificity of the urban environment and its importance for the narration, plot and construction of protagonists in novels has not been, so far, thoroughly discussed.[1] This study focuses on literary representations of the metropolises New York and London in novels written after 9/11 whose plots allude to the events of that day. It positions these texts within the context of the genre of the city novel, rooted in and deriving from the urban and industrial developments of modernity. In these novels fictional characters are placed in a real life cosmos, the streets of which can be marked on a map of the "real" city in question. The city in many of these texts is given a personality and can become the primary focus, itself the main character[2] (Gelfant, Klotz, et al.). Fictional characters can, furthermore, interfere with urban reality outside of the fictional text: places invented as significant in a text can materialize as attached to these protagonists in the real city, for

5

instance 221B Baker Street in London became the Sherlock Holmes Museum and the graveyard of the Trinity Church in Lower Manhattan is where the grave of the fictional character Charlotte Temple can be found.[3] The "simulacral" city (Groes *The Making of London* 3), i.e., this "doubling up upon itself," is the most dramatic example of the mutual interference of reality and fiction within an urban setting (Wirth-Nesher 11). This book focuses on the way 9/11 is perceived and "dealt with" in spatial terms, i.e., on how the event and its repercussions become inscribed into the urban reality that then has to be made walkable, livable and readable again.

The action of all of the chosen texts is set in either New York City or London (or in both as in Joseph O'Neill's *Netherland*) and in all of them the urban setting and context plays a crucial role. In some of the texts the metropolis is looked at from outside and in retrospective (Mohsin Hamid's *The Reluctant Fundamentalist*) and in others its perception is shaped by visiting other places and returning with new insights and additional, richer urban knowledge (Brussels in Teju Cole's *Open City*). Urban individuals and city dwellers in what I call post–9/11 city novels change the city through the way they live, through their movements and actions, just like the metropolis co-shaped by other individuals, observers and flâneurs becomes an inseparable part of their lives. I deliberately use the term "flâneur" referring to the modern concept of the "passionate spectator" and "the painter of the passing moment" in search for modernity (Baudelaire *The Painter of Modern Life* 15) in order to point to the artistic dimension of finding new meanings in a city and to show it as rooted in a long tradition of writing and experiencing urbanity. This creative practice plays an important role in the process of storytelling which the characters of post–9/11 fiction perform and which often enables them to address the otherwise unspeakable and ungraspable reality.

The specific relation between a literary protagonist and the wounded, frightened and vulnerable city is marked by reciprocity. This also involves contact between individuals connected by the fact of living in and hence sharing the same urban space. In 1903 Georg Simmel wrote about the nature and characteristics of the "typical metropolitan resident." He characterized this specific urban being as one whose "relationships and concerns ... are so manifold and complex that, especially as a result of the agglomeration of so many persons with such differentiated interests, their relationships and activities intertwine with one another into a many-membered organism" (Simmel 3). This powerful metaphor of seeing cities as organic structures will be traced and examined as it features prominently in post–9/11 fiction and has a long history of representation. How does an urban organism act and react in case of a major social crisis? Established and seemingly secure links, relations of power and hierarchy in such an urban body when it is being exposed to and attacked by the virus of fear and paranoia do not seem to function any more. The city in the analyzed novels is often anthropomorphized, referred to as a living creature that can feel and become an object of emotional importance and attachment. Perceiving the city as a body also involves, as Antje Dallmann points out, the motif and tendency of seeing processes taking place within it as evolutional or even "natural" (Dallmann 31). These processes include the changing character of particular areas, the general social and urban development, spreading out of city limits.

Post–9/11 city fiction draws on a number of traditions of perceiving and shaping the city, deriving from both literary theory and the sociology of urban spaces. It alludes to the 19th century tradition of experiencing the modern metropolis through walking, aimless strolling, wandering, i.e., to the strictly male, in its original concept, figure of the flâneur. The post–9/11 stroller walks through different parts of the "wounded" city and discovers its changing character. The discoveries made while walking are private and individual experiences conducted in public spaces and therefore crucial for establishing a relation with the city. Post–9/11 fiction reflects the altering nature of parts of the city, marking its social development which is not necessarily portrayed as natural or organic. The urban stroller walks through gentrified areas (for instance Julius in Cole's *Open City*) and notices social segregation that gentrification triggers. Further separation and isolation of the already gentrified areas after September 11 is justified through the neoliberal discourse of "securitization of urban spaces" leading to "political intensification of social inequality" (Schillings and Vormann 160). This segregation is based solely on economic factors as these white collar areas are considered more vulnerable and hence, according to the discourse, deserve more protection and security measures than others.

The analyzed city novels produce cultural knowledge about the attacks of September 11 and their impact on society, individuals and the metropolis, which becomes the central setting of all of the plots chosen for this study. The narratives "behave" similarly to many non-fictional philosophical texts produced in response to 9/11 which try to grasp and explain the specificity of that day (as a historical world event, as a beginning of a new war and new meanings, etc.). Post–9/11 fiction serves as a reservoir of sentiments and responses, a mirror, a "seismographic register of the cultural imaginary of our time" (Däwes *Ground Zero Fiction* 411) and forms a public space, a "Speaker's Corner of the imagination," as Sebastian Groes called it when referring to contemporary London writers, "masters" of the city (*The Making of London* 4–5). Post–9/11 (city) fiction is self-referential, highly intertextual and provides a space for an unlimited multitude of voices.

The post–9/11 novel is preeminently a city novel and as such it is organized, written and to be read through (the urban) space. It is not only inscribed in the city but it also creates new spaces within the urban context and reassigns meanings within the city cosmos. The analyzed novels not only reflect the post–9/11 city, but they also create, produce, celebrate and *write* it. Through these fictional texts, a cultural knowledge and work is produced that serves to tame the city and make it more approachable. Each of the novels is an attempt at remapping the city in question and through this process at controlling the unpredictable body of the metropolis.

The following chapters focus on different spatial remappings in the context of post–9/11 writing. The book is set within the multidimensional frame of spatial interventions, i.e., walking, strolling, moving through the city and writing it, all in the context of 9/11 and aimed at spatial and symbolic remapping of the post–9/11 reality. Remapping also means establishing new reading patterns and rules which have to be explained, i.e., a new map requires a new legend which has to be written and adjusted to the post–9/11 urban reality. Combining these dynamic elements makes it possible to find traces of 9/11 in the city through walking and through writing. In other words, it becomes possible not only to write and walk the post–9/11 metropolis but the events of 9/11 and their reminiscences traceable in the city can be contextualized through space and on an abstract level become walkable themselves.

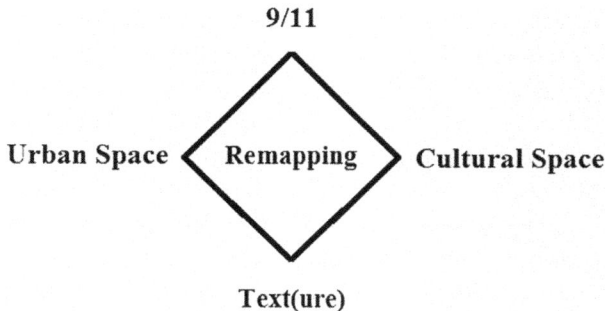

9/11

Urban Space ◁ **Remapping** ▷ **Cultural Space**

Text(ure)

Remarkably, characters of the novels set in London are not as eager to explore their city as their New York based counterparts are. In responding to 9/11, British fiction anticipates a metropolitan catastrophe floating in the London air and mirrored in all of the analyzed texts. All three London novels analyzed here, project a dystopian or catastrophic scenario of some sort in order to prevent the city from an unknown and unwritten act of urban terror. Covered with "New York dust" (Ali 368) and surrounded by fear that was blown together with it over the Atlantic, characters of post–9/11 London novels hardly ever leave the safety zone of their boroughs. Partly subconsciously, even while walking and in that way contemplating the city, they remain close to the endangered comfort zone of "home."

Writing the City: City as Text as City

The city is not only a language but also a practice (Lefebvre *Writings on Cities* 143)

Apart from the level of content and the meaning of the attacks and their consequences for the plots, the book enters and explores the meta-level of writing a city, i.e., of the way narration and the imaginary shape the real city and of how fiction contributes to reality. In fact, we cannot live outside of representation since urban space requires a dialogue—it is mobile and alive; it becomes "filled with politics and ideology" (Soja 6) and cannot be experienced without mediation as the city is itself a "text that is partly composed of literary and artistic tropes" (Wirth-Nesher 11). This text can then be read, reread and rewritten in a number of ways which are strongly linked to and dependent on the subject exposed to it. There is hence a strong relation of interdependence between an individual and the city which influences the construction and identification of the "self." As Eveline Kilian puts it, "The self can be changed in its encounter with the city, just like the city is reshaped and reorganized in the mind during each excursion" (*Exploring London* 281). The given metropolis is the source of literary energy in all of the analyzed novels. It provides ways of self-identification and redefinition in times of a major political, social, urban and always personal crisis.

As a non-exchangeable social space for the literary setting, the city can simultaneously become universalized through its microcosmic character. It is always unmistakably New York or London—each extraordinary in its metropolitan character, but at the same time there is always a symbolic dimension in the way they stand for all Western post–9/11 cities terrorized by fear and suddenly vulnerable. I examine the way both the metropolis and its people (individually and as a society) act and react after the events of 9/11 in the chosen literary representations. The book explores the emergence of new post–9/11 life cartographies of the featured characters, i.e., how they attach emotions, memories and feelings to a specific place/city and transform it into their unique personal space. This private space, inaccessible to the crowd, marks a particular phase of the featured characters' lives which ends when they leave or when this space is being transformed by external factors, as it was in the case of 9/11. In this instance, the city requires a "remapping," an important process featured in all of the novels presented here.

The focus is on fiction written in English and the aim is to establish a multidimensional trans-metropolitan (New York City versus London) paradigm. All of these texts classify as "historiographic metafiction" in Linda Hutcheon's terms; they are both "intensely self-reflexive and yet paradoxically also lay claim to historical events and personages" (*A Poetics of Postmodernism* 4). The relation and interdependence of fiction and history is discussed or "investigated" (Däwes *Ground Zero Fiction* 348) in all of them. Choosing the novel as a genre places this study in the research tradition and analysis of the city novel and follows Volker Klotz's argument that the novel and the city appear as two similarly constituted systems:

> The novel and the city appear as two similarly assessed systems. As systems which to a large extent correspond to each other in their wholeness as well as in their particular parts and their relations to one another. This means that the city finds in the novel the most appropriate instrument thanks to which it can enter the literary status without radical loss of substance. Also the other way round, the novel finds in the city an object, which stubbornly like no other, demands and exhausts its full capacities [*Die Erzählte Stadt* 438, my translation].

It also corresponds to the notion of the novel being the modern literary genre *par excellence* and hence the literary place most suitable for the city, "the principal theater of bourgeois life and also the form of collective existence that undergoes the most spectacular, dynamic growth throughout the modern period" (Alter ix). Arin Keeble adds that "it is undoubtedly the novel ... that has the most capacity to attempt, at least, to both internalize and contextualize traumatic or catastrophic events" (6) and, as I argue, it is as such the most relevant genre for this study. The book examines how geographical, social and political characteristics of a metropolis are linked to portraits of individuals in order to address the notion of trauma, memory and the construction of the Other after September 11. The relation between a fictional character standing for an individual and the city can be used to illustrate processes like racism, discrimination, fear as a collective experience and social phenomenon and general confusion that emerge as reactions to the terrorist attacks.

Both of the cities can be perceived as symbolic spaces; as "capitals" and headquarters of the politically allied (post)imperial capitalist world powers and as "global cities."[4] As faces of these two countries and societies, they have become terrorist targets (9/11 and 7/7) and in this context the media quintessence of all things American and British. It comes as no surprise that most of Ground Zero fiction[5] is set in either of the two metropolises. As Birgit Däwes points out, most of the American plots are set either in New York or Washington,

D.C. (*Ground Zero Fiction*). According to my research, the vast majority of British texts that respond to 9/11 and anticipate 7/7 is set in London.[6] The metropolises are special, but, on the other hand, the symbolism and literary power of each of the cities is based on their universality, as Ian McEwan puts it in case of the UK capital: "London lies wide open, impossible to defend, waiting for its bomb, like a hundred other cities" (*Saturday* 276).

Different literary associations and constellations emerge after 9/11, specific to each of the cities, according to their history and cultural contextualization, since, as Rolf Lindner points out, "a city is not a neutral container, which can be arbitrarily filled, but a historically saturated, culturally coded space already stuffed with meanings and mental images" (210). Analyzing spatial transformations and developments in post–9/11 fiction allows for a wider discussion of how places in general come to mean something and on how this meaning of particular places in these particular metropolises changed after 9/11. This book analyzes and compares post–9/11 depictions of New York and London as living, changing and identity shaping and confusing places and spaces.

New York and London after 9/11 become ultimate stages for storytelling; they are filled with stories told by different voices that are all rooted, inspired by and centered on one of the cities. Hence these cities can be "read" in the given context which establishes a strong link to literature and especially to the genre of a novel with its plurality of perspectives and possible multiple narrators. It also spurs the discussion about the new urban Other whose presence emerged after 9/11 and contributed to social changes in the metropolitan and literary environment. It is in this context that the monograph focuses on texts written in English by authors of different origins and creeds that feature characters of different cultural, racial and religious backgrounds. This wide range of American and British white and non-white literary voices contributes towards and shapes the pluralistic post–9/11 metropolitan discourse.

Characters in the chosen novels are strongly attached to the cities they live in. The scale of this emotional, social and cultural attachment becomes clear to many of them only after the fall of the towers. The urban confusion they come to experience is expressed in different ways but in most cases it is set around the individually tailored process of reclaiming the given urban space after the attacks. Some of the characters start walking excessively, with or without a plan, according to the same pattern (e.g., Chuck in Naqvi's *Home Boy*) following a differently planned route every time (Oskar in Foer's *Extremely Loud and Incredibly Close* or Lilian in DeLillo's *Falling Man*) or getting lost in the city (Chuck in Naqvi's novel, Julius in Cole's *Open City*). Others move through the city using the subway or other means of transportation in order to explore its different parts and to escape the well-known and spatially limited neighborhoods where they live and work (Hans in O'Neill's *Netherland*). Out of all means of travelling through the city in order to experience it, walking as the "pre-eminent spatial practice" (Pile 4) is considered the most prominent one by scholars and philosophers examining cities and urban processes (Benjamin, Baudelaire, De Certeau, Sennett, Soja, Sinclair).

Walking makes connections within the city clear; it provides understanding of the urban structure. "Walking, moving across a retreating townscape, stitches it all together: the illicit cocktail of bodily exhaustion and a raging carbon monoxide high" (Sinclair *Lights Out for the Territory* 4). But all movement and the feeling of being immersed in a city are inspiring and become crucial in the process of storytelling in the analyzed novels. During their city escapades, the characters come across personal memories strongly linked to the urban space (Changez in Hamid's *The Reluctant Fundamentalist*) or the history of the city which reveals itself to them in places they visit (Julius in Cole's *Open City*). Some of them feel excluded, "othered," discriminated against and as a consequence decide to leave the city and country (Chuck in *Home Boy*, Changez in *The Reluctant Fundamentalist*, Chanu in Ali's *Brick Lane*, Mo in Waldman's *The Submission*: all of these characters are Muslim and feel "othered" on this very basis). All of them take the attacks personally and seek help in the urban environment that surrounds them. This turns out to be a very individual experience too: in some texts the city is portrayed as a friendly, vivid presence which never sleeps and can always provide company. In others it is frightening, unpredictable, loud, inescapable, overwhelming and hostile, symbolizing the ruthless rules of capitalism and responding to the fearful and paranoid sentiments of the society.

Such mapping and remapping has different forms and yet it always is a process that seeks to tame the urban space, to name it or to rename it, to explore or to re-explore it, to find out more about it, to become more familiar with it and finally and most importantly to control it for one's own purposes and emotional comfort. It happens on various levels: linguistically, when places are renamed and hence recreated to be introduced to the urban vocabulary (for instance the imaginary phenomena of "New Yorkistan," "Londonstani," "Ground Zero" discussed in greater detail in the next chapter); visually, when the city landscape changes in the process and when spaces come to serve new purposes (e.g., information board memorials of posters of missing people after 9/11); and semantically, through movement which encourages emergence of new meanings and a different, always individual perception of the urban space. Remapping in the post–9/11 context is always a very personal process and involves reclaiming memories attached to places. It is also connected to storytelling which is an important feature of the therapeutic character of the process.

Remapping the Post–9/11 Metropolis: Mapping the Other in the City

After the Twin Towers fell, the city lost an important orientation and reference point. Before 9/11 the towers were visible from Lower and Midtown Manhattan and marked the geographic direction when looked at from a distance. The suddenly altered urban space made people feel disoriented; they lost their reference point and so, metaphorically, did the city. These complex processes are reflected in fiction which features many disoriented characters, geographically and emotionally. Following established and seemingly appropriate patterns is in many cases no longer possible after September 11. Accordingly, marriages and relationships dissolve (for instance in Ken Kalfuss's *A Disorder Peculiar to the Country*, LaBute's play *The Mercy Seat*), apartments are abandoned or changed (O'Neill's *Netherland*), long forgotten acquaintances and old friendships are being traced back and refreshed (Naqvi's *Home Boy*), estranged family or unclear common pasts are searched for, readdressed and restored (Schwartz's *The Writing on the Wall*, Foer's *Extremely Loud and Incredibly Close*).

Together with the general spatial and symbolic disorientation, the sense and meaning of "home" has been lost, as Judith Greenberg points out: "The attacks freshly complicated those terms—'home' and 'New York'—and proved anew that they signify not just location but also a relation to identity" and hence location (also the exact one within the city) produced a sense of vulnerability (*Wounded New York* 22–23). The farther away from downtown, the more distance in perceiving what happened was possible. As Thomas Pynchon puts it in *Bleeding Edge*, "the farther uptown, the more secondhand the moment" (327) and the more controlled the narrative of the attacks. This applies on a different scale to the whole country: the more geographical distance from ground zero, the less "troubled the sense of home" (Greenberg 23) and hence a possibility of emotional remoteness. This is something that according to Joseph O'Neill's *Netherland* but also to Chris Cleave's *Incendiary* did not happen to London after 7/7. It was "a frightening but not a disorienting occurrence" and "Londoners remain[ed] in the business of rowing their boats gently down the stream" (O'Neill 236).

In the context of identity, Judith Greenberg refers to what I call disorientation, as a "profound dislocation" (*Wounded New York* 25) that emerges when a part of a well-known, homely landscape is missing. Novels reacting to 9/11 published before 7/7 that are set in London are concerned with the city's future, draw catastrophic visions and reflect the intensity of metropolitan life dominated by constant fear (McEwan's *Saturday*, Cleave's *Incendiary*). A specific form of discrimination derives out of this fear and insecurity which, as a consequence, produces the urban Other rooted in the British cultural context (Ali's *Brick*

Lane) and leads to a thorough reexamination and reframing of the notion and sense of home. According to Hana Wirth-Nesher, the interpretation of the concept of "home" is also what distinguishes the modern urban novel from its pre-modern predecessors (*City Codes* 18). Home is no longer associated with separateness from the world outside or with privacy; characters of the modern urban novel often perceive the city as their home and feel most comfortable when immersed in it. The border between private and public blurs and "home" itself becomes a subject of redefinition; it is "no longer a haven, no longer clearly demarcated" (Wirth-Nesher 19) and in the urban reality of home everybody is always exposed to the sight of a stranger; in other words, in a city everybody is somebody else's stranger.

Postmodern New York City has not only always been "young" and constantly changing, but as Joseph O'Neill points out, it also used to be a place where death, up to 9/11, was invisible:

> It had quite recently struck me with force that I did not want to join the New York dead. I associated this multitude with the vast burying grounds that may be glimpsed from the expressways of Queens, in particular that shabbily crowded graveyard with the monuments and tombs rising, as thousands of motorists are daily made to contemplate, in a necropolitan replica of the Manhattan skyline in the background.... I was reminded of the tradition of oblivion in force in this city—in which, howling ambulances aside, I went for years without ever seeing a sign of funerary activity. (The moment came, as everybody knows, when that changed.) [204].

The sudden and overwhelming presence of death is mirrored in all analyzed texts and often is the reason for remapping. In both New York and London novels, mapping the city and putting it into (new) frames is presented as an attempt of placing oneself within this mapped cosmos (Foer's *Extremely Loud and Incredibly Close*, DeLillo's *Falling Man*, Waldman's *The Submission*). This mapping can evolve through movement that leads to discovering the urban space anew; through looking at the city from above in order to gain a wider perspective; through naming places and through any other way of establishing a personal relation with the city.

Both of the metropolises have also been (re)mapped literarily/linguistically in the post–9/11 media which signalized that the changes that occur in the cities required a new graphical and linguistic reflection. *New Yorkistan* (Figure 1), the cover of *The New Yorker* from December 10, 2001, by Maira Kalman and Rick Meyerowitz, shows a map of Manhattan, Brooklyn and parts of Queens divided into areas that carry new names that are both familiar and foreign: Lower Manhattan is called "Moolahs," the east part of Queens is turned to "Outerperturbia" and "Cold Turkeystan." According to Timothy Krause, it is a "pivotal, liminal document that records an ambivalent response to September 11 and its attendant events" ("Covering 9/11" 21). The imaginary cartography helps to address the multitude of social problems. By merging English words with prefixes or suffixes that are somehow in the common Western understanding associated with the Middle East, it locates the post–9/11 Other within the city. It is an uncanny piece in Freudian sense—it is familiar and strange at the same time; comforting and provocative, a document that familiarizes the unknown while estranging the familiar. Maps chart cultural space; they are "aesthetic lenses and ideological prisms, prone to exaggerations, distortions, and other narrative fictions" (Krause 22), so in this context a map becomes a genre which has many similarities with a cartoon which also works with exaggerations and humor to address serious and problematic political and social issues. *New Yorkistan* is a "colonialist pastiche of the newly conquered foreign lands" (Krause 23). This way of dealing with a well-known, yet suddenly changed space reflects the nature of the reactions to the attacks of 9/11.

Similar linguistic mergers are to be observed in the case of London: Rushdie's "Babylondon" from *The Satanic Verses* (459) becomes "Londonistan." The book *Londonistan: How Britain Is Creating a Terror State Within* (2006) written by the British journalist Melanie Phillips tries to trace the motives of the young men who were made responsible for the London bombings of 7/7 and who grew up in Great Britain. The second reference here is Guatam Malkani's novel *Londonstani* (also 2006) about a gang of four boys from South Asia. It features a non-existent slang generated for the purpose of the book. It combines English, Punjabi and rap. All titles are based on the same concept: to linguistically connect London and New York with Afghanistan and to, symbolically, bring the Other into the Western metropolis. No other Western city has become subject to such a linguistic and semantic hybridization as a part of the post–9/11 discourse.

"Young" New York versus "Old" London: Memory and the Urban Ruin

It is a modern concept that New York City grows older in order to become younger again. In the "perpetual cycle of de- and reconstruction" (Baer 5), it changes constantly and does not get sentimental, unlike London whose past very much contributes to the present. The architect Mark Wigley claims that a city that was able to "so completely forget that a third of it was destroyed by a deadly downtown fire in 1776 … and forget that a quarter of it was destroyed by another downtown fire in 1835" (52–53) will also be able to get over the

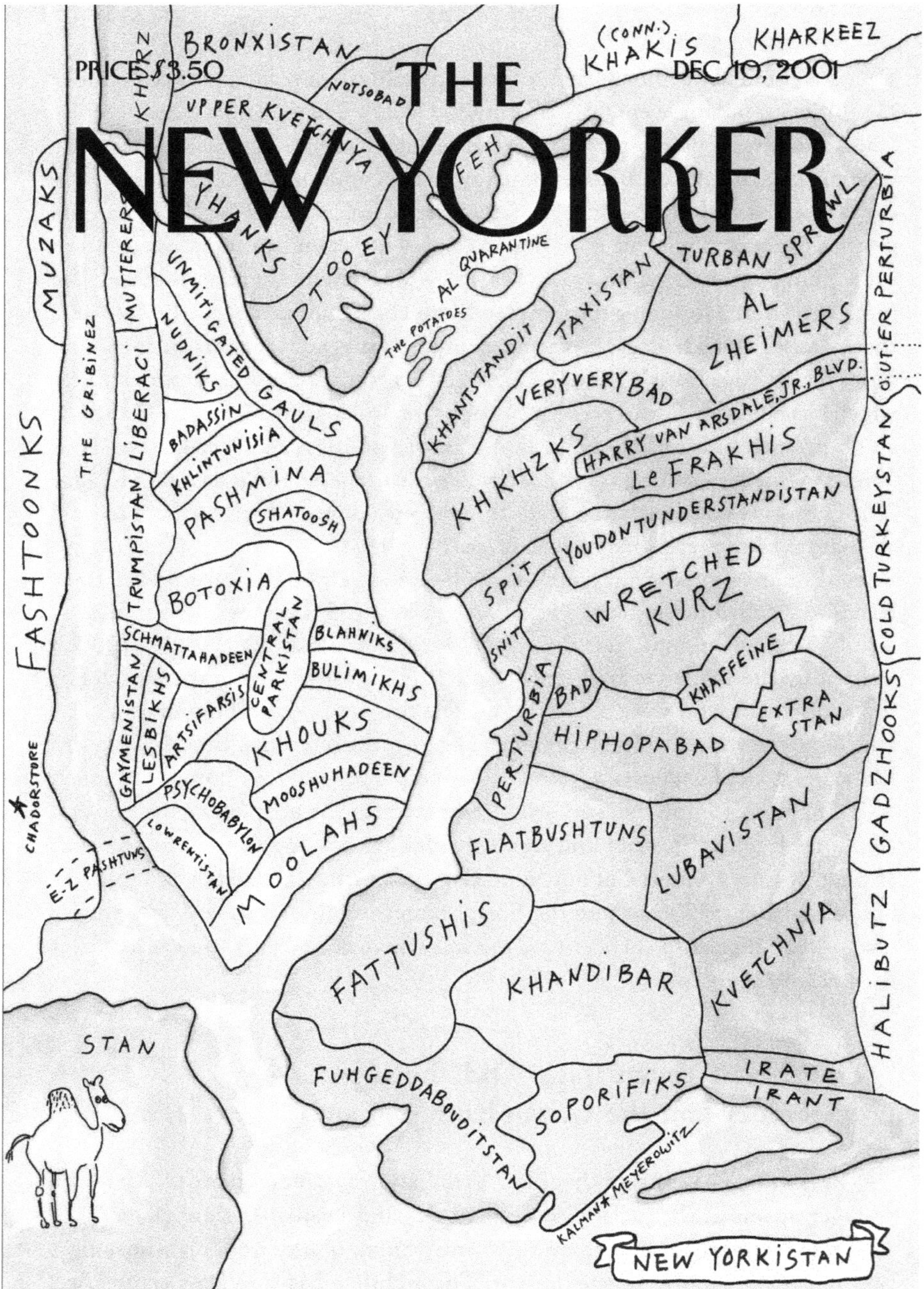

Figure 1: *New Yorkistan*. An attempt at familiarizing the unknown Other. Maira Kalman and Rick Meryerowitz/The New Yorker. *The New Yorker*, December 10, 2001, cover, "New Yorkistan."

traumatic events of 9/11 quickly. But as Ulrich Baer points out, in the instant "when event becomes tale" (Baer ii), when stories emerge as reactions to a disaster, in a consequence, the disaster is not only preserved but also becomes inscribed in the city and its altered reality. Michel de Certeau described New York as a "concept-city"—it constantly changes, develops, and is being "enriched by new attributes." For him it is the machinery and at the same time the product ("hero") of modernity (90). Multiculturalism, new "contact zones of cultural translation" (Lenz *Postmodern New York City* 13) and the presence of new "otherness" as well as a redefinition of public and private space characterize the postmodern metropolis and require new cultural responses and approaches. 9/11 led to a certain reconstruction of this postmodern otherness and again requires a redefinition of urban spaces and notions.

According to Michel de Certeau, "unlike Rome, New York has never learned the art of growing old by playing on all its pasts. Its present invents itself, from hour to hour, in the act of throwing away its previous accomplishments and challenging the future" (*The Practice of Everyday Life* 91). Incorporating the pasts into the present is a process that can be observed in most, if not all European metropolises when compared to their American counterparts and when looked at the way they are represented through medial images. It seems that the imagery of New York does not accept any "gaps"—again, unlike in the case of London. The narrator of Chris Cleave's novel *Incendiary* refers to the architectonic gaps (missing buildings) that have remained in London since World War II as holes in the teeth of the city. London, here again, is hence metaphorically portrayed as a body, as a "smiling liar" whose back teeth are rotten (Cleave 5). In New York City's urban structure, the old is replaced with the new, without being given the chance to grow truly old and to as such carry meaning. There is no place for rotten teeth or gaps. Until recently buildings were destroyed regularly in order to be replaced by taller ones, as for instance in the case of Fifth Avenue, where within sixty years all houses from Greenwich Village to the north of Central Park were replaced by "a new generation of their taller heirs" (Sennett *Flesh and Stone* 360). In fact, in order for the World Trade Center to be built, the whole small businesses area Radio Row had to be demolished. The city—this "chameleon urban fabric" (Sennett 360)—has repeatedly destroyed itself in order to grow more and more. Eliminating old buildings however does not support urban and social diversity (Jacobs *The Death and Life* 200). New ideas need old spaces in order to develop; creativity requires diversity and hence homogenized urban spaces do not contribute to the health and well-being of a diverse society. In 1961 Jacobs named Brooklyn as an example of a space that attracted a lot of small businesses, Manhattan being too expensive and too exclusive for startups (209).

This tendency to look only forward that dominated media depictions and promotion of New York as the city of the future, shows the space as one that lacks memory and does not preserve anything from its past for next generations. This "willed amnesia" (Kennedy 36) associated with late capitalism successfully eliminated the past from the present and in the metropolitan context resulted in Americans' uneasy attitude towards the urban ruin. The emptiness that remains after the destruction of the Twin Towers becomes a new space in downtown Manhattan; it acquires a new meaning and importance. This sudden gap and the absence of the buildings signify. As Jean Baudrillard puts it, the towers which were "the symbol of omnipotence, have become, by their absence, the symbol of the possible disappearance of that omnipotence" (51).

Remaining parts of the destroyed buildings and their material content collected at Ground Zero in the weeks after the attacks were stored in a hangar at JFK airport in Queens forming a bizarre kind of museum or collection of evidence that remains closed to the public. The ruin itself has been preserved, but then removed from public sight, i.e., it was not reclaimed for any kind of cultural attention and will not contribute to shaping of the collective memory.[7] The other site within the urban space that was used to accommodate the debris from Ground Zero is Fresh Kills Landfill on Staten Island—a dumping ground for New York City waste since 1948, which reopened in 2001 as a "graveyard" for the remains of the towers and indirectly for what used to be the Manhattan skyline. A project called "Lifescape" was launched to transform the world's biggest domestic waste landfill. Its aim is to revive an existing dead space (C. Lindner 301) so to create a new space that will emerge out of the ruin without eliminating the past from the future. The full scope of the project which is at the same time a "place and a process" (Corner 15) including the environmental recovery is supposed to be visible in thirty years (C. Lindner 301). Lifescape as a space and a cultural concept does not appear in post–9/11 fiction which, with the exception of Joseph O'Neill's *Netherland* and Jonathan Safran Foer's *Extremely Loud and Incredibly Close* where the borough is mentioned and travelled to, generally does not focus on Staten Island.

The debate about a memorial for the victims of the attacks of 9/11 and about the new architectural design for the "gap" in Lower Manhattan has shown Ground Zero as a temporary space that has already been physically and symbolically transformed. However, Ground Zero as a concept that joins the symbolic and spatial dimensions "continues to readjust the collective self-image of New York City as the metropolitan, global city of the 21st century" (Lenz, Ulfers and Dallmann *Toward a New Metropolitanism* 23) and plays an important role in perceiving and reclaiming the city in post–9/11 fiction. The process of organizing and preserving the collective memory of the towers is the central motif of Amy Waldman's novel *The Submission* where the discussion about the 9/11 memorial is used to address old and deeply rooted internal conflicts, discrimination, collective paranoia and fear that dominated the life of the city after 9/11. It is also being used to address the general condition of the American society in times of national grief (published in 2011, the action of the novel is set in 2003).

New York City and the History of Disaster Fantasies

Two slightly opposite statements emerging from September 11 2001, which dominated the public discourse in the immediate aftermath, were that what happened was "unimaginable" and that "it was like a movie." The sight of the towers falling was both "utterly incomprehensible" and "wholly recognizable" (Page 4). All kinds of New York-related destruction fantasies have been part of the American pop culture, so according to Slavoj Žižek, "America got what it fantasized about and that was the biggest surprise" (*Welcome to the Desert of the Real* 16). September 11 was then New York's own form of an ultimate disaster movie (Page 202) that was followed by a shift in imagining and picturing the city. After 9/11 "suddenly, everyone loved New York […] it became a blameless victim" (Page 202) and to imagine its destruction—a motif that had been present in American culture pretty much since the beginning of the 20th century[8]—became tasteless and insensitive.

In fact many old and well-known motifs became taboos; a man falling out of a skyscraper as part of the promotion of the AMC series *Mad Men* was highly criticized. The fact that some of the characters of DeLillo's *Falling Man* live in a building called "Godzilla Apartments" is an intended provocation that clearly alludes to the perverse history of imagining New York disasters caused by imaginary monsters. That however shows that fantasies of the city's end have not stopped after 9/11 and remain present in U.S. culture. What Page calls "late 20th century American lust for disaster porn" (2) and Mark Seltzer America's "wound culture"[9] (*Serial Killers* 21) as well as the obsession with fantasizing about the destruction of New York have been part of the national narrative, inscribed in culture.[10] "To destroy New York is to strike symbolically at the heart of the United States. No city has been more often destroyed on paper, film, or canvas, and no city's destruction has been more often watched and read about than New York's" (Page 14). 9/11 marks a tremendous shift in this narrative also in regard to the complex relation of the collective spectacle of violence and representations of individual bodies. Birgit Däwes talks in this context about a turning point in America's wound culture:

With the public spectacle of the burning and collapsing World Trade Center, the disfigured individual body—so central to the late twentieth-century cultural imaginary—was replaced by "wounded" towers in an assault that was as much an act of communication as it was an act of violence.... Post 9/11 literature turns away from the public spectacles of slaughter and symbolically rewrites the anxiety of death into interior and (semi-) private spaces [*Ground Zero Fiction* 299–300].

9/11 was followed by an unofficial auto-censorship among popular culture producers but "disaster porn" survived and according to Max Page it is reassuring to see that these fantasies continue as they are a sign of the city getting back to its normal *modus operandi*: of recovering. New York was rediscovered as a fragile community "built on a delicate mix of people and buildings, the solace of anonymity and the thrill of cosmopolitanism" (231). Page also adds that "if New York is no longer the setting of our worst fears, then it may no longer be the home of our greatest hopes. And that would be the beginning of the city's end" (Page 231). Remarkably, in reacting to 9/11 not only New York (as in, for instance, Masha Hamilton's novel *31 Hours*) but also London becomes the setting of imagined disasters: in Cleave's *Incendiary* a football stadium is attacked by eleven suicide bombers; in the dark comedy *Four Lions* directed by Chris Morris the London marathon becomes a terrorist target.

Buildings to Love and Hate: Vulnerable Cities

Not only the city but also its skyline and its buildings often become anthropomorphized and felt for in post–9/11 fiction. They are subjects to emotional reactions and attachments. New York is often referred to as the "wounded" city, the towers as "twins." This process is reflected in, among others, Don DeLillo's *Falling Man* where the already mentioned "Godzilla Apartments" are described as a building that has a "face" and its own weather systems created by its height. Godzilla's wind currents "can knock old people to the pavement" (DeLillo 71). An emotional attachment to buildings is a motif that appears in Jonathan Safran Foer's *Extremely Loud and Incredibly Close*: Oskar on his quest through New York encounters Mrs. Black who lives in the Empire State Building and quite literally takes care of it. Also in Mohsin Hamid's *The Reluctant Fundamentalist* the Empire State Building is referred to as one of "expressive beauty" and its description is highly emotional. In Amy Waldman's *The Submission*, when lit up red and white and seen from the Brooklyn Bridge, it is compared to a parfait (211). As Mark Wigley points out, in the simplest terms "buildings are seen as a form of protection and insulation from danger" (46), designed and constructed by humans to give shelter. It is in these terms that "to be hurt by a building is unacceptable" (Wigley 46) and against the primary role and obligation of architecture. Wigley alludes to the relation between a building and human body: buildings are our witnesses, they are supposed to live longer than we do and bear witness to generations using, watching and identifying with them. Hurting a building in this context means hurting an entire piece of cultural heritage and memory assigned to it.

Destroying the towers meant destroying not only a physical part of the city of New York but also interrupting the city's sense of memory and time. The buildings became victims, and as a consequence "victimized those who watched them suffer" (Wigley 48). Amy Waldman in her novel *The Submission* refers to the towers as "generational continuities" and calls a city skyline an intergenerational collaboration that seems "no less natural than a mountain range that had shuddered up from the earth. This new gap in space reversed time" (29). This imagery of a skyline for a city is hence something as natural as mountains for a landscape. The attacks of September 11 were not only symbolic offenses on American values, capitalism and progress but also, as Peter Eisinger puts it "assaults on cities as urban places" ("The American City in the Age of Terror" 115).

The fascination with the enormous structures of the World Trade Center has been present since their very beginning, even before they were built.[11] The danger of falling inscribed in their very existence (just like it is inscribed into the existence of any so overwhelmingly high architectonical structure) has been a motif worked with repeatedly. Philippe Petit—the tightrope walker who in 1974 walked between them was playing with the possibility of falling with every step he made. Numerous filmic scenes of people jumping or falling from New York skyscrapers follow, for instance in Brothers Cohen's 1992 *Hudsucker Proxy*. Petit's tightrope act is reconnected with the fall of the towers and brought back to public attention through media, the documentary *Man on Wire* (2008) and Colum McCann's novel *Let the Great World Spin* (2009) which places Petit at the center of the fragmentarily constructed plot.

According to Paul Virilio and Chris Turner, September 11 marked the beginning of a "new war" the front of which (symbolically and physically) became the Manhattan skyline (*Ground Zero* 82). This skyline, fragile and vulnerable, becomes a very important motif in post–9/11 fiction and its shape contributes to the urban character of the city. Metaphorically it becomes the city's face, which through different expressions reflects the moods of the city and communicates them to the outside world. Christoph Lindner claims that "New York's skyline is a site of instability and change distinguished in the contemporary urban imaginary by visions caught somewhere between the sublime and the uncanny" (304). This urban imaginary corresponds to the feelings and emotional condition of many of the characters of post–9/11 city novels who often in their urban existence are caught between the impressive and the fearful, between uncomfortable and scary. The new symbolism of skyscrapers in this context—as matching the general atmosphere of the wounded metropolis and its people—appears in Jonathan Safran Foer's *Extremely Loud and Incredibly Close*, Don DeLillo's *Falling Man* and Joseph O'Neill's *Netherland*—from a synecdoche of progress and bursting capitalism, they become primarily associated with fear, fragility and vulnerability of the seemingly powerful supermetropolis. The frightened city also frequently enters the characters' minds: Chuck, the narrator of Naqvi's *Home Boy*, when recalling his New York past in the context of 9/11, talks about the "skyline of [his] memory" (17) and admits that the city has forever influenced his life and perception of the rest of the world.

The city itself proves more vulnerable than expected or thought, as Art Spiegelman puts it: "I took my city, and those homely, arrogant towers, for granted. It's actually all as transient and ephemeral as, say, old newspapers."[12] On the other hand, the Twin Towers were *post factum* referred to as first and most vulnerable targets in New York, "almost waiting to topple over onto the rest of the city" (Page 190); as architectural monsters committing suicide (Baudrillard 47) reflecting the attackers' desire for a suicidal death in "the most monumental figure of western urban development ... in the atopia-utopia of optical knowledge that has long had the ambition of surmounting and articulating the contradictions arising from urban agglomeration" (de Certeau 93). Also their twining, a form of doubling of power and hegemony that they came to symbolize is discussed and used as a reference point in fiction, e.g., in forms of doubling of motifs or parallel stories—like in DeLillo's *Falling Man* where Nina's lover Martin has an RAF past and lives under a false name, so has a double identity. Additionally, his story functions as a parallel to the one of Mohamed Atta also told in the novel. Lynne Sharon Schwartz's novel *The Writing on the Wall* features twins as characters, even more explicitly referring to the doubling of motifs and meanings complimenting each other.

Jean Baudrillard argues that the fact that there were two of the towers signifies "the end of any original reference" (*Spirit* 43). Built in Lower Manhattan, the sense of exposure, precariousness and vulnerability was crucial to their historical experience (Burrows *Manhattan at War* 23).[13] Marshall Berman calls them "a brutal and overbearing ... expression of an urbanism that disdained the city and its people" pointing out their isolation from the downtown street system and unfriendly pseudo-public spaces within the World Trade Center complex (*When Bad Buildings Happen to Good People* 6). Their absence is equally if not more overwhelming.

The collapse of the towers caused damage to other buildings in Lower Manhattan proving that, like in a human body,[14] if something happens in one part of the city, it always has an influence on the entire rest of the urban system. The post–9/11 dust, the smell of which made Art Spiegelman understand what the horror of Auschwitz smelled like,[15] settled on facades, walls and windows of buildings surrounding the World Trade Center. These neighboring buildings became silent witnesses to the tragedy and the dust was preserved on their surfaces and interiors for years. As the report of the New York City Department of Health and Mental Hygiene from September 2002 shows, the dust sampled in various parts of Lower Manhattan contained toxic substances[16] dangerous for the people who inhaled it. The "wounded" area turned out to be much larger than originally thought since the exposure of buildings and people in this dense urban environment was enormous. This is a theme reflected in Joseph O'Neill's *Netherland* where the protagonists abandon their Manhattan loft after 9/11 out of fear of exposure to toxic substances. The fact that breathing in New York becomes dangerous makes life there impossible for the wife of the main character.

Completely paranoid, she eventually escapes to London which she considers a safer place, leaving her husband behind and almost destroying their marriage. But London too becomes very fragile which can be observed in Ian McEwan's paranoid reality of *Saturday* and in Chris Cleave's disastrous vision of a terrorist attack in *Incendiary*. Here London changes into a fearful and xenophobic city where bridges are being blocked, tourists arrested, a curfew introduced and the word "multiculturalism" together with the legacy of postcolonialism eliminated from people's vocabulary and understanding. Both of the mentioned British novels in reacting to 9/11 anticipate the events of 7/7. Bitterly enough, Cleave's novel was published on July 7, 2005.

London-based fiction reacting to 9/11 mirrors the latent but omnipresent fear of a vague anticipation and draws possible scenarios to describe the unknown. On the other hand, fiction reacting to 7/7 wanders away from London and becomes geographically more "liberated" and diverse, as the attacked capital can now recover. Llewellyn's *Eleven*, for instance, published in 2006 and set on September 11, 2001 is set in Cardiff and is a statement about the symbolic distance from the remote and isolated metropolitan world. Even more importantly, after 7/7 the focus shifts away from the metropolis in order to find out more about its enemies—terrorist cells operating in the British province, for instance, in Sunjeev Sahota's novel *Ours Are the Streets*. Projections fed by the desire to satisfy the tragic curiosity are no longer necessary.

Although also "covered with New York dust" (Ali 368) post–9/11 London is a very different place to New York to be written. The fear and paranoia that this writing draws from and reflects is of a different kind, despite sharing an origin. None of the other European metropolises has such a large variety of literary responses to the fear of a potential act of terrorism anticipated after the events of 9/11, as London does. Accordingly, in the analyzed post–9/11 London novels, apocalyptic fear of an approaching disaster caused by an unknown Other, impossible to define or locate, floats in the metropolitan air. Not knowing becomes a source of disastrous fantasies set in London in all of the texts: in Cleave's *Incendiary* it is a terrorist attack on a football stadium; in McEwan's *Saturday* Henry Perowne imagines a disastrous scenario while watching a burning plane through his bedroom window. In Ali's *Brick Lane* the disaster is imagined as a process originating within, shown as a self-destroying march of violent masses in East London.

The state of blurry anticipation is unbearable for the city which becomes vulnerable. In *Incendiary* it is portrayed as a hysterical woman who gets drunk regularly, in *Saturday* as a brain which requires medical treatment, and in *Brick Lane* as a dangerous creature one should try to stay away from. The general metropolitan geographical imagination is darker, and the characters featured in the novels are not as keen to explore or reclaim the city as their New York based counterparts. Reasons for this apocalyptic behavior can be located in the city itself and in its post–9/11 and pre–7/7 depictions, personifications and literary geographies.

In analyzing projections of disasters situated in these two metropolises, it strikes that neither New York, nor London has a clearly defined center. New York—the urban grid, "an expanding chessboard" (Sennett *Flesh and Stone* 359) was designed in advance to being inhabited, on a mostly empty land. Equality of each building and area made land act like money. Exactly because of the intended equality of space, this grid lacked a superior space that a center could become. London's map is "messy with few unifying features: no ring road (except the outer orbital M25 motorway), no axial boulevards, no consistent street grid, and no clearly defined 'downtown'" (Hebbert 4). This contributes to the general confusion of the modern urban individual but stands also for the size and density of the metropolises, impossible to be "centered" in a single area.

Urban disasters projected on such a wide decentralized space are impossible to channel or control. This lack of means and impossibility to control the city are phenomena strongly reflected by fiction reacting to the events of 9/11. It is highly incongruous with modern digital city mappings technology, street views, GPS tracking and hence very difficult to accept. Many of the fictional characters do not comply and try to regain control over the metropolis, since they hope that to subdue the city would bring back a structure to their post–9/11 lives.

Emergence of New Urban Spaces in Post–9/11 New York and Its Fiction

Analyzed cultural representations reflect the physical and symbolic changes that occurred in New York after the attacks of 9/11. The absence of the Twin Towers resulted in the emergence of new spaces which carried new meanings and turned into new reference points within the city. Probably the most apparent of these new spaces is Ground Zero itself which also, very importantly, has constantly changed since 9/11, and which all of the novels set in New York and discussed here, refer to. It is here where the geography of the disaster of 9/11 begins—Ground Zero is its epicenter. Other new spaces are the already mentioned Hangar 17 at the JFK airport that became known best through Francesco Torres's photography,[17] the 9/11 memorial and museum as well as the new not yet completed World Trade Center the presence of which already radically changed downtown Manhattan. The Observatory placed on top of One World Trade Center offers new vistas over Manhattan for which the most natural reference featured in press reviews seems to be the view from the no longer existing restaurant and observation deck Windows of the World. But before all this began to happen, in the very first days and weeks after the attacks, the surrounding streets and buildings were turned into new public spaces: when they were transformed into urban information boards, where people were putting photos of their missing relatives and friends.

Every missing-poster told a story and contributed to the production of the post–9/11 "counter narrative" (DeLillo *In the Ruins*) responding to the one plotted and imposed on the city by the terrorists. New York was full of hope-generating stories which through their (visual) presence became literarily inscribed into the city and its character. The whole city was transformed into "a regime of memory" (Zukin 15) and mirrored the shock and mourning of its people. The missing individuals whose photographed faces covered the streets in most cases did not know each other while still alive. They were symbolically united by the tragedy; they became the united victimized face of 9/11 brought together by those who mourned for them. *Post-mortem* they were given a collective identity; they were integrated into a "collective life" (Berman 4) in an artificial "center" of mourning. Most of the photos came from family albums and provided an intimacy with the missing people. The private collective traces and memories of life interfering with the urban environment (re)formed the post–9/11 public space. The line between public and private blurred or as the main character in Don DeLillo's novel *Falling Man* puts it: "since that day in September all life had become public" (182). These individual stories made streets readable in the process of collective mourning. The capacity to mourn is, according to Judith Butler, crucial also in terms of political decisions and actions as it is strongly linked to opposing violence in what becomes a vicious circle of attacking and mourning—the circle of war in our times:

> Without the capacity to mourn, we lose that keener sense of life we need in order to oppose violence. And though for some, mourning can only be resolved through violence, it seems clear that violence only brings on more loss, and the failure to heed the claim of precarious life only leads, again and again, to the dry grief of an endless political rage [Butler xviii-xix].

Collective mourning precisely localized and condensed in particular physical spaces becomes hence the city's reaction and answer to violence.

The term "ground zero"—used in an attempt to name the new space that emerged from the sudden absence of the Twin Towers—refers in its original meaning to a nuclear catastrophe and according to the Oxford English Dictionary describes: "the ground situated immediately under an exploding bomb, especially an atomic one." It specifically signifies the tragic consequences of American attacks on Hiroshima and Nagasaki (Däwes "Celluloid Recoveries" 286). The American post–9/11 rhetoric is hence strongly linked to World War II (Melnick *9/11 Culture*), the Cold War and America's "cultural obsession with nuclear imagery" (DeRosa 60). This linkage can also be observed in fictional representations of the conditions of post–9/11 cities. The bombing of Dresden during World War II and a survivor's account of the Hiroshima bombing appear as important references in Jonathan Safran Foer's *Extremely Loud and Incredibly Close*; Chris Cleave's *Incendiary* draws a link between bombs dropped on London by Nazi Germany and the fictional terrorist attack on a football stadium. In Don DeLillo's *Falling Man* Ground Zero is describes as a "bombed-out city" (58). In Teju Cole's *Open City* the place becomes a metonym of the disaster: the main protagonist who is also the first person narrator of this novel encounters a tourist who asks him about the "way to 9/11." What he means is Ground Zero:

> The place has become a metonym of its disaster: I remembered a tourist who once asked me how he could get to 9/11: not the site of the events of 9/11 but to 9/11 itself, the date petrified into broken stones [Cole 52].

The meaning of the place melted with collective memory of the attacks; it became incorporated into the complex image of that day. The novel draws further on that image and Teju Cole describes a subway train passing by the work site as a "livid vein drawn across the neck of 9/11" (Cole 58).

Used in this context, the term "ground zero" promotes a discourse of American exceptionalism (Sturken 167; Däwes *Ground Zero Fiction* 414), one that "proclaims the events of 9/11 to be unique in the history of violent acts"

(Sturken 167) and also puts the crash of American Airlines 77 at the Pentagon and the crash of flight 93 in Shanksville aside. Marita Sturken discusses this phenomenon together with the Oklahoma City bombing of 1995, where the term "ground zero" was also used but immediately lost its status after the attacks of 9/11. The 21st century Ground Zero is a site of cultural memory production; it is "the primary space in the U.S. that defines 9/11" (Sturken 169) but it also shows that remembering 9/11 is marked by "a need for repetition and analogy" (Däwes "Celluloid Recoveries" 286). From a site of destruction and loss, it rapidly changed into a constantly mediated battlefield over which the families of the dead want to claim ownership.[18] The space was "created" by and to be experienced through media. It became attached to the collective memory of the events of September 11 which as such is always an inherently mediated phenomenon (Neiger 3).

Ground Zero has been constantly reshaped and mediated through images marking the general obsession with visual representations of this tragedy and memory, the "iconomania" (Sturken 186) that contributed to our perception of the terrorist attacks. This marks a tremendous difference between 9/11 and 7/7: the London bombings were not about images. The entire aspect of performativity so important in the case of 9/11 was left out. It was not a staged tragedy; it took place partly underground with no daylight. One of the most important issues that dominated the post–7/7 discourse in Great Britain is the fact that the suicide bombers were all British; they did not come from outside to attack the country or symbolically the Western World—they were already a part of it. They managed to operate as sleeper cells in the UK province.

This defiance coming from within and not from outside is a central motif of textual representations responding to the attacks, for instance in Sunjeev Sahota's novel *Ours Are the Streets* (2011), Salman Rushdie's *Shalimar the Clown* (2006) or Ed Husain's autobiography *The Islamist* (2007) or the film comedy *Four Lions* (2010). All of the mentioned texts set the Muslim Other in the center of the plot. They all describe a personal development of young men who become religious fundamentalists in small British towns, with the exception of *The Islamist* which is set in East London but which describes exactly the same process. This pseudo-religious rebellion happens against the spirit of British multiculturalism contextualized in the postcolonial past of the country and viewed as its legacy. Melanie Phillips claims that 7/7 was far more alarming and dangerous to America's long term future than 9/11. According to her, the London bombings "finally lifted the veil on Britain's dirty secret in the war on terrorism—that for more than a decade London has been the epicenter of Islamic militancy in Europe" (Phillips *Londonistan* x). She further claims that "kicked out of or repressed within their own countries, *they* streamed in their thousands to the British capital because *they* found it to be more hospitable and tolerant than any other place on the globe" (Phillips *Londonistan* 19, all emphasis mine) setting up a clear post–7/7 us versus them dichotomous discourse, *them* being "Islamist terrorists and jihadi ideologues" (19).

Slightly different in this respect is Rachid Bouhareb's film *London River* (2009) set in East London straight after the attacks of 7/7. It shows an encounter of two people from very different cultural and religious backgrounds who come to London to search for their children. They represent both sides of Phillips's dichotomy and their individual worlds do clash at first, in order to then form a base for a joint quest full of respect for one another. Through portraying common sorrow, grief, pain and loss as cross-cultural and cross-religious, the film questions the legitimacy of and shows alternatives to "othering" as a cultural practice.

Ground Zero can also be read metaphorically, as a new starting point. It is, in its constitution a space of a temporary character (Sturken 167), a space between the past and the future, a very temporary "gap" in the city and in people's perception and comprehension of it. It is a common understanding that only by building something greater, taller and better than the towers, the U.S. could make a point in responding to the terrorists—a mechanism of a "reflexive machismo" (Sorkin and Zukin x). Ground Zero then functions primarily as a concept rather than a place and as such it is reflected in fiction. It is to be anticipated that soon the term will be used in a historical context only.

The emptiness, the gap in the Manhattan skyline and the 9/11 Memorial as new trauma-related spaces in New York play an important role in the remapping of the city in fiction. They influence the way literary characters identify with the city, comprehend, explore and rename its parts and places. Birgit Däwes in her typology of post–9/11 fiction uses the term "Ground Zero Fiction"[19] in spite of the "conceptual intricacies, echoing the senses of exceptionalism and historical amnesia that prevailed after the attacks" (Däwes *Ground Zero Fiction* 15). Däwes shows that the relationship between fiction and history works both ways: fiction not only shows the different 9/11 imaginaries but also redefines that very imaginary and opens space for the creation of new meanings. This is also true for urban spaces that are being redefined, reinvented and remapped in post–9/11 fiction.

The Urban Other After 9/11

All of the analyzed novels address the post–9/11 phenomenon of the emergence of the Other in the urban context. They do so to different degrees and from different perspectives. In order to embrace the process of "othering" defined as disrespect for the Other (Versluys 150), they situate the Other in different urban structures, environments and situations. It is in the metropolis, the zone of daily cultural coexistences and plurality, that the radicalized anti–Muslim sentiments deriving from fear and lack of knowledge are most visible and most immediate. The post–9/11 Other is clearly profiled as a Muslim with potential inclinations to Islamic terrorism, "headscarves on the women, beards on the men, dark skin" (Waldman 152). This profiling marks a certain shift in patterns of discrimination, as one of the characters in Amy Waldman's *The Submission* points out: "The police used to stop African Americans solely for 'driving while black.' Now it's acceptable to single us out for 'flying while Muslim'?" (41). On a similar note Chuck, the main character and first person narrator of Naqvi's *Home Boy*, states: "[I] understood that just like three black men were gang-bangers, and three Jews a conspiracy, three Muslims had become a sleeper cell" (Naqvi 153). All of the texts show the process of "othering" as racist generalization and gradual exclusion from social and urban structures and forms.

The discrepancy between the picture of the Muslim Other fabricated by the media and an individual human being is most explicitly addressed in Waldman's *The Submission* where the othered "subject" can no longer recognize himself in the media projections which use his face to literally create a brand (in economic and commercial terms) for the evil enemy. According to Kristiaan Versluys who in his work on the post–9/11 Other draws from Emmanuel Levinas and from postcolonial studies with Said's *Orientalism* as a point of departure, the Other as a concept has never been considered or described as a pejorative phenomenon; it is the process of "othering" that embodies ignorance and prejudice:

> The Other (upper-case) as a concept involves the recognition of the singular and self-generated identity of someone else, in particular someone belonging to a different ethnicity or culture. By contrast "othering" is an act of exclusion, whereby, through prejudice, ignorance, or both, one refuses to treat someone else fully as an individual [Versluys 150].

Many theoreticians and philosophers want to see the Other as a reflection of the self; constructed to embody what we are not, the concept can only exist in relation to ourselves who construct it. Emerged as a product and result of dichotomizing after the attacks of September 11 and in their aftermath, the (evil) Other embodies the deepest fears, prejudices and insecurities of its creator(s) and is hence a reflection of those. The concept is hence in its very foundations grounded in the self as the need for such a construct rises in its threatened inventor.

Kristiaan Versluys talks about the "inextricable implication of the self with the Other" (163) when analyzing Martin Amis's portrayal of Muhammad Atta in his short story entitled "Last Days of Muhammad Atta." In this text Amis tries to imagine the day preceding the attacks of 9/11 in the life of the terrorist—the "ultimate Other." His portrayal of Atta works on the assumption that the terrorist must have gone through phases of religious reluctance, also or especially during his last days. According to Versluys, exactly at this point, i.e., in his assumed religious reluctance, Atta in this short story resembles Amis himself and is hence as the imagined Other, inevitably a reflection of its creator. The possibilities of imagining the Other are grounded in and limited by the self which is shaped and influenced by a given cultural context. Julia Kristeva calls for recognition of the foreigner/the Other in ourselves in order to avoid dangerous patters of "othering":

> Strangely, the foreigner lives within us: he is the hidden face of our identity, the space that wrecks our abode, the time in which understanding and affinity founder. By recognizing him within ourselves, we are spared detesting him in himself.... The foreigner comes in when the consciousness of my difference arises, and he disappears when we all acknowledge ourselves as foreigners, unamenable to bonds and communities [1].

While Jacques Rancière claims that 9/11 "did not mark any rupture in the symbolic order [but only] brought to light the new dominant form of symbolizing the Same and the Other" (104), Kristiaan Versluys in his study of post– 9/11 fiction suggests that September 11 did rupture normalcy and "created opportunities to come face to face with the Other" (182). Facing this confrontation, writers continuously see it as their task to try not to dichotomize the events, to provide the other perspective than the one they themselves could identify with, i.e., to stand face to face with the Other on one level; to acknowledge the power structures but to see them as inter-relational, changing and potentially reciprocal. Consequently novels like John Updike's *Terrorist*, Don DeLillo's *Falling Man*, Masha Hamilton's *31 Hours* or the British novel by Sunjeev Sahota *Ours Are the Streets* make the attempt to provide the perspective of the ultimate Other, the terrorist, not the victim. Monica Ali's *Brick Lane* and Teju Cole's *Open City* work more on the level of the collective and try to explain and imagine how radical Islamic movements come to existence in the context of a Western metropolis (London in Ali's text, Brussels in Cole's).

Masha Hamilton's novel *31 Hours* aims at twisting the image of the stereotypical Other and shows him as a young white American man fascinated with Islam and at the same time lost in his search for a religion and a cultural context.[20] This approach works as a social and political provocation; a disruption in what Judith Butler calls the "hegemonic grammar" according to which "words like *terrorist* and *slaughter* [...] should be reserved for unjustified acts of violence against First World nations" (Butler 13) performed by intruders coming from outside of that First World. Masoud, Jonas's mentor in Hamilton's novel reflects on exactly this one-sided Western pseudo-logic which makes some lives more "grievable" (Butler 20) than others: "Jonas was the prize, the blond-haired, Western-raised Wahhabi. *Let's see*, Masoud thought, *if the media will call* him *a terrorist*" (99, emphasis mine). Jonas's motives are linked to the ones of the European IRA. DeLillo's *Falling Man* offers in this context a link to the German Red Army Faction which is meant to westernize the (post-)9/11 terrorist, to bring him closer to the Western public. In Waldman's *The Submission* the post–9/11 Other becomes a universally applicable threat with which, e.g., daughters of one of the characters blackmail her: when things do not go according to their will, they threaten her with marrying a Muslim (164). The effect is humor, which softens the novel's message but intensifies social criticism.

Hamid's *The Reluctant Fundamentalist* "plays" with the notion of the Other and provokes with its ambiguity; the tension here shifts constantly between a white American man to the Pakistani narrator and the intentions of both are at least unclear. In Ian McEwan's *Saturday* the Other is personified as a white British psychopath, aggressive and intrusive, disturbing with his presence the normalcy of everyday life of the other characters. Quite surprisingly, sensitive to poetry, he is "a fellow creature whose very vulnerability comprises an appeal to closeness and solidarity" (Versluys 193). In Foer's *Extremely Loud and Incredibly Close* the nine-year-old Oskar genuinely approaches strangers he encounters in the city and tries to befriend them, make New York City his family, with no exceptions.

All of the texts address the phenomenon of the Other through space as it is crucial in establishing norms and exclusions. The Other is sensitive to location and hence non-transferable, non-adjustable to a different cultural coding. Selected novels show that in the context of New York City and London after 9/11 the images of the urban Other can be very similar despite the geographical distance and cultural differences, as equally motivated fear invades both of the cities and minds. Fiction mirrors this tendency and patterns of discrimination and "othering" against Muslims can be found in texts written on both sides of the Atlantic and set in either of the cities, e.g., headscarves being pulled (*Brick Lane* and *The Submission*), Muslim characters losing jobs (Cleave's *Incendiary*, Alis' *Brick Lane*, Naqvi's *Home Boy*) and in consequence leaving the country (H.M. Naqvi's *Home Boy*, Ali's *Brick Lane*).

Georg Simmel proposes to view the distance to the stranger as ambiguous in the context of city space and the relations with him/her as positive, as a form of interaction necessary for the metropolitan coexistence:

> The unity of nearness and remoteness involved in every human relation is organ
> ized, in the phenomenon of the stranger, in a way which may be most briefly for
> mulated by saying that in the relationship to him, distance means that he, who is
> close by, is far, and strangeness means that he, who also is far, is actually near. For,
> to be a stranger is naturally a very positive relation; it is a specific form of inter
> action ["The Stranger" 146].

All of the texts which work with the metaphor of the city as a body and
all it incorporates, latently suggest that the city itself, dangerous, unpredictable
and omnipresent can take the form of the Other. Literary characters sharing a
metropolis become mistrustful towards one another, avoid public or crowded
spaces and seek shelter at home, in seemingly isolated spaces, or, in most radical
cases, leave or consider leaving the city (e.g., Rachel in O'Neill's *Netherland* or
Lianne in DeLillo's *Falling Man*). The city interferes with their lives and participates in all social processes after 9/11. New York enters Changez's room in
Hamid's novel to keep him company but also to observe him. Its constant presence is reassuring and frightening at the same time. In Hamid's novel, in which
the dichotomous positions are assigned to cities, Lahore is shown as the Other
(city) to New York and vice versa. Also here, the one is shown as a reflection of
the other. Seemingly entirely different, the cities turn to have many similarities.

Inscribing the phenomenon of the Other into the cityscape means that
the metropolis has to be (re)claimed and redefined in one way or another. Areas
considered safe zones by a given group turn against them, e.g., Little Pakistan
in Brooklyn suddenly becomes empty in Naqvi's novel which results in the
streets turning longer, eerie and uncanny. Similarly Kensington in Waldman's
The Submission changes its character: the Bangladeshi community is scared to
leave their houses anxious of being harassed or deported. In other words, to
"other" a certain group of people means to "other" entire parts of the city, i.e.,
to eliminate them and in so doing to potentially change the city structure.

Cartography of the Book: Structure Overview

This monograph is divided spatially into two parts, "New York City" and
"London," and proposes a map of post–9/11 American and British city novel.
(With "American" in the context of this book I mean strictly the United States.)
The texts analyzed in the first part are set primarily in New York City (some
of the characters travel) and deal with remapping of this urban space. The study
of the remapping starts with accompanying nine-year-old Oskar Schell, the
main protagonist of Jonathan Safran Foer's *Extremely Loud and Incredibly Close*
on his quest through the boroughs of the city and spaces in between them. Oskar

remaps the metropolis through walking according to a very precisely prepared plan and pursuing a particular aim. Looking for a lock that a key found in his deceased father's cabinet would open, Oskar is also looking for signs and instructions of how to live.

"New York" continues with following the post–9/11 flâneur Julius in Teju Cole's *Open City* ten years after September 11, 2001. The professional psychiatrist, stroller, and hobbyist historian learns about the city and its history through walking, reading and listening to stories attached to places he discovers. As the 21st century embodiment of the Benjaminian Angel of History he sees the past as inscribed into the city's present and the distinction between the two becomes blurry. His walks are fully intuitive and their length and the obtained route depend on loose associations with which Julius gradually reveals what feels like the urban subconscious. The novel touches upon social rules of racial exclusion and belonging in a metropolitan context and describes a community of "brothers"—young black men who without knowing each other feel the sense of community and anticipate mutual past and history of oppression. Julius without realizing or wanting to, becomes a part of this parallel society which does not only deprive him of his anonymity but also makes him feel marked as a non-white Other.

The ambiguity of the urban Other is also one of the main aspects in Mohsin Hamid's *The Reluctant Fundamentalist*, the key to which is the urban space itself, addressed through the dichotomous character of New York City and Lahore. The cities connected through the main character and narrator function as synechdoches of whole societies and cultures and on the urban level point to many similarities of the seemingly opposite poles. H.M. Naqvi's *Home Boy* traces the nature of post–9/11 "othering" within the urban grid of Manhattan which, first liberating and easily accessible through its seemingly predictable geographical nature, after 9/11 becomes claustrophobic, restricted, controlling and offers no place to hide.

The part "New York" finishes with a study of an architectonic project aimed as a submission to a fictional competition for the post–9/11 memorial and a contribution to shaping of the post–9/11 city in Amy Waldman's *The Submission*. The attempt at participating in the recreation of wounded New York turns to a conflict set around race, religion, and the eligibility of "othering" in the post–9/11 context. The characters of Waldman's novel are spread within and beyond the city limits and all contribute to shaping the post–9/11 discourse through active interaction with the metropolis and with one another.

The second part of the monograph is devoted to London. It is divided according to geographical and historical divisions within London, as mirrored by the analyzed post–9/11 British novels: into East and West. Unlike the texts discussed earlier, whose characters circulate within New York City and other metropolises eager to explore it and to contribute to establishing their new textual geographies, the characters in the three texts presented here hardly ever leave their London neighborhoods. They actively engage with the city but, they do not leave their safety zones, preferring to remain with the well-known, unsurprising, and safe (a geographical equivalent of comfort food made so prominent in, e.g., *Brick Lane* or *The Submission*). Restricting the "natural" territorial frames of their lives influences their perception of London and its post- and at the same time pre-disaster cartography, as literary depictions of post–9/11 London mirror the fear of becoming the next target. All of the texts to some extent anticipate an approaching metropolitan tragedy; they try to write it in order to prevent it from happening, and to save London through this writing. The characters remaining in their respective boroughs subconsciously prepare for a disaster and instinctively keep close to home. Exploring and reclaiming spaces through remapping—the process addressed in nearly all of the previous chapters—is a reaction that has its roots in a previous disaster and its consequences.

London in the analyzed literary reflections becomes a vulnerable body which is anxious and furious. Constructed as a letter, Chris Cleave's novel is an attempt at writing the city out of trauma and healing its wounded and hysterical body. *Incendiary* published on July 7, 2005—the day of the terrorist attacks on the London underground and buses—is yet another example of the reciprocity of reality and fiction; of writing and walking the city. The novel features Osama bin Laden—the ultimate Other of the time—whom the letter is addressed to. This disaster fantasy is followed by a study of the city in Monica Ali's *Brick Lane*, set just like *Incendiary* in the East London borough Tower Hamlets. The process described here is one leading from urban claustrophobia to personal liberation, so a reverse course to the one addressed in Naqvi's *Home Boy*.

In *Brick Lane*, the attacks of 9/11 and the urban "othering" which enters London together with the "New York dust" (Ali 368), are the ultimate reasons for leaving the city. Chanu, just like the other male Muslim characters in Waldman's *The Submission*, Hamid's *The Reluctant Fundamentalist* and Naqvi's *Home Boy* abandons the Western metropolis and returns "home," to Bangladesh. His decision is a contribution to his wife's liberation from the limitations of an arranged marriage and a last step to her independence. The city as viewed through her kitchen window facing Brick Lane enters her life and adopts her. She becomes a part of it and is no longer a silent observer isolated in the vacuum of her flat.

The focus of the next chapter shifts spatially from East to West London and lies on the character Henry Perowne observed in Ian McEwan's *Saturday* throughout one full day in London. This novel, which draws from modernist techniques of approaching time and linking it to space, is another important contribution to the nature of post–9/11 racial profiling and "othering." The city in this novel has little in common with Tower Hamlets in *Incendiary* or *Brick Lane* and matches the exclusiveness of Perowne's privileged life.

The book ends with a form of a spatial synthesis provided by an analysis of Joseph O'Neill's *Netherland* which features both New York City and London. The main protagonist Hans, alone in paranoid post–9/11 Manhattan remaps the city and his life through a new passion: cricket. His obsession with this sport, very much unfitting to the urban character of New York City, makes him establish an entirely new cartography of the already well-known space. The center of it, similarly to the center of Hans's life, shifts dramatically. When Hans returns to London, he realizes that the process of remapping New York has also influenced the way he perceives the British capital. He realizes that he misses the other city and that it has become a part of his life, reappropriated and turned into home after and through the events of September 11 which as the text suggests, have Americanized him.

Part One

New York

I

Remapping New York City in Jonathan Safran Foer's *Extremely Loud and Incredibly Close*

Inventing the Post–9/11 City

Foer narrates his novel with three equally prominent[1] voices, whose first-person accounts alternate throughout the text and create a fragmented and complex story line. Birgit Däwes calls the novel a "postmodernist pastiche of genres—combining *bildungsroman* and anti-detective novel, epistolary novel and memoir, as well as documentary and picaresque elements" (*Ground Zero Fiction* 379) and Krstiaan Versluys refers to the alteration of voices as a "materialization of the condition of abnormality as a result of a devastating loss, projected against the family's larger losses and further abnormalities" (Versluys 101). In this chapter I claim that in this textual world of abnormalities the city is the key to understanding the relation between these three characters whose narrative voices are used to tell the fragmented lives that combined, form the mentioned reality.

The reader first encounters the nine-year old Oskar Schell, a boy who has lost his father on September 11. Then the other two narrators make their appearances: his paternal grandparents, survivors of the World War II Dresden bombing who reunite after the loss of their son in the terrorist attack.[2] All three individuals are traumatized and the process of writing has for all of them a therapeutic character. Foer's novel universalizes trauma by illustrating the way historical events come together in an inter-generational encounter of members of a single family. As Kristiaan Versluys points out, these three characters try to reach out to one another and "the novel consists of their attempts to establish contact" (80), although what they write is not necessarily addressed to the other two. Oskar's grandfather, Thomas Schell, Sr., continuously writes letters to his "unborn son"; Oskar writes a diary titled "Stuff That Happened to Me" which does not seem to be intended for an audience. Only Oskar's Grandma's letter is clearly addressed to her grandson. They all meet in New York City and are symbolically united by grief caused by the events of September 11 and their common loss. Trauma becomes an impulse to establish a cross-generational communication that exceeds physical, geographical and emotional boundaries. In consequence trauma also generates the need to explore the city in order to constitute and understand its new geography. This process, different in case of each of the protagonists, is possible only due to the newly emerged communication between them and unconditional acceptance within it.

Oskar talks about the "worst day" when, after returning home from school, he finds five messages that his father has left on the answering machine calling from one of the burning towers. After he has listened to all of them, the phone rings again and although Oskar can see his father's number, he does not pick up and lets him leave another message. He decides not to tell anyone about the recordings and keeps listening to them over and over again in secret. His father's desperate voice gives Oskar "heavy boots" and makes him feel guilty of not having picked up the phone and of not being able to tell anyone about the messages. This voice recorded and preserved belongs to Oscar only; it becomes emotional baggage, a heavy stone of guilt rather than a fetish.

The boy's world changes dramatically after the attacks—everything that he does now has a new meaning and importance. According to Oskar, his fear and unease originate from his bad conscience and from the fact that he is consistently prevented from finding out how exactly his father died. He starts inventing in order not to think. He invents things that are closely related to the city of New York and are intended to improve the lives of the people connected by a collective trauma and united within the city by pain and loss:

> In bed that night I invented a special drain that would be underneath every pillow in New York, and would connect to the reservoir. Whenever people cried themselves to sleep, the tears would all go to the same place, and in the morning the weatherman could report if the water level of the Reservoir of Tears had gone up or down, and you could know if New York was in heavy boots. And when something really terrible happened—like a nuclear bomb or at least a biological weapons attack—an extremely loud siren would go off, telling everyone to get to Central Park to put sandbags around the reservoir [38].

Being aware of the danger skyscrapers pose to birds overwhelmed by their monstrous presence, Oskar invents a device that saves them from dying. There is a parallel between birds and people, equally helpless in the face of a disaster when confronted with the height of an unnaturally tall building. Skyscrapers become constructions that surpass their creators.

> Yeah, so I invented a device that would detect when a bird is incredibly close to a building, and that would trigger an extremely loud birdcall from another sky-

scraper, and they'd be drawn to that. They'd bounce from one to another.... But the birds would never leave Manhattan [250].

In Foer's novel, being "incredibly close" signifies an approaching death, which can be interrupted by an "extremely loud" lifesaving birdcall, something that was not possible on 9/11 because planes crashed into the World Trade Center, not birds. The title of the novel signals the impossibility of naming the actual occurrence. It is beyond comprehension and beyond existing vocabulary.

Oskar also invents things related to microcosms of his world, for example the apartment he lives in:

> As I walked to the kitchen, I invented a lever that could be on the front door, which would trigger a huge spoked wheel in the living room to turn against metal teeth that would hang down from the ceiling, so that it would play beautiful music, like maybe "Fixing a Hole" or "I Want to Tell You," and the apartment would be a huge music box [14].

Both of the songs by the Beatles that Oskar mentions here refer to his state of mind and contribute to a number of intertextual references in this novel.

Scholars analyzing this novel often refer to Günter Grass's *The Tin Drum* published in 1959 in which the protagonist, also a young boy called Oskar, decides to stop growing as a symbolic protest against the world that surrounds him when the Second World War is about to start (Uytterschout, *An Extremely Loud Tin Drum*; Däwes *Ground Zero Fiction* 387). In both novels a drum becomes an attribute assigned to the main character. Drumming becomes a means of self-protection and seems to serve a therapeutic function. Other references discussed in the context of *Extremely Loud and Incredibly Close* include Kurt Vonnegut's *Slaughterhouse Five*, in which the memory of the bombing of Dresden is used in tandem with transnational memory to reconnect with another traumatic event, as it is in Foer's novel (Hornung 177, Däwes *Ground Zero Fiction* 387).

Inventing and exploring the city are Oskar's ways of locating and finding himself in the changed metropolis that he has not had the chance to discover on his own before 9/11. According to Kritiaan Versluys, the inventions "speak to [Oskar's] intent to reinvent the world, to live in a world that has remained free from trauma, in which the unthinkable has not yet happened" (Versluys 102). His father's death marks Oskar's loss of confidence, balance, internal peace and coherence. It also marks the end of carefree childhood. "Being with my dad made my brain quiet. I didn't have to invent a thing" (12). Inventing becomes a way to address Oskar's fears, but instead of calming him down, the process of invention prevents him from sleeping and, in addition to writing letters to famous people like Stephen Hawking, it becomes "a proof of a morbid obsession" (Versluys 103).

Oskar desperately wants to find out how exactly his father died and is interested in anything that has anything to do with him. He therefore leaves the microcosm of his and his grandma's Upper West Side apartments and begins an expedition: a thorough process of exploring and of establishing a personal, very accurate map of the city. Unlike previous expeditions that have been a game that he played with his father, this one is not limited to any particular area of the city—the whole New York becomes an empty space, a *tabula rasa* that has to be filled by Oskar's discoveries, stories and experiences. There is no "master" of the game, nobody who could give Oskar any clues as to whether he is going in the right direction. The aim of the mission is to find a lock that fits a key Oskar found in a blue vase in his father's closet after his death. He believes that the word "Black" written on the envelope in which the key was placed is a sign or a hint left by his father.

Another motto of his quest is "never stop looking," a phrase Oskar's father circled in red in the *New York Times*. The boy decides to visit all people named Black within the five boroughs of New York in order to ask them about the key. He hopes that finding a person who knows something about the lock and his father would contribute to his memories of him and give him new facts to hold on to. As the expedition proceeds, the urban space becomes a map of his father's life, full of traces that he left moving from one place to another and talking to people he knew. Oskar, the flâneur-detective,[3] to use Walter Benjamin's term, leaves traces and marks the city with his own experiences and encounters while moving through it. Particular places in New York then become associated with particular people who Oskar meets along his journey. All of them share the same surname and in this way become universalized—they represent all of the people living in New York and the diversity of the metropolis.

A person called "Black" becomes an everyman in Foer's novel; they can be found everywhere, they have different skin colors, creeds, jobs, etc. On the other hand, they are chosen to be part of Oskar's quest and eventually provide him with a seeming solution, a lock that fits his key. "Black" is a popular name in the United States but Foer's use of it is quite purposeful. "Black" is obviously also a color loaded with meaning in the context of U.S. racial politics. "Black" is also the color of mourning in Western cultures and a category that racially and culturally marks Julius in Cole's novel *Open City*, and makes him unwillingly enter a pseudo-community of "Brothers" which he cannot escape. All the characters called "Black" in Foer's novel also form a structure resembling a community of individuals, quite randomly put together on the basis of an assumed common denominator. Read in the context of race studies and together with Cole's novel, the choice of the name "Black" in *Extremely Loud* conveys a criticism of the shallowness of social constructs used to categorize and distinguish.

Remarkably, Oskar befriends many of these everyman-figures, which deconstructs the tendency of superficial secondary contacts that dominate the life of the postmodern metropolis (Deny *Lost in the Postmodern Metropolis*). Martina Deny discusses the changing quality of social bonds as marking the postmodern urban environment. In Foer's novel, New York City becomes a symbolically smaller and a more familiar place where all doors open if you knock, which points to the changed nature of the post–9/11 city immersed in collective trauma and grief. Furthermore, the fact that a nine-year-old walks through New York alone shows the city as a safe place, and serves as a literary portrayal of the city as sensitive and vulnerable after 9/11. It is also an attempt to bring the city closer to Oskar, to make it a welcoming space where people are open for non-superficial and non-pragmatic relations and bonds. In Foer's post–9/11 New York people exposed to the medial discourse of fear need each other's physical presence. They are very much unlike the modern crowd in which this presence feels threatening and in which a freely moving individual body lacks physical awareness of other human bodies (Sennett *Flesh and Stone* 21–23).

The setting becomes innocent and magical. During one encounter Oskar is embraced fifteen times. Peter Black from Harlem lets him hold his newborn baby. Ada Black orders a cab for Oskar and kisses him goodbye. All of the Blacks seem to need "real" contact with one another after 9/11, as each of the novel's three narrators do. New Yorkers have been hurt together with the city; the absence of the Twin Towers created an absence in their individual lives, the novel suggests. The experience of 9/11 creates a bond between them and makes them feel responsible for one another.[4] It is significant that the quest's treasure and the solution of the riddle lie in Greenwich Village, in the narrowest house in New York where Abby Black lives. She knows that the key opens a safety deposit box and that it does not have anything to do with Oskar's father.

The smallest of houses "in a city that prizes bigness" (Versluys 115) symbolically refers to and brings to mind Oskar's father's words about the importance of the smallest things in life. This loop of symbols and meanings that reappears in Oskar's life through his city encounters makes him feel closer to his father and gives him the comfort of knowing that there is so much of him in the city. The helpers that Oskar encounters during his quest also very often need help themselves and long for love. Schell's neighbor A.R. Black had not left his apartment since the death of his wife twenty-four years earlier, and isolated himself from the world by turning off his hearing aids. It is Oskar who convinces him to help him look for the lock and hence makes him go outside to listen to the world. This confrontation with the reality he wanted to tune out slowly eventually liberates him from his grief and years of mourning. William Black, Abby's ex-husband whose deceased father had left him a blue vase with a key to a safety deposit box inside, is a sad person still in love with his estranged wife. The encounter with Oskar, whose father bought the vase from him, is also the end of the quest of looking for the key and functions as a spiritual awakening that helps William realize what is really important. The character Fo Black, a man mistakenly obsessed with the "I♥NY" slogan, makes a significant contribution to the notion of love in a metropolis. Fo Black misunderstands "NY," thereby pointing out the fragility of meaning and the multitude of interpretations and possibilities inscribed in the metropolis:

> I asked him did he really love New York or was he just wearing the shirt. He smiled, like he was nervous. I could tell he didn't understand, which made me feel guilty for speaking English, for some reason. I pointed at his shirt. "Do? You? Really? Love? New York?" I said, "Your. Shirt." He looked at his shirt. I pointed at the N and said "New," and the Y and said "York." He looked confused, or embarrassed, or surprised, or maybe even mad. I couldn't tell what he was feeling, because I couldn't speak the language of his feelings. "I not know was New York. In Chinese, *ny* mean 'you.' Thought was 'I love you.'" It was then that I noticed the I♥NY poster on the wall, and the I♥NY flag over the door, and the I♥NY dishtowel, and the I♥NY lunchbox on the kitchen table. I asked him, "Well, then why do you love everybody so much?" [239].

Love is important in a city that lives and moves fast and that changes constantly; it is a possibility of regaining orientation, of not feeling lost. Here it is confronted with a commercial slogan used as a part of the city's branding, of its media image. This superficiality of love in this context is almost offensive to Oskar, for whom post–9/11 New York is not an easily lovable but rather a highly confusing and problematic place. Love is the solution in Foer's novel, but only if it finds ways to overcome trauma. As Versluys puts it, "through the act of speaking, love conquers the suffering of generations" (118). The quote refers to the inability to speak about trauma that resists any form of representation, including spoken words, as it is the case with Oskar's grandfather, Thomas Schell, Sr., who has refused to speak since the bombing of Dresden. This act of speaking as a liberating practice is also the literary force that shapes this novel, that names the unnamable, that processes and helps to address trauma.

What bothers Oskar throughout his entire quest is the fact that the coffin symbolically buried at his father's funeral was empty. The body was never found and Oskar feels that the ashes have forever become an invisible part of New York. The city is then everything: a collective symbolic graveyard for the victims of 9/11, a personal link between Oskar and his deceased father, and also the starting point for all new things that could possibly happen after the tragedy. For Oskar, the only way to find out how to live, the only way out of the trauma of his loss, is befriending the city. Kristiaan Versluys points out that "ttrauma must be given a place within one's recollection in order to heal.... Traumatic memory must be turned into narrative memory" (79). Oskar creates meaningful places by moving through the city. His journeys narrate his traumatic experience; he describes them in a scrapbook, which puts them into a temporal and spatial order—into a narrative, into a plot. He is often scared of things he has to confront along the way, which makes this process difficult to accomplish and requires both self-determination and courage:

> Even after a year, I still had an extremely difficult time doing certain things, like taking showers, for some reason, and getting into elevators, obviously. There was a lot of stuff that made me panicky, like suspension bridges, germs, airplanes, fireworks, Arab people on the subway (even though I'm not racist), Arab people in restaurants and coffee shops and other public places, scaffolding, sewers and subway grates, bags without owners, shoes, people with mustaches, smoke, knots, tall buildings, turbans. A lot of the time I'd get that feeling like I was in the middle of a huge black ocean, or in deep space, but not in the fascinating way. It's just everything was incredibly far from me [36].

This mixture of associations is clearly a response to the post–9/11 media discourse. The well-known images of potential threat disseminated by mass media are combined with Oskar's personal fears and form whole sequences of seemingly random notions that make him feel scared and uneasy. People he meets on his quest and tasks he sets for himself to accomplish make his travels to different parts of the city seem like a computer game, in which the protagonist needs to fulfill tasks using tools he finds on his way in order to reach a further level. In its magical fairy-tale depiction, the whole process aims at symbolically remapping and reclaiming the metropolis.

The city in *Extremely Loud and Incredibly Close* becomes a very specific place: one that at the end of the journey, along with the stories he collects, belongs to Oskar—it is his New York that sometimes becomes personified, as in case of the Sixth Borough story his father tells him, in which a whole borough of New York and its inhabitants decides to separate from the rest of the city to circulate around the world independently, breaking all spatial and temporal limitations. According to the story, the only reminiscence of the Sixth Borough in contemporary New York is Central Park, which was dragged from the Sixth Borough to Manhattan. This magic place "saved" from escape almost entirely constitutes Oskar's pre–9/11 urban experience, as the expeditions he played with his father before "the worst day" all took place there.

> They liked their lives and didn't want to change. So they floated away, one millimeter at a time.... Central Park didn't use to be where it is now.... It used to rest squarely in the center of the Sixth Borough. It was the joy of the borough, its heart. But once it was clear that the Sixth Borough was receding for good, that it

couldn't be saved or detained, it was decided, by New York City referendum, to salvage the park.... Enormous hooks were driven through the easternmost grounds, and the park was pulled by the people of New York, like a rug across a floor, from the Sixth Borough into Manhattan [221].

The Sixth Borough functions as a utopian island that given the possibility of making choices and the freedom to move, decides to abandon the city and to become its own cosmos; safe, independent and without metropolitan ambitions, physically and symbolically detached, and constantly moving, therefore difficult to follow or attack. This story remains important to Oskar because it was told by his father and therefore belongs to a world that does not exist anymore. The story marks the shift between Oskar's childhood and his mature quest in which there seems to be no place for imaginary stories invented by parents for their children.

Kristiaan Versluys quotes Georg Simmel to point out that the multitude of options that a metropolitan urban environment offers can lead to deep confusion and the "unimaginable psychic state" of an individual overwhelmed by possibilities (108). Eventually Oskar realizes that his search for the right lock in such a huge city is a Sisyphean labor:

> When I got home that afternoon, after eight months of searching New York, I was exhausted and frustrated and pessimistic, even though what I wanted to be was happy [287].

But he also recognizes that his quest is a process and that the search itself has a tremendous therapeutic importance. The effort not to stop looking is the purpose of the endless journey.

One of the possible deaths he imagines for his father is jumping out of the burning building. This thought occupies a central place in Oskar's mind. He tries to find photos of people who jumped and is offended that he does not have access to the internet pages that show the "falling man." Oskar feels a certain ownership over the tragedy since it happened in his city and made him lose his father. He perceives it as unfair that people in Europe can see what he cannot although he lives in New York and the city is everything that was left after his father:

> I found a bunch of videos on the Internet of bodies falling. They were on a Portuguese site, where there was all sorts of stuff they weren't showing here, even though it happened here. Whenever I want to learn about how Dad died, I have to go to a translator program and find out how to say things in different languages, like "September," which is "Wrzesień," or 'people jumping from burning buildings' which is 'Menschen, die aus brennenden Gebäuden springen." Then I google those words. It makes me incredibly angry that people all over the world can know

things that I can't, because it happened *here*, and happened to *me*, so shouldn't it be *mine*? [256].

It is somewhat similar to the I♥NY T-shirts: people who wear them claim the right to love the city which in fact, as Oskar states, is not theirs and not for them to love. He prints out pictures of a man falling down a skyscraper[5] and puts them in a backward order in form of a flip-book so that the man is not falling down but up, back into the open window. This sequence is printed at the very end of the novel and marks an attempt at turning back time in order to revert to normalcy. Oskar fantasizes about what it would be like if the whole day of September 11 had never happened, if his father did not leave the apartment that morning, etc., a vision that makes Oskar feel safe but is not a viable solution.

Oskar, like most of the characters in post–9/11 city fiction discussed in this book, interferes with the metropolis in various ways: through walking, looking at it from above to put it into perspective, eventually even by taking underground trains, which disorients him. Oskar's and Thomas Schell, Sr.'s individual daily urban interventions bring them closer to one another and evoke a symbolic transnational memory of earlier (in this case European) disasters which "bring comfort and sustenance to the American character" (Hornung 173). The need for an individual remapping of New York is shared and therefore makes them reach out to one another.

Walking 1: Making Places Meaningful

By walking alone through different boroughs, Oskar learns to understand the city and with each step or newly acquitted neighborhood, tries to get closer to his father, who once told him that one's mark in life is not a question of "painting the *Mona Lisa* or curing cancer" but of "simply moving one gram of sand one millimeter" (86). In this exhausting process achieved by small steps he also gets closer to himself. Out of the fragments of the city he develops a personal map of the space his father used to live in. In order for Oskar to adopt this space as his own, he needs his own memories and experiences attached to it. The city then becomes a subjective concept dependent on his individual perception which is shaped by memory, dreams, legends and interpretations. It requires individual mapping in order to become bearable. At the same time the process of mapping the city constantly overlaps with Oskar's own life mapping and the process of identity formation. These two developments are intertwined. By inventing his own New York, Oskar becomes a different person. New York becomes a labyrinth of stories and places to discover in order for Oskar to understand what has happened.

Walking is an important practice in the city performed by people who shape it. Michel de Certeau wants to see the process of constant singular movement as a "space of enunciation" (98). Walking is the pedestrian's process of "appropriation of the topographical system," just as speaking is an appropriation of a language performed by its user or speaker. De Certeau compares walking in the city to linguistic formations; a city would not exist without pedestrians, without movement, just as language would not exist if people did not use it. Walkers decode urban structures and give them meaning. At the same time, according to de Certeau, "to walk is to lack a place. It is the indefinite process of being absent and in search of a proper" (103), which corresponds to Oskar's own motivations and state of mind. Moving makes the city a social experience. Names of places are an "impetus of movements" (de Certeau 103); they give meaning and direction to movement. These names can become ideas or tourist emblems; they "direct and decorate," which is significant in the case of establishing new places with new names that the events of 9/11 ultimately led to.

Just like other post–9/11 urban strollers, Oskar seeks solace in the city through movement. Unlike most of the other protagonists presented in this monograph though, Oskar always walks according to a precisely prepared plan. He is never aimless or lost. Unlike Julius in Teju Cole's *Open City*, Oskar never loses track of time and tries to keep control at all times, in an attempt to bring order back to an abruptly altered everyday life. Despite the desire for control and precise mapping of New York boroughs, Oskar's strolls, too, are intuitive and often exhausting, as he develops a subway-phobia and hardly ever takes trains. Through walking he creates personal paths within the city. Gradually Oskar claims the city for himself, changing unknown and frightening spaces to places of his own. He does not want to escape the city, like Rachel in O'Neill's *Netherland*, but rather seeks relief and emotional escape through the process of place making, by marking his life on the map of the metropolis.

Looking at the City from Above: The Empire State Building and the Symbolism of Skyscrapers

Oskar's New York is a place in which skyscrapers are similar to people; they are fragile and fearful and need "air bags" (160) that Oskar invents for them. He fears tall buildings and they become one of the objects he fantasizes about while obsessively inventing. In fact, the novel begins with an invention strongly linked to New York City's skyline:

So what about skyscrapers for dead people that were built down? They could be underneath the skyscrapers for living people that are built up. You could burry people one hundred floors down, and a whole dead world could be underneath the living one. Sometimes I think it would be weird if there were a skyscraper that moved up and down while its elevator stayed in place. So if you wanted to go to the ninety-fifth floor, you'd just press the 95 button and the ninety-fifth floor would come to you. Also, that could be extremely useful, because if you're on the ninety-fifth floor, and a plane hits below you, the building could take you to the ground, and everyone could be safe, even if you left your birdseed shirt at home that day [3].

It is only when Oskar discovers that one of the individuals called Black lives in the Empire State Building that he forces himself to go and visit her there, thereby overcoming his fear. Ruth Black and her life are so strongly connected to the building that they become synonymous—for Oskar she becomes the Empire State Building. She tells him lots of facts about the skyscraper while they stand on the observation deck and watch New York from above. She tells him that the building was made with materials "from just about everywhere but New York, in much the same way that the city itself was made great by immigrants" (248). Ruth also says that she knows so much about the building because she loves it (251). The fact that they too are actually lovable makes tall constructions less scary for Oskar.

According to Michel de Certeau, when seeing a city from above one becomes a spectator and can read in that city, "a universe that is constantly exploding" (91), a "stage of concrete, steel and glass, cut out between two oceans …, a *migrational*, or metaphorical, city thus slips into the clear text of the planned and readable" (93, emphasis original). For Oskar, New York City becomes not only more legible but also more bearable when viewed from above. The motif of looking at the post–9/11 city from above as an attempt to become closer to the tragedy of 9/11 is frequently exploited in post–9/11 fiction; in Frédéric Beigbeder's novel *Windows on the World* published in France in 2003 the narrator, based in Paris, writes from the Tower of Montparnasse. The height functions as a transatlantic bridge and brings him closer to New York City and to the victims locked in the World Trade Center towers. Another prominent example of a literal "elevation" of characters that is significant for the plot is Cole's *Open City* in which the sight of New York from a plane in the air changes Julius's perception of the metropolis.

Oskar too has the impression of becoming closer to his father and to the attacks of 9/11 when on top of the Empire State Building. Similarly to Julius in Cole's novel, he also feels like watching a model and losing sight of the "realness" of New York. At the same time the fact of being so far away from the city

which he is desperately trying to make sense of makes him feel very detached
and lonely:

> You can see the most beautiful things from the observation deck of the Empire
> State Building. I read somewhere that people on the street are supposed to look
> like ants, but that's not true. They look like little people. And the cars look like
> little cars. And even the buildings look little. It's like New York is a miniature
> replica of New York, which is nice, because you can see what it's really like, instead
> of how it feels when you're in the middle of it. It's extremely lonely up there, and
> you feel far away from everything [245].

Being so high up, Oskar comes to understand the temporality of all things,
including New York's architecture, which drawn by financial reasons makes it
impossible for a "regime of memory" that requires permanence to be established
(Zukin 15) as buildings have been built, rebuilt, torn down and replaced by
new once ever since. Oskar wants to see skyscrapers as people: "Everything
that's born has to die, which means our lives are like skyscrapers. The smoke
rises at different speeds, but they're all on fire, and we're all trapped" (245).
Subconsciously he feels the urge to preserve some of his own history inscribed
in the city. He keeps inventing things that would save the frightening but fragile
structures from dying and from disappearing:

> What about windmills in the roof of every skyscraper? What about a kite-string
> bracelet? A fishing-line bracelet? What if skyscrapers had roots? What if you had
> to water skyscrapers, and play classical music to them, and know if they like sun
> or shade? [323].

According to de Certeau, legends and memories tie people to places and
assign meaning to them. This meaning can be personal and/or collective. "Stories diversify, rumors totalize" (de Certeau 108) as they are private and often
remain local or secluded, while rumors are propagated by the media and are
omnipresent, making it impossible to escape. Rumors cover everything and
"gathered under the figure of the City, the masterword of an anonymous law,
the substitute for all proper names, they wipe out or combat any superstitions
guilty of still resisting the figure" (108). De Certeau calls memory an "anti-
museum"; it is not localizable and not exposable to others. Fragments of it come
out in legends, which assign meaning to places and which all flâneur figures in
post–9/11 fiction encounter and confront. Collective memory merges with the
one of an individual stroller to form a new perception and understanding of
the suddenly changed metropolis. Choosing a child protagonist for the post–
9/11 flâneur is a way of marking and communicating a genuine desire for cities
to be their own history and museums. Oskar's attitude is a demanding one: he
sees it as the city's duty to preserve the memory of individuals who contributed

to building, destroying and rebuilding it; the memory of his father and of his own urban quest.

Walking 2: Looking for One's Past, Memory as Anti–Museum

9/11 is the ultimate reason for Thomas Schell, Sr., to return to New York from Dresden, where he has lived after his wife became pregnant with Oskar's father and he felt too scared to become a parent. His entire life has played out in the two cities, Dresden and New York, each of which gave him shelter when he felt he had to escape the other one. This mirrors Oskar's image of birds being called from an opposite direction in order to be saved from the ultimate danger and also from themselves. After the loss of his love Anna in the bombing of Dresden, Thomas encounters Oskar's grandma, Anna's sister, in a New York café. They are brought together by shared grief and a history of survival, but not by love. The loss of Anna, pregnant at the time, makes Thomas's life a constant and tiresome retreat from people he is scared of hurting or who might hurt him. The events of September 11 force him to come back to New York and face his trauma again. His life is divided by tragedies of loss. His reactions are marked by his refusal to love, which he uses as a mechanism of a self-defense. He decides not to love in order not to be hurt. He also stops talking and communicates by writing or showing the words "yes" and "no" tattooed on his hands. The loss of the son he refused to have is no less painful; it becomes the longing for an abandoned love for which it is no longer possible to fight. He rediscovers his past by walking through the city and noticing changes, comparing it to his memories. He returns to something he escaped, to a relationship based on the common experience of survival, to a lack of love that is for him spatially linked to New York.

He recognizes the space and tries to contextualize himself within the transformed city, a process that reminds him of the time that has passed. These places are familiar yet strange, changed, with new functions and attributes, not always welcoming. The encounters with seemingly familiar shops, buildings and parks remind him of the gap of forty years that is not erasable. In fact, this is all the reader learns about the forty years between his times in New York which he spent in Dresden—these two cities function as two separate realities that do not overlap.

Dresden is not touched upon as a place significant for Thomas's perception of the new New York. It is a place symbolically meaningful for his past, associated with trauma, a spatial self-penalty that reminds Thomas Shell of all his losses on a daily basis. It also serves as a spatial frame that isolates his New York past in a form of an emotional vacuum. When back in New York, still refusing to speak, he writes about the process of remapping his own past in the city:

> I spent most of my days walking around the city, getting to know it again, I went to the old Columbian Bakery but it wasn't there anymore, in its place was a ninety-nine-cent store where everything cost more than ninety-nine cents. I went by the tailor shop where I used to get my pants taken in, but there was a bank, you needed a card just to open the door, I walked for hours, down one side of Broadway and up the other, where there had been a watch repairman there was a video store, where there had been a flower market there was a store for video games, where there had been a butcher there was sushi, what's sushi, and what happens to all of the broken watches? [278].

My general application and usage of the concepts[6] of "place" and "space" here follows Tim Cresswell's argument that a "place is a way of understanding the world" (*Place* 11). It is a personalized *space* shaped by memories, intertextual references and cultural knowledge. Furthermore, not only are places created "through social processes but [they] also fulfill an important array of social needs ...: identity, community, and security" (Chen 8). Places have different meanings according to the experience, age and expectations of people who explore and approach them.

Paradoxically, this clash of perceptions and associations with places within New York contributes to communication between Thomas Schell, Sr., and Oskar. These two traumatized individuals, two generations apart, walk the same grid of streets in search for new and old meanings. Both seek the sense of life after a great tragedy. Broadway has a different meaning for Thomas Schell looking for his lost past than it has for Oskar, who discovers the street and many other places for the first time. Confronting the city, Oskar's grandfather acknowledges the presence of various absences in his life. He has to cope with memories of places that no longer exist. For Oskar, many places mean something because his father referred to them in some way:

> As we drove, I imagined we were standing still and the world was coming toward us.... I saw the Trump Tower, which Dad thought was the ugliest building in America, and the United Nations, which Dad thought was incredibly beautiful [316].

In order to become independent from the overwhelming memories of his father, Oskar needs to explore these places on his own. This echoes the experience of Thomas Schell, Sr., who has to remap his memories of pre–9/11 New York. Unlike Oskar, he can only recall and refer to memories that are painfully connected to the wife he abandoned.

Oskar thinks about the city, its different boroughs, names, and places in between that do not belong to any borough and that do not exist on maps as such:

> When I was exactly halfway across the Fifty-ninth Street Bridge, I thought about how a millimeter behind me was Manhattan and a millimeter in front of me was Queens. So what's the name of the parts of New York—exactly halfway through the Midtown Tunnel, exactly halfway over the Brooklyn Bridge, the exact middle of the Staten Island Ferry when it's exactly halfway between Manhattan and Staten Island—that aren't in any borough? [88].

This concept of in-between places that are not recognized or acknowledged by others, but which Oskar sees and feels, relates closely to the notion of "Nothing Places" that Oskar's grandparents constructed in their shared apartment, in order to establish rules for living together. Nothing Places, just like places in-between, are fundamentally private; they allow an individual to "temporarily cease to exist" (110), to become invisible. As long as the apartment consisted of many Something Places and only one Nothing Place, the relationship was in a framework of rules that made it controllable; that made it function despite the lack of love. When Nothing Places started to dominate the common space, it became more and more difficult to live together and Thomas eventually escaped to Dresden.

The idea of Something and Nothing Places is a way of simplifying reality, as is the reduction of language to the words "yes" and "no" tattooed on Thomas Schell's hands. The attempt to control reality by establishing boundaries in communication and within the living space is motivated by traumatic experience and fear. This radical, minimalistic and seemingly efficient approach influences the perception of reality and narrows it down to what seems to be essential but in fact generates more difficult binaries, impossible to cross. Thomas Schell's reality becomes very narrow. Finding ways of liberation from the self-built borders of expression and perception turns out to be very difficult.

Alone in Dresden he writes letters to his unknown and unwanted son, which he "wasn't able to send to him while he was alive"[7] (268). The letters occupy a very prominent position in the novel. They constitute Thomas Schell, Sr.'s narration and the story of his life. Writing becomes an integral part of his lonely existence; a confession through which he tries to explain and justify to himself his decision to leave. All these letters are stored in a drawer in Oskar's grandma's apartment. The very end of the quest is marked not by finding the lock but by digging out Oskar's father's grave and placing the letters in the empty coffin. This heroic and symbolically liberating act is conducted by Oskar and his grandfather. When asked why, Oskar answers: "Because it's the truth, and Dad loved the truth. 'What truth?' 'That he's dead'" (321). The dramatic process of digging-up his father's grave at night is described by Oskar as an adventure—as a requiem to his quest that marks the end of searching, the end of mourning, the end of visiting different people called "Black." Oskar is surprised by how wet and empty the coffin is. Eventually he is relieved that his father is not under "all that dirt" (320), a weight so heavy that it has caused the coffin to crack, and finds solace in this discovery.

Foer's novel provides different scenarios of inventing and reinventing a city and makes it to the most important process in post–9/11 recovery of its protagonists. Two featured postmodern flâneur figures—one wearing the "mask" of a child, the other one of an old, emotionally broken man—map the city and project their sorrows, desires and grief on it. The places they make while walking through New York contribute to shaping of the post–9/11 urban reality and function as starting points for a life after September 11. Each of them through forming a new personal urban foundation approaches the other one and contributes towards a mutual understanding. In other words, the city becomes a basis and a tool for communication; a set of signs, a meta-language that remains when, while facing the unspeakable, other communication systems fail. The metropolis is what keeps the characters alive because it gives them a purpose to act and possibilities of expression. It also provides them, and consequently the fictional text these characters are constructions of, with a spectacular literary energy.

II

Metropolis as Source of Literary Energy: Teju Cole's *Open City*

I remembered a tourist who once asked me how he could get to 9/11:
not the site of the events of 9/11 but to 9/11 itself, the date petrified
into broken stones (Cole *Open City* 52).

Uncovering the Urban Subconscious

In Teju Cole's *Open City*, published in 2011, the metropolis is crucial for the plot as it encourages the narrator to tell his story, gives the story a structure and a direction. The novel is set around the very personal urban cartography of the main character–Julius. The extraordinary relation between him and New York City which, ten years later, still carries many traces of the attacks of 9/11, is a set of reciprocal influences, developments and racial provocations. Julius, originally from Nigeria, explores the city to gain an understanding of it but also to learn more about himself; to contemplate the nature of the past, the absence of people who were once important to him, and the inevitability of death which latently accompanies him during his walks. Walking is for him, among other aspects, a form of meditation; an exceptional physical and mental state. Wandering through the streets aimlessly and endlessly, he actively interferes with the metropolitan environment; and immediately becomes a part of it. New York on the other hand slowly "works itself into [his] life at walking pace" (3).

While walking through the streets of New York, the city reveals its history to Julius—the trained psychiatrist. The way he approaches the city reminds of psychoanalysis in classical Freudian sense. What Julius performs in the city is an analysis of the urban psycho—a deep, long, exhausting and emotional process for both sides involved, which functions as a commitment and as a bond between him and the city. The aim of the analysis is to understand 9/11 and the way it is inscribed in the city and becomes walkable as place. Jim Hopkins points to the importance of "mappings" in psychoanalysis which establish connections between the past and the present and between desires, dreams and memories attached to the timely dimensions. Julius maps the city through movement which as a form of mediation can also be considered "cognitive and metaphorical" to use Hopkins's phrasing in regards to the Freudian concept (16).[1] In analyzing the city, Julius follows his own free associations which combine unfiltered and unorganized thoughts, memories and impulses into a kaleidoscopic perspective. Freud describes this method as an analyst's device and suggests instructing the patient to "act as though [they were] a traveler sitting next to the window of a railway carriage [and were to describe] the changing views which they see outside" (135). Through random and fragmented uncovering of the different layers of the city's history, Julius himself in a chaotic trance of endless walking and associations, tries to approach the urban subconscious. While revealing itself to him, the city forces Julius to go through his own past—the process turns out to be not only intense but also addictive. The city's subconscious is its past and history—traces of which have been often hidden and expelled from the urban surface by each and every generation. The desire to understand 9/11 and how it became inscribed in the texture of New York and in fact of every city provides a motivation for reaching out to particular places which reveal their story, their political, economic and social meaning to the analyst.

This chapter demonstrates how walking reveals the city to the post–9/11 flâneur who while strolling through New York City, Brussels and the history of these places mixed with his own history, during one of his walks literally and symbolically enters 9/11. This revelation makes him understand how the place (Ground Zero) through a certain doubling upon itself became a metonymy of the day; of an emergency in general and of the disaster it came to symbolize. September 11, 2001, becomes located and inscribed into the map of New York City and symbolically into the meta-map of the global metropolis. It becomes walkable—a motif also prominently used in the 9/11 Museum in New York where visitors literally enter the day—September 11—through a revolving door and are led through it, minute by minute and step by step. Time becomes space and space is marked by time. Both, merged, are walkable.

Julius the Flâneur

Julius is a character who embodies the idea of changing the city through movement and specific urban behavior. While walking, he silently observes, makes mental notes and creates meanings which he then attaches to given urban spaces. He is a "passionate spectator" (Baudelaire 15), a philosopher and a psychoanalyst. Connecting his observations through associations and own memories, he tries to put together the broken parts of the urban body. He fills the gaps of the unknown with his own contexts and historical knowledge. The city poses a challenge to Julius and revealing its past step by step marks a progress in Julius's urban investigation and analysis.

In Teju Cole's novel the city is portrayed as a fragmented and constantly changing organism that ultimately becomes an inspiration for Julius, and the source of literary energy of the text. Remarkably, the post–9/11 metropolis in this novel, very specific in its characteristics and features, is also clearly a global city; it stretches way beyond its GPS data, it influences perception of other places and incorporates all other cities. Post–9/11 metropolis is hence a global space, impossible to escape or to sets limits to. As Julius wanders through New York, he understands that the post–9/11 city is no longer traceable on a map, as it trespasses all physical borders and lines. As a concept it is transnational and at the same time perceivable through senses, so individually tailored, read and interpreted.

Similarly to Oskar in Foer's *Extremely Loud and Incredibly Close*, Julius exercises an "appropriation of the topographical system" through walking (de Certeau 98) and at the same time he is constantly lacking a place. Moreover, walking is a solitary experience which paradoxically makes Julius separate from other people whom he observes but avoids personal contact with, very much unlike Oskar who claims the city by befriending people he meets during his quest. Moving makes the city for Julius a distant social experience but it enhances the feeling of loneliness. His evening walks, after a day spent at the hospital offer a form of an emotional asylum, although the city, wounded and vulnerable often appears to him as dangerous and aggressive. While walking, Julius forgets about time, does not feel hungry and often realizes very late that the distance to his apartment is no longer walkable. Then he returns by subway in which the closeness of other people paradoxically intensifies his solitude.

> Aboveground I was with thousands of others in their solitude, but in the subway, standing close to strangers, jostling them and being jostled by them for space and breathing room, all of us reenacting unacknowledged traumas, the solitude intensified [7].

Walking aboveground brings him into a state of contemplation and isolation while being surrounded by other individuals, traffic and urban noise. When spatially and sensually restricted by a subway train, the character feels like a bird in a cage: claustrophobic, uncomfortable and lonely in the collective lack of freedom; unable to listen to the city and its stories.

Before he starts following the desire to walk without a clear purpose or destination, Julius observes birds, and what he calls their natural immigration (4). "Not long before my aimless wandering began, I had fallen into the habit of watching bird migrations from my apartment, and I wonder now if the two are connected" (3–4). The motif of birds and other flying creatures overwhelmed by Manhattan and especially by its skyscrapers keeps reappearing in post–9/11 New York-based novels. It serves as an ultimate reference to the smallness and fragility of human beings, dominated and endangered by monstrous architectonic structures they themselves created, for instance birds in Foer's *Extremely Loud and Incredibly Close* or a firefly in Mohsin Hamid's *The Reluctant Fundamentalist*.

Similarly to the London-based neurosurgeon Henry Perowne in McEwan's *Saturday*, Julius connects the city to his work on the human brain and mind as he can never fully detach from his professional life and passion. Semantic connections in New York City operate on different levels, all of which are based on sings. The way in which they are linked and brought together establishes meaning and discourse.

The city perceived as an urban brain is a set of connections between urban neurons/actors transmitting meaning and operating within the system. Roland Barthes talks in this context about urban semiology and analyzes the city as a language, i.e., also a set of signs, through which connections and meanings are being established. Different parts of the city are connected to one another and to its inhabitants. Accordingly, the discursive aspect of a metropolis builds bridges between its different signs and actors, and generates meaning. This creation of meaning is an important part of the process of place-making and remapping, i.e., shifting the meaning within existing urban spaces.

> The city is a discourse and this discourse is truly a language: the city speaks, its inhabitants, we speak our city, the city where we are, simply by living in it, by wandering through it, by looking at it [Barthes 92].

Consequently, New York in *Open City* needs to be examined and explored in order to be understood and tamed, just like a language needs to be learned in order to be able to communicate within a given system. Walking, the repetitiveness of moves it involves, its rhythm, and the freedom it offers, function for Julius as a way of examination and analysis and, remarkably, also as a cure. Aimless wandering quickly becomes so much attached to his life that Julius cannot imagine living without it anymore. Walking is inscribed in his New York experience. It gives him the feeling of independence and of a certain control which he cannot do without:

> Every decision—where to turn left, how long to remain lost in thought in front of an abandoned building, whether to watch the sun set over New Jersey, or to lope in the shadows on the East Side looking across to Queens—was inconsequential, and was for that reason a reminder of freedom [7].

Walking is refreshing and soothing. The city responds and contributes to Julius's moods and in the form of mutual analysis brings him to different stories from his own past. The hidden twist or maybe even a form of a joke of this otherwise rather serious novel is the fact that Julius is a psychiatrist who does not speak to his mother.

Measuring Time through Space

The notion of time in this novel is attached to and defined by space. Walking through New York which stands for the present is an attempt at establishing a coherent and livable life cartography—a map which would give sense to all events and experience in the main character's life. Nigeria and carefree runs through Lagos symbolize the past, and Julius considers it a closed chapter of his life associated with childhood. But people, motives, stories and memories from Nigeria keep reappearing in Julius's New York life and connect these two spatial and temporal dimensions. The past that lies beyond tamed and appropriated places and people attached to them is very blurry and intangible:

> We experience life as a continuity, and only after it falls away, after it becomes the past, do we see its discontinuities. The past, if there is such a thing, is mostly empty space, great expanses of nothing, in which significant persons and events float. Nigeria was like that for me: mostly forgotten, except for those few things that I remembered with an outsize intensity. These were the things that had been solidified in my mind by reiteration, that recurred in dreams and daily thoughts: certain faces, certain conversations, which, taken as a group, represented a secure version of the past that I had been constructing since 1992. But there was another, irruptive, sense of things past. The sudden reencounter, in the present, of something or someone long forgotten, some part of myself I had relegated to childhood and to Africa [155–156].

These different spaces perceived sensually have their smells, tastes, sounds and unique atmospheres which in memories become attached to specific events. Once recalled through one of the senses, the memories of these places stand for something very complex and unique. Nigeria is the taste of Coca Cola which as all good things in Julius's childhood has been rationed (132). Other children believed that drinking it would make their skin darker and so refrained from doing so. For young Julius the meaning of his skin color is abstract. He likes Coca-Cola because it tastes like nothing else in the world and becoming darker is the least of his worries (132). Later on in his New York life, his skin color begins to matter.

In the novel it is significant and important that Julius, the first person narrator, is a black man. Race and gender are crucial for the urban setting of the novel—they signify and have their unique, New York-specific meaning. The skin color alone makes Julius involuntarily enter a community of "brothers," young black men, who without knowing each other, recognize the ethnic otherness they are marked with and use it as bonding. They beckon or briefly greet one another on the streets as if they all knew each other although in fact they do not. This community-like experience of being a black man in New York in *Open City* is based on assumed preconditioned common legacy of oppression; it indicates responsibility and features exclusiveness. It is nothing formal or outspoken; it is rather a form of a race and gender-based "club," a parallel society based on exclusion; a city within the city. One belongs to it because of one's gender and skin color and it is impossible to quit it because of exactly these very reasons.

> There had earlier been, it occurred to me, only the most tenuous of connections between us, looks on a street corner by strangers, a gesture of mutual respect based on our being young, black, male; based, in other words, on our being *brothers*. These glances were exchanged between black men all over the city every minute of the day, a quick solidarity worked into the weave of each man's mundane pursuits, a nod or smile or quick greeting. It was a little way of saying, I know something of what life is like for you out here [212].

Sharing the fate of being black in New York and the symbolic experience of survival inscribed into it are enough to start a conversation, or to potentially become close or emotional. This happens to Julius once in a cab when the cabdriver is furious because Julius has not greeted him like a "brother" and once at a bar when Kenneth, a black museum guard, recognizes him. Basing his argument on the fact that both of them are African, he positions himself in opposition to Americans, most of whom "don't know anyplace other than what's right in front of their noses" (53). The inescapable requirement to fully submit to the community of "brothers" overwhelms Julius who feels obliged to apologize to Kenneth before he leaves. The bar is in downtown Manhattan, close to the ruins of the World Trade Center and the Hudson. Julius, confused and lost in thought decides to walk towards the water and reflects on the strange phenomenon of a city based on an island that turns away from the water surrounding it.

The machinery of freely drifting thoughts and links sets in motion and Julius recovers from the ambiguity of the "brotherly" encounter. "Everything was built up, in concrete and stone, and the millions who lived on the tiny interior had scant sense about what flowed around them. The water was a kind of embarrassing secret, the unloved daughter, neglected, while the parks were doted on, fussed over, overused" (54). In order to calm down after the confusing encounter, Julius subconsciously returns to associating freely. The process starts with looking at Ellis Island. The symbolic place for the mostly European refugees brings him back to the specific nature of the racial solidarity he is being exposed to. "Blacks, we blacks, had known rougher ports of entry" (55). Julius realizes that this historical experience which they have been marked with generations earlier, functions as a basis of mandatory acknowledgment between all of the "brothers" within the geographical limits of the metropolis. Then again his thoughts float away to other loosely related issues.

Ethnic Identity versus Anonymity in the Metropolitan Context

The obliging, seemingly concerned and care-taking environment of "brothers" turns out to be dangerous and self-destructive. One evening Julius, walking in the darkness in Harlem on 124th Street toward Morningside Park is attacked by a group of young black men, beaten heavily and robbed. Back home, Julius reflects upon all the clichés associated with black people in the U.S. and this fills him with disgust and bitterness:

> Then the campus police, who would put up a sign by the elevator announcing (as so often before, in all the previous instances when I wasn't the victim) that someone had recently been attacked in the neighborhood, and that the suspects were male, black, and young, of average height and weight [214].

The disturbing issue here is the fact that Julius himself could match the description of his attackers. The community of "brothers" has betrayed him but at the same time it has betrayed itself. Equally unsettling is the fact that Julius cannot simply quit the community.

The incident brings him to the subject of praying which in his understanding is placed not far from regular and concentrated city walking. After he returns home, he watches his neighbor pray through the window and admits to himself that he too, sometimes prays. The act itself, its mysticism and intimacy seem more important that the reason or beliefs behind it. Praying in this novel is a way of formulating thoughts and acknowledging desires and dreams. "Prayer was, I had long settled in my mind, no kind of promise, no device for getting what one wanted out of life; it was the mere practice of presence, that was all, a therapy of being present, of giving a name to the heart's desires, the fully formed ones, the as yet formless ones" (215). Endless and repetitive wandering through the streets is then a form of urban prayer and of worshipping the city.

The novel suggests that this experience of urban violence is too a part of a New York life. Julius does not mention this experience again in his narrative and blocks it in the depths of his mind; they remain unavailable, even for free association. The text signals the frequency of violent acts in the city when placing the main character among colleagues who have already been mugged in New York. This aspect of the metropolis comes across as a taboo in the cosmos of a passionate analyst but also belongs to its subconscious.

At a later point in the novel, after Julius's return from Europe, another "brother" starts a conversation with him, a much longer one that Julius would appreciate. It is a post office worker who introduces himself as a poet and writer and who asks Julius where he was from. He refers to Africa as the "motherland" and to Julius as a messenger of old values (185). Despite the undoubtedly good intentions of the speaker, Julius immediately develops a reaction of annoyance placed dangerously close to aggression. Stigmatized by the previous experience of violence, he starts to avoid black men in New York.

A denial of a group one forcefully and pre-conditionally belongs to (due to nationality, gender, skin color, mother tongue, etc.) is an experience that can lead to an identity crisis. Being unable to escape this issue within New York, Julius escapes entirely and goes to Brussels for several weeks. The European urban time is marked by different historical experience and different collective memory. It is free from the "brotherly" obligation of acknowledgment and functions as an antidote to New York.

Brussels versus New York: The Dual Urban Setting

As in many post–9/11 city novels, also here the spatial frame spans two urban settings—one of which is supposed to function as an antidote to the other one.[2] New York is linked to Brussels where the main character goes to look for his grandmother and indirectly for his own past. The city serves as a complimentary component to understanding the urban space as such. Brussels is the title *open city*—a term which derives from its status during the Second World War and which symbolizes its experience of surrender in order to survive. "Had Brussels's rulers not opted to declare it an open city and thereby exempt it from bombardment …, it might have been reduced to rubble. It might have been another Dresden" (97). The city opens Julius to new experiences of belonging and provides him with a new attitude with which he returns to the U.S. New York in this novel stands for seriousness; it is about lost love, death, destruction and pain. Brussels is serenity; it offers rest and peace with which Julius returns to New York changed; he is longing for the city and returns feeling more American than ever before. Setting the novel in two cities is also a means to show that the post–9/11 metropolis is a global space that stretches way beyond the geographical limits of New York City. In fact, every metropolis is marked by traces of 9/11, the novel suggests.

The "peculiar European oldness" (97) and traces of world history he encounters in the Belgian capital, give his walks a different significance. Walking in New York has been soothing for his freshly broken heart and has made him reevaluate different stages of his past attached to different places. In New York he develops a desire to search for his grandmother whom he has lost contact with many years before and who supposedly lives in Brussels. She becomes the ultimate reason for Julius to go. Pursuing the goal of finding his "oma" turns out to be a utopian idea and Julius ends up walking aimlessly again. The main character wants to see Brussels as an antidote to New York. It is filled with his grandmother's latent (or imaginary) presence.

> Every now and again, looking into the faces of the women huddled at the tram stops, I imagined that one of them might be my oma. It was a possibility that has come to me each time I was out in the city, that I might see her, that I might be tracing paths she had followed for years, that she might indeed be one of the old women with their orthopedic shoes and crinkly shopping bags, wondering from time to time how her only daughter's son was doing [115].

Julius continues walking and spends a lot of time on his own but he is more open and susceptible to other people. The city is marked by random encounters which together reshape Julius's perspective on New York. He spends four weeks in Brussels and remains a tourist; he does not attempt to make this city his home or to map it with meaning or emotions. Brussels is free of commitments and so are the mentioned encounters. Without a plan and with the original reason of going to Belgium turning into just an excuse, he wanders aimlessly, but this time, unlike in New York, he is not searching for solitude.

When a young Muslim man in a conversation with Julius does not deny supporting Hamas and Hezbollah, an important mechanism sets into motion. The novel shows how geographical distance from a given place and culture empowers the notion of belonging. It is only when confronted with anti–American sentiments coming from and while being outside of the country that the protagonist starts feeling geographically attached to New York. He experiences a notion of belonging to the city and at this moment identifies with what it stands for, despite the fact of not being American. When Julius provocatively asks his conversation partner about Al-Qaeda, he replies:

> Let me tell you a story from our tradition, a story about King Solomon. King Solomon gave a teaching once about the snake and the bee. The snake, King Solomon said, defends itself by killing. But the bee defends itself by dying. You know how a bee dies after a sting? Like that. It dies to defend. So each creature

has a method that is suitable to its strength. I don't agree with what Al-Qaeda did, they use a method I would not use, so I cannot say the word support. But I don't cast a judgment on them [121].

The statement makes Julius feel sad rather than angry, more than he would have expected or wanted to (120). Remarkably, while in Brussels he identifies as an American more than he does in New York.

Another random encounter which leads to discovering new facets about the self is marked by casual sex and anonymity. Julius introduces himself as Jeff, an accountant from New York—in other words, he wears a mask which grants him a random identity. The woman in her fifties whom he meets at a café tells him her name but he forgets it immediately and somewhat programmatically. They never see each other again but this experience becomes attached to Brussels in Julius's memory and opens a previously blocked aspect of his life. Consequently, his return to New York marks the beginning of the second and last part of the novel entitled "I have searched myself" and giving an end to "Death is a perfection of the eye." Finding a balance in the urban cosmos requires a second pole, an input from outside. Being elsewhere opens new perspectives and provides the post-modern flâneur with global knowledge necessary to make sense of the interconnected and interdependent post–9/11 metropolis.

Traces of 9/11

While descending for New York after a month in Brussels, Julius, still on the plane, recognizes the city immediately but associates it not with New York itself but with a memory of a model built for the World Exhibition of 1964 he has once seen in the Queens Museum of Art. The real urban space in this moment comes to represent the representation of itself which in consequence makes it less real. The city matches the model, not the other way round. It appears familiar to Julius but seems more abstract than the city he has encountered and explored while walking. He recalls the day he has first seen the panorama. The following quote indicates one important feature of it: it needs to be updated regularly in order to keep up with the changing city and so the model has been worked on since 1964 to mirror urban developments of the metropolis:

On the day I had seen the Panorama, I had been impressed by the many fine details it presented: the rivulets of roads snaking across a velvety Central Park, the boomerang of the Bronx curving up to the north, the elegant beige spire of the Empire State Building, the white tablets of the Brooklyn piers, and the pair of gray blocks on the southern tip of Manhattan, each about a foot high, representing the persistence, in the model, of the World Trade Center towers, which, in reality, had already been destroyed [151].

In the case of 9/11 this means a capacity of stopping time and freezing the city in its innocence, openness, serenity and natural exposure from before the attacks. It is the presence of the Towers in the model that marks a symbolic rupture and not their absence in the real city. The fact that they are still there is unsettling because it does not correspond to the notion of reality. The World Trade Center towers have become a symbol of their own destruction, of the horrors of 9/11—seeing them again in Manhattan is uncanny rather than evoking sentiments. The model represents the old pre–9/11 New York that Julius has in fact never known, but which was regularly updated to match reality and is yet frozen in time. Having the impression of approaching the model, Julius subconsciously keeps looking for the Towers.

The metropolis Julius walks through is, almost a decade later, still marked with the wounds and pain of September 11. He is being confronted with different aspects of the 9/11-related urban reality. The new space that emerged out of the destruction of the Twin Towers—the new Ground Zero[3]—together with the date used in order to refer to the attacks become in Cole's novel the urban metonymy of the disaster:

> The place has become a metonym of its disaster: I remembered a tourist who once asked me how he could get to 9/11: not the site of the events of 9/11 but to 9/11 itself, the date petrified into broken stones [52].

9/11 localized on the city's map and symbolically inscribed in it becomes a place and can as such be approached in spatial terms. It can be walked and rewalked, written and rewritten, claimed and reclaimed but as the novel suggests, it cannot disappear as it is "petrified" into the very core of the city.

Julius, who is confronted with death at work in the hospital, who treats depressed and emotionally lost people, walks through New York to recover. The city is full of life and energy, but there also is death in the Manhattan air. Skyscrapers which are meant to symbolize power and progress become dangerous structures that make people who are locked in them vulnerable and helpless. It strikes the narrator that no bodies were visible on September 11, except of the falling ones, the ones liberating themselves out of the cages, the "sarcophagi of concrete and steel" (Baudrillard 45) to death. Atrocity is nothing new, says Julius but "the difference is that in our time it is uniquely well-organized, carried out with pens, train carriages, ledgers, barbed wire" (58). Lacking bodies is its new component.

Regular conversations with Dr. Saito, an old teacher, whom Julius visits, contribute to the understanding of time, past and death. Saito is the oldest man

Julius knows (9) and Julius becomes a regular listener of his monologues. Dr. Saito is dying alone surrounded by the lively metropolis full of people and urban noises which enter his Manhattan apartment every day. This bothers Julius who starts noticing the presence of death in the vibrant city regularly. Once he hears music played by a brass orchestra that passes him by and continues walking interfering with the city noise. The music evokes memories connected to Nigeria and becomes a strong emotional experience for Julius, for whom in this moment the past, the present and all places attached to them become one—a unified blurred and infinite sequence of reflections. To live means to struggle for the notion of the original which is difficult as motifs keep reappearing and no place can guarantee a uniqueness of experience:

> Whether it expressed some civic pride or solemnized a funeral I could not tell, but so closely did the melody match my memory of those boyhood morning assemblies that I experienced the sudden disorientation and bliss of one who, in a stately old house and at a great distance from its mirrored wall, could clearly see the world doubled in on itself. I could no longer tell where the tangible universe ended and the reflected one began. This point-for-point imitation, of each porcelain vase, of each dull spot of shine on each stained teak chair, extended as far as where my reversed self had, at that precise moment, begun to tussle with the same problem as its equally confused original. To be alive, it seemed to me, as I stood there in all kinds of sorrow, was to be both original and reflection, and to be dead was to be split off, to be reflection alone [192].

Julius, who is interested in history, thinks about all the transnational memories and experiences of cruelty and bloodshed. He thinks of 19th century Europe, West Africa and the United States and comes to the conclusion that Western societies in 21st century, spoiled by the secure environment they created, are the first ones in the history of mankind who are completely unprepared for disaster (200). Omnipresent security results in vulnerability, lack of memory and a notion of exceptionalism and superiority which combined can be fatal.

> For us, the concept of three million New Yorkers dead from illness within the first five years of the millennium is impossible to grasp. We think it would be total dystopia; so we think of such historical realities only as footnotes. We try to forget that other cities in other times have seen worse, that there isn't anything that immunizes us from a plague of one kind or another, that we are just as susceptible as any of those past civilizations were, but we are especially unready for it. Even in the way we speak about what little has happened to us, we have already exhausted ourselves with hyperbole [201].

Pointing to the repetitiveness of history, emotions and fears which, as the novel suggests, is consequently ignored by politics, media and individuals overwhelmed with the amount of information, is a form of a strong social criticism.

The analysis of the city's subconscious conducted by the main character shows that much effort has been done in depriving the city from resourceful memory.

Julius the Historian

During his walks through New York and Brussels and those imaginary ones through Nigeria, Julius provides the readers—his imaginary audience—with historical facts about the places he visits. The links between world's history and his personal life story inscribed to particular historical circumstances of the era he happens to live in, preoccupy and concern him. The cities and their histories that Julius encounters during his walks are linked to the present; they provide reasons and explanations for various processes. Similarly to the Benjaminian "Angel of History," Julius cannot stop seeing the past in the presence and future. He "records the constellation in which his own epoch comes into contact with that of an earlier one … and establishes a concept of the present as that of the here-and-now, in which splinters of messianic time are shot through" (*On the Concept of History* VI). In other words, he succeeds at something impossible for individuals rooted in space and time: he sees the city with all the dreams, projects, plans, successes and failures of all the generations, from first settlers and their New Amsterdam to the 21st century with its fears and obsessions of securitization invading the urban spaces. This is the moment in the text in which the protagonist approaches the urban subconscious.

In the process of projecting all of the timely dimensions at the same time, the city, despite efforts of removing all debris of history from within its geographical limits, becomes its own museum and to a certain degree also its own ruin; a living testimony of buildings replacing other buildings. Julius the chronicler recounts his encounters and impressions that emerge out of the confrontation with the urban spaces. In his walks history reveals itself in the presence— "wreckage upon wreckage" (Benjamin)—the concealments of the city's history become visible. They overlap with memories of people and stories linked to other places. When one of his friends from Nigeria suddenly appears in his New York life and tells him a story from their common past, Julius refuses to remember it. She tells him that when they were teenagers at a party hosted by her brother, he has forced himself on her. Julius does not comment on this; in fact, the story does not seem to evoke any feelings in him, no scrutiny or guilt. Also here, by not acknowledging the story flashing back at him from the past, he behaves similarly to the historian in Benjamin's work. "To articulate what is past does not mean to recognize *how it really was*. It means to take control of a memory, as it flashes in a moment of danger" (*On the Concept of History* VI, emphasis mine). Julius does not return to the story, nor does he direct his analytical eye of a city stroller, archivist, passionate historian and psychiatrist towards its meaning or importance. Instead he turns into some very remote divagation about Nitzsche changing the subject entirely.

The city as such and the two particular ones in which the action of the novel takes place—New York and Brussels are the beginning, the center of, and the answer to everything that happens in the plot. They embody world history and come to form and symbolize different stages of the life of an individual—the literary protagonist whose personal life cartography is shaped by city maps and urban spaces. His life, divided into phases marked by the presence or absence of particular people is being contextualized through the cities and urban experiences he is confronted with. Elements and motifs from his childhood in Lagos, Nigeria reappear in his adult life in New York and often find reflection in Brussels connecting these seemingly remote places with one another.

The metropolis in Cole's novel is a powerful body, an extraordinary social phenomenon and space which even if destroyed, wounded, or dangerous can provide a solution, generate energy. Its streets are soothing and walking through them is a form of a mutual therapy for both: Julius, the main character and New York itself. Brussels functions temporarily as an antidote; Julius recovers there. Lagos attached to the carefree childhood and marked by racial innocence will be reflected in any city to which Julius decides to go and its memories will contribute to each new urban experience.

Finding strength and solace in walking through the city and unraveling the different layers of its urban memory and subconscious makes the city the source of creative and artistic potential and energy for Julius—the analyst. It reconnects him with the modern figure of the artist-flâneur, the lonely observer among crowds. This shows a continuity of the motif in post–9/11 city fiction that reflects and represents the altered, traumatized urban space which requires remapping so that its new cartography can be adjusted to match reality.

Many characters[4] in post–9/11 city novels undergo the process of taming a city in order to make it livable in the changed reality. In other words: remapping the city is a way of restructuring their lives, reestablishing their personal cartographies. In Cole's novel this process is symbolically addressed through the confusion over a reverse reflection of a city model from the 1964's World Exhibition in "real" New York. It is no longer clear what is real and what is its potential reflection; where does reality end and representation begin. The one seems to be as easily destroyable as the other. This corresponds to the confusion that the attacks of September 11 and their medially staged character evoked. The traces of the destruction of that day are visible only in the real city, i.e., its artistic reflections need to be adjusted to its new post–9/11 cartography. Teju

Cole's novel features a character who as artist-flâneur tries to adjust his reflexive eye and in fact the novel itself is an attempt at an adjusted reflection of the changed city. The ability to adjust lies, as Cole seems to suggest, in the timely distance from 9/11.

The following chapter discusses two novels set in closer proximity to September 11. In both of them the characters in order to cope with the events of 9/11 and with the altered urban space eventually escape New York permanently to look for different means to see the city from outside.

III

The Ambiguity of the
Other in Mohsin Hamid's
The Reluctant Fundamentalist
and H.M. Naqvi's *Home Boy*

This chapter is devoted to two literary responses that explore perspectives on post–9/11 New York City from the position of the Other: Mohsin Hamid's *The Reluctant Fundamentalist* and H.M. Naqvi's *Home Boy*. They belong to the category defined by Birgit Däwes as "ethnic responses" (Däwes *Ground Zero Fiction* 410), many of which have gone largely unnoticed and been excluded from the post–9/11 literary canon; more so in this particular setting in the case of the latter novel. They present non-Caucasian American, non-Western, Muslim perspectives on the September 11 attacks. Both of the texts are strongly linked to New York City and therefore of great relevance to this study.

The novels often use non-Western spatial and intertextual references and as such contribute an important perspective on perceiving, understanding, remapping and inhabiting the multicultural post–9/11 Western metropolis. Together with O'Neill's *Netherland*, Cole's *Open City* and Ali's *Brick Lane*, the texts feature characters foreign to their urban settings, whose approaches and cultural knowledge are made rich and engaging precisely because they do not formally belong. As Richard Sennett points out, the foreigner is more than "the most threatening figure in the theater of society"; through their ability to question that society's rules, "the foreigner may also gain another knowledge through his or her own exile, denied to those who remain rooted to home" (Sennett "The Foreigner" 191). Their experience of displacement gives these characters new insights to the city which post–9/11 fiction provides space for. Both novels feature plots focused on the time in New York between arrival and departure—the experience of urban space is therefore limited by time, which in both cases is linked to the events of September 11. This triggers the need of storytelling, the need to preserve the memory of a space within a given time.

Both Hamid's and Naqvi's novels feature other places and use the spatial dimension to address post–9/11 "othering" and the East-West dichotomy. In *The Reluctant Fundamentalist* Hamid divides the tension between New York and Lahore, and in *Home Boy* Karachi constitutes the "other" place. These cities serve as synecdoches for the societies and cultures they are placed within and thereby relate to different levels of the dichotomous reality.

In Love with (Am)Erica: Dramatic Encounters with the Past in Mohsin Hamid's *The Reluctant Fundamentalist*

Published in 2007 and written by the Lahore born Pakistani writer Mohsin Hamid, *The Reluctant Fundamentalist*, takes the form of a dramatic monologue.[1] Accordingly, it is entirely narrated in the first person by Changez, a Pakistani native, and addressed to an American man visiting Lahore who has agreed to have dinner with the narrator. These two men become symbolic agents of the opposites in the highly problematic "us versus them" or "the West versus the rest" post–9/11 dichotomy. As the narration progresses it becomes clear that these figures transcend any representation of real individuals. Hamid's addresses this religious, cultural and political binary by constructing his protagonists as meta-allegorical figures representing both sides. This creates a possibly divided readership, as each position is made plausible and potentially identifiable with.

Changez, who announces himself as a lover of America on the very first page of the novel, tells the newly arrived stranger the story of his life in the United States. He establishes a narrative distance between the person he is in the story he is telling and his new present self in Lahore. His tale is narrated chronologically and shows him as a young, talented and ambitious student at Princeton who is well received by his mostly white American peers. He is known for his hard work, politeness, and a British accent that is considered sophisticated and associated with the affluent upper class. However, he is on a scholarship and holds three on campus jobs in unpopular locations (12) in order to afford his stay at Princeton and to avoid witnesses to his financial struggle. The microcosm of the university campus is the first face of the United States that Changez encounters. He is surprised by the fake Gothic architecture and artificial oldness that suggest a past that has never been: "When I first arrived, I looked around me at the Gothic buildings—younger, I later learned, than many of the mosques of this city [Lahore], but made through acid treatment and ingenious stonemasonry to look older" (3).

Princeton is portrayed as the quintessence of artificiality, a vacuum bubble for the privileged. In Changez's story the university also becomes gendered, as America does later on, but with a clearly negative connotation: "Every year,

Princeton raised her skirt for the corporate recruiters and ... showed them some skin" (5). University life gives Changez a sense of competitiveness and self-esteem; it makes him feel confident of getting any job he wants. After a highly selective recruitment process, he begins a professional career in a management consultancy immediately after graduating, which fills him with pride and satisfaction: "I was in my own eyes, a veritable James Bond—only younger, darker, and possibly better paid" (73). According to Anna Hartnell, the management consultancy called Underwood Samson, and abbreviated U.S., reflects American state power and represents its "pragmatic face" (Hartnell 340). The company propagates the philosophy of sticking to its money-driven "fundamentals," something that Changez becomes reluctant to after 9/11.

As in O'Neill's *Netherland*, DeLillo's *Falling Man* and many other post–9/11 novels, the spatial setting of *The Reluctant Fundamentalist* is manifold: in the monologue of the one evening on which the men meet, New York is considered from Lahore, Pakistan. The retrospective narrative makes the geographical scope of this novel extraordinarily wide, and embraces locations on different continents. It includes a vacation in Greece, business travels to Manila in the Philippines and Valparaiso in Chile. Their incorporation into the story provides a better understanding of the global situation and Changez's position within it. All of the places play an important role, by marking the shifts and changes in either the symbolic world order or in Changez's perception of it. Geographical distance encourages and supports emotional remoteness by assigning some clarity to the past. These places function as catalysts for change and are always connected to particular people who contribute to this process. The retrospective is embedded in what the reader is presented with as the present. The spatial distance enables Changez to talk about the past but it does not deprive him of sentiment.

Telling the story to an American stranger, whose intentions are unclear, makes Changez recapitulate his past relationships with New York and (Am)Erica—the country and the woman that merge in his narrative into one extraordinary hybrid—the love of his young life that has abandoned him and broken his heart. In his story, (Am)Erica hates to be alone and rarely is. She attracts people to her and rivets their attention. Her presence is marked with "an uncommon *magnetism*" (24, emphasis original); she is a "lioness: strong, sleek, and invariably surrounded by her pride" (24). She has great beauty to which Changez is extremely sensitive—a mechanism that he uses to point to severe cultural differences: "It is remarkable, I must say, how being in Pakistan heightens one's sensitivity to the sight of a woman's body" (29). (Am)Erica's white female body appears as exotically attractive and Changez's fascination with it comes across as a reverse colonial gaze, pointing to the perpetual reciprocity of cultural influence.

After 9/11 Erica is overwhelmed with a reoccurring nostalgia and memories of her deceased boyfriend Chris. She falls into a depression that leaves Changez helpless. His one-sided love for Erica mirrors his fascination with the U.S. and the disappointment brought by the radical shift after 9/11. To Changez the country is clearly gendered, and his feelings towards it are as tempestuous as they are towards the woman he loves. Changez admits that a part of him has been left in the U.S. when he talks about Erica: "[I] lost something of myself to her that I was unable to relocate in the city of my birth" (195). Although when talking to his listener he refers to America as "your country," part of him clearly belongs there—to what after 9/11 has become the "other" side which he has decided to escape. The way Changez reflects on world politics and his own changing attitude towards it suggests that more time has passed than it in fact has. When at the end of the novel he reveals his age—twenty-five, it comes as a surprise. His New York past is not so remote after all.

Throughout the novel Changez refers to himself first as an "exotic acquaintance" for his Princeton friends (19), then as a "Western-educated urbanite" (61) equipped with a "Third-World sensibility" (77) and also as an "emotional madman." He reflects on his narrative and on (hi)story-telling as such:

> [T]o be honest, I cannot now recall many of the details of the events I have been relating to you. But surely it is the *gist* that matters; I am, after all, telling you a history, and in history, as I suspect you—an American—will agree, it is the thrust of one's narrative that counts, not the accuracy of one's details [135].

Saying this, the fictional character touches upon the nature of historiographic metafiction, in which fictional characters are surrounded by real world events, and reality and fiction constantly reflect and complement one another. The dramatic monologue form creates an unreliable situation: the narrator misjudges himself, addresses his own confusion and questions his own decisions and motives. However, as Alan Sinfield points out, in a dramatic monologue "to comprehend even the simplest factors of time and place we must look through the speaker's eyes and enter his mind, and this requires an exercise in sympathy which influences our attitude to him" (Sinfield 8). Although Changez undermines his own narrative authority and thereby his credibility, his emotional struggle with himself maintains the reader's sympathy. In these circumstances the question of reliability does not seem prominent, as it is the *gist* that matters.

From Lahore to New York City and Back: Cities as Synecdoches of Cultures and Societies

The cities in *The Reluctant Fundamentalist* provide unique lenses through which the political, social and cultural dynamics in the post–9/11 world are seen and addressed. New York and Lahore form a transnational axis in which the story is set and through which the narrator controls the narrative. Changez talks to his silent listener about his family and his hometown Lahore, using transnational references to make the spatial dimensions and meanings understandable for the American. He always tries to put them into perspective and to thereby show his erudition, at times infantilizing or embarrassing the listener:

> Our situation is, perhaps, not so different from that of the old European aristocracy in the nineteenth century, confronted by the ascendance of the bourgeoisie. Except, of course, that we are part of a broader malaise afflicting not only the formerly rich but much of the formerly middle-class as well: a growing inability to purchase what we previously could [12].

When talking about Lahore and Pakistan's socioeconomic situation, Changez becomes bitter and reproachful. With eyes trained at Princeton and at Underwood Samson, he sees the tremendous unfairness of the fate his country has to suffer. He feels personally betrayed by American political action and more generally by everything America embodies. He reflects upon Pakistan's long history of constant occupation and suffering that America lacks. Lahore, the "ancient capital of the Punjab, home to nearly as many people as New York, layered like a sedimentary plain with the accreted history of invaders from the Aryans to the Mongols to the British" (8).

He describes many similarities between the two cities, both of which he feels emotionally attached to. Lahore and New York—cities which represent two binary poles in the post–9/11 discourse of dichotomies, have, in Changez's description, a lot in common. This elevates them to an urban meta-level, beyond the notion of countries and nations. Both have parts that are walkable, i.e., pedestrian-friendly and those "degrading man on foot"—parts that favor of people in cars. Changez refers in this context to "urban democracy" of places in the first category in which everybody can become a part of the crowd, and its lack in older parts of Lahore. An immediate reference to Manhattan follows:

> You will have noticed that the newer districts of Lahore are poorly suited to the needs of those who must walk. In their spaciousness—with their public parks and wide, tree-lined boulevards—they enforce an ancient hierarchy that comes to us from the countryside: the superiority of the mounted man over the man on foot. But here, where we sit…. Lahore is more democratically *urban*. Indeed, in these places it is the man with four wheels who is forced to dismount and become part of the crowd. Like Manhattan? Yes, precisely! And that was one of the reasons why for me moving to New York felt—so unexpectedly—like coming home [36].

New York and Lahore—the two antipodes of the novel's dual urban setting are connected and interlinked. The one finds reflection in and reflects the other. Many of the arguments brought up by Changez gain strength precisely through comparison with the other city or the condition of the country in general. Changez is a lover of urban space and life. He understands cities and the processes that occur in them. Knowing both New York and Lahore gives him the potential not only to compare, but also to see each place through the lens of the other. Visiting New York for the first time, Changez realizes he had been familiar with the metropolis even before his arrival. He has known it through cultural, mostly filmic representations:

> Seventy-Seventh Street, in the heart of the Upper East Side. This area—with its charming bistros, exclusive shops and attractive women in short skirts walking tiny dogs—felt surprisingly familiar, although I have never been there before; I realized later that I owed my sense of familiarity to the many films that have used it as a setting [56].

Fictional, filmic or artistic depictions of New York not only reflect the city but also create its primary image, *make it* what it is, and preserve the memory of buildings, streets, squares, parks and other urban places which in reality keep changing. Literature and film function then as photo albums do, as chronicles of memory, collecting images and stories attached to particular places. Changez is conscious of the unique character of the different urban spaces that surround him and lives the metropolitan life of a "successful urban dweller" (72). When the outdoor area of the Lahore restaurant empties, he reflects on the power of emptiness in big cities designed for the presence of crowds. Solitude in this context is literarily out of place, and becomes a disturbing factor: "The fact that we are all but alone despite being in the heart of a city" (176). The city does not only have a heart but it also has lungs with which it breathes. In Changez's story, New York becomes a beautiful body, pulsing with life and energy.

> It was one of those glorious late-July afternoons in New York when a stiff wind off the Atlantic makes the trees swell and the clouds race across the sky. You know them well? Yes, precisely: the humidity vanishes as the city fills its lungs with cooler, briny air [67].

It is a city of possibility filled with "magical vibrancy and sense of excitement" (179). Changez's perspective on New York evolves from a fascinated stranger to a New Yorker who, eventually, feeling betrayed and used, chooses to abandon the city. This progression is visible in the retrospective narrative. When Erica shows Changez parts of Manhattan, he refers to New York as Erica's city (129). Erica lives in a fancy apartment on the Upper East Side, and her spacious bedroom is, according to Changez, "the socioeconomic equivalent of a spacious bedroom in a prestigious house in Gulberg" (58) where he grew up. When they lose contact, New York becomes Changez's only faithful companion. When he cannot sleep at nights it is the city that enters through his windows (128) and joins him in his loneliness and sudden detachment. When things fall apart with Erica, Changez seeks comfort in the city. During his walking hours he revisits the places attached to memory of Erica, in order to be closer to her. This process echoes the remapping and re-establishment of the urban context by Jonathan Safran Foer's protagonist Oskar in *Extremely Loud and Incredibly Close*, who begins a quest for traces of his deceased father in post–9/11 New York. Also in this text walking has a therapeutic character. The city has the extraordinary ability to preserve moments and memories when they are attached to particular places. These moments become a part of the city and shape the way it is perceived and understood by the narrator. As these emotionally loaded spaces vanish or are replaced with others, the memories too disappear.

> I wandered about the city revisiting places she [Erica] had taken me to, whether because I thought I might see her or because I thought I might see something of us, I am not now certain. A few of these places—such as the gallery in Chelsea we had visited on the night of our first date—I proved unable to find; they had vanished as though they had never existed. Others, like the spot in Central Park where we had gone on our picnic, were easy to locate but seemed to have altered. Perhaps this was the effect of a change in season; perhaps also it was in the city's nature to be inconstant [187].

After 9/11 the city becomes a stage on which Changez manifests his feeling of otherness and displacement. He attempts provocation in order to generate a reaction, when in fact he is depressed and desperate. New York absorbs his anger. His walking is an aggressive movement that represents his rage against the outside world.

> [S]ometimes I would find myself walking the streets, flaunting my beard as a provocation, craving conflict with anyone foolhardy enough to antagonize me. Affronts were everywhere; the rhetoric emerging from your country at that moment of history—not just from the government, but from the media and supposedly critical journalists as well—provided a ready and constant fuel for my anger [190].

The process of finding new ways in the city without Erica and without the admiration for Underwood Samson is difficult. Wandering in search for traces of her in the city, Changez recalls "diving" into his New York life in the significant September of 2001, shortly after the attacks of 9/11. He and Erica walk through the streets of Manhattan on a warm sunny day and notice a firefly, lost between the monstrous skyscrapers, overwhelmed and disoriented:

> [A] tiny greenish glow visible up close but overwhelmed by the city's luminance when viewed from even a modest distance. We watched as it crossed Fourteenth Street, headed south…. "Do you think he made it?" she [Erica] asked me. "I have no idea," I said, "but I hope so" [188].

This tiny creature symbolizes the vulnerability of man surrounded by architectonic constructions he himself created. Especially in the light of 9/11 these buildings come to overwhelm and threaten. When "locked" in a skyscraper and dependent on technology, individual freedom of movement and decision-making become limited. Throughout the novel Changez reflects on the nature of extremely tall buildings and construes them not only as a potential threat but also as aesthetic objects, artistic achievements. Skyscrapers reflect the sun, influence the wind and hence interfere with nature to become a part of the landscape. They evoke emotion and contribute to the city's extraordinariness:

> Think of the expressive beauty of the Empire State Building, illuminated green for St. Patrick's Day, or pale blue on the evening of Frank Sinatra's death. Surely, New York by night must be one of the greatest sights in the world [54–55].

The sense of stability and power generated by their size interfere with notions of insecurity and unease derived from their overwhelming presence. The confrontation with the old pre-skyscrapers world, symbolically represented here by a firefly and in Foer's novel by birds, reminds of the urban death of these flying beings, expelled from the city by monstrous buildings. Other flying creatures that appear in the novel's metropolitan settings are Lahorian bats that remind Changez of a pre-skyscraper *"dreamier* world" (71, emphasis original) in which even the Himalayas seem less dramatic than extremely tall buildings are now (38). Bats are "incompatible with the pollution and congestion of a modern metropolis" (71) but are at the same time, like Changez, "successful urban dwellers ... swift enough to escape detection and canny enough to hunt among the crowd" (72). They have a sense of direction. Unlike butterflies or fireflies they can navigate in order to escape and survive. Skyscrapers and metropolitan modernity have chased these creatures out of New York, but they, like Changez, have found shelter in Lahore.

Underwood Samson and the Universal Nowhere

Fundamentalism in the novel is, as Birgit Däwes points out, connected not with religion but with reluctance (Däwes 2011: 335). The word is used in the context of a company that embodies American capitalism and whose motto it is "stick to the fundamentals." Hamid's novel mentions Islam only in passing; religion and religious fundamentalism stay outside of the narrative. By contrast, Naqvi's *Home Boy* addresses Islam directly and the religion plays an important role in confronting the city. However, despite its centrality, Naqvi's novel also treats religion with a certain distance, possibly derived from the impact of the diverse metropolis. The first time the word "jihad" is mentioned is in reference to gardening (Naqvi 67).

With ruthlessness inscribed into its rules and tasks, Underwood Samson represents authority, superiority, and certain ignorance towards its clients and indirectly towards foreign countries whose economies it rates. Underwood Samson's employees are evaluated like the companies they rate, through highly competitive comparisons in the result of which individuals become exchangeable and replaceable. The entire mechanism is driven by money and the only person who softens it in this novel is Jim, Changez's supervisor and mentor who employs him. Jim likes Changez and claims to understand him because he believes to see in him a reflection of his young self: "I never let on that I felt like I didn't belong to this world. Just like you" (80). Jim is the exemplary personification of the American Dream in this novel; he is The Great Gatsby figure, faithful to his dreams, and similar to Chuck Ramkissoon in O'Neill's *Netherland*, who tries to pursue the nonsensical idea of building a cricket stadium in New York despite all obstacles. Jim has managed to work his way up the career ladder, thus proving, to others but most importantly to himself, that the transition from rags to riches is indeed possible in America. He talks openly about his poor background and shows off his wealth by inviting his team to a summer party at his house in the Hamptons. In the city he lives in a fancy loft in Tribeca. Changez is struck by the attention paid to design and art, and a "not insignificant number of male nudes" (136). Jim laughs at the question of whether he is married or has children. When at a bar in Manila he sits with his arm around the back of Changez's chair, it makes Changez feel literally like being taken "under his wing" (81).

The novel suggests a homoerotic element in the relationship between those two men. Their acquaintance is inscribed in the hierarchy of the company but clearly extends beyond the strictly professional. Jim—the patronizing mentor who calls Changez "a kid" when assigning him to a new project—recognizes himself in the young Pakistani and is at the same time intrigued and moved by his "otherness," which stands out in Underwood Samson's homogenous working environment. Changez shares his observations about Jim with the white, male American stranger in Lahore without comment, as if he was gradually revealing the insights of the acquaintance and there was more to come.

The relationship between the young, ambitious Pakistani Princeton graduate and his American mentor can be construed as a metaphor for the illusory and never fully graspable love affair between the East and the West. It is marked by disappointments on both sides. Jim certainly is, next to Erica, the other figure who emotionally chains Changez to America. At the same time Jim "belongs" to Underwood Samson and disappears from Changez's life after he stops working for the company. Sacrificing a part of the self's autonomy to the wild and ruthless capitalism embodied by Underwood Samson is requisite for the acquaintance. It cannot exist outside of the professional constellation of the mentor-protégée, which, on a global scale reflects the power relations inscribed in international (inter)dependencies.

In the globalized everyday environment of Underwood Samson its employees even look alike; they conform to the same dress code and have the same haircuts. After 9/11, when Changez returns from his visit in Lahore with a beard, it is considered a pointed political statement. The company employs only one other non-white analyst and from the beginning there is mutual understanding and sympathy between this character and Changez. They share a legacy of being the "colonized subjects" and they talk about cricket, a game that becomes a metonymy for their childhoods or is simply used as a metaphor in their everyday New York vocabulary. This brings these two characters close to Naqvi's Chuck, who also refers to cricket when recalling his childhood in Karachi. Once Wainwright asks Changez while they share a cab downtown:

> "Hey man, do you *get* cricket?" I asked him what he meant. "My dad's nuts about it. He's from Barbados. West Indies versus Pakistan ... best damn test match I ever saw." "That must have been in the eighties," I said. "Neither team is quite so good now" [43–44].

Changez also uses a cricket metaphor to refer to his boss's open, friendly, and honest attitude, which for him seems to equal a confession, something far too intimate for a strictly professional conversation: "The confession that implicates its audience is—as we say in cricket—a devilishly difficult ball to play. Reject it and you slight the confessor; accept it and you admit your own guilt" (80). The postcolonial context is critical as Changez alludes to it as to an aspect that America and Pakistan have in common—the only reference made on a national and not city level: "Like Pakistan, America is, after all, a former British colony, and it stands to reason, therefore, that an Anglicized accent may in your country continue to be associated with wealth and power, just as it is in mine" (47). Chuck, the main character of H.M. Naqvi's *Home Boy*, recalls playing cricket as a boy in Karachi. In Chuck's memory his father's death is marked by moving into a new apartment and by the end of the cricket games in the garden. Symbolically, the absence of cricket marks the end of careless childhood linked in Chuck's memory to an end of a space (the house and the garden).

Underwood Samson is a corporation that works to unify businesses around the world and achieve full international exchange of sources, resources and people, and therefore also aims to establish a value system which could be applicable to all of the mentioned factors. In so contributing to globalization, its offices—which all look the same—are beyond the categories of space, distance and time. The company has its own rules and priorities that do not always have much to do with the real world. Its employees are supposed to feel at home everywhere they go in the "globalized world" that is narrowed down for them through the vacuum bubble character of the corporation. "The company is simple. It has only one service line: instantaneous travel. You step into its terminal in New York, and you immediately reappear in its terminal in London. Like transporter on *Star Trek*" (13–14). It aims at creating the universal nowhere, an anti-place, free from cultural coding, specificities, memories, burdens or character. Consequently, Underwood Samson is future-oriented and pays little attention to the past (132).

Being a part of this machinery is connected with social status and respect in America, but not necessarily in the other countries Changez becomes exposed to during his business travels. The view from the lobby of Underwood Samson in Manhattan makes Changez for the first time reflect on the state of the cities in the U.S. and those of Pakistan. The comparison is troublesome and at this stage makes him feel ashamed rather than angry:

> Four thousand years ago, we, the people of the Indus River basin, had cities that were laid out on grids and boasted underground sewers, while the ancestors of those who would invade and colonize America were illiterate barbarians. Now our cities were largely unplanned, unsanitary affairs, and America had universities with individual endowment greater that our national budget for education. To be reminded of this vast disparity was, for me, to be ashamed [38].

The question of identity, linked to the city rather than to the country or a nation, contributes to the importance of the urban space in this novel. "I was, in four and a half years, never an American; I was *immediately* a New Yorker," claims Changez (37, emphasis original). When after 9/11 the city is "invaded" by American flags, it strikes him as inappropriate—for Changez, being a New Yorker is very different from being an American. The city embodies for him values and phenomena that until 9/11 stayed on a post-national level. Its cosmopolitan character is unique and hence it cannot stand for or represent the entire country or nation. Accordingly, in Changez's understanding, not all New Yorkers are Americans and not all Americans are New Yorkers:

> Small flags stuck on toothpicks featured in the shrines; stickers of flags adorned windshields and windows; large flags fluttered from buildings. They all seemed to proclaim: *We are America*—not New York, which, in my opinion, means something quite different—*the mightiest civilization the world has ever known; you have slighted us; beware our wrath* [90, emphasis original].

Amy Waldman's novel *The Submission* exploits a similar motif; one of the characters makes a clear distinction between New Yorkers, their tolerance and sense of multiculturalism and the rest of the "much more narrow-minded heartland" (Waldman 18).

Remarkably though, when working on an Underwood Samson project in the Philippines, Changez's understanding of belonging changes. When asked where he is from, his answer is New York. He realizes that this statement, just like any other identity-related claim is sensitive to a given location and can mean different things depending on where it is being revealed. The concept of feeling more American when outside the country appears in several post–9/11 novels which involve the immigrant experience, for example the already discussed *Open City* by Teju Cole or Joseph O'Neill's *Netherland*. When taken outside of the cultural context, the need to position oneself in relation to that context emerges and seems inescapable. Julius and Hans—the protagonists and narrators of the mentioned novels, respectively—feel a stronger bond with the U.S. when they travel to Europe. Julius feels more attached to its values when he talks to two Muslim men he encounters in Brussels. Hans feels an almost natural need to speak up for the U.S. in a critical political discussion with his wife's British friends in a London pub. For Changez, saying "New Yorker" in the Philippines means being an American and a traitor. Manila, like Valparaiso in Chile later in the plot, plays an interesting role in the process of shifting sentiment further away from America.

Interaction with people in the two cities Changez visits on business trips for Underwood Samson makes him very conscious of the superior attitude he, as an ambassador of his company, promotes. This knowledge makes him feel like a hypocrite and is highly confusing. Once he discovers he feels like he has more in common with the Philippinos than with his American colleagues, the struggle for a more coherent identity begins. New York, where the feelings of exclusiveness and superiority are rooted, becomes a more and more ambiguous place for Changez. It is not only the city, but also and more significantly the company that provided the enthusiasm at the beginning and it is the same company that takes it away from Changez. 9/11 happens in the background of that process and ultimately functions as a catalyst. Its consequences intensify Changez's unease about his position in the United States.

Monologue of Sarcasm and Fear

The interaction between Changez and his American listener and addressee remains "exclusively intradiegetic" (Däwes *Ground Zero Fiction* 328). Changez, the narrator and storyteller, is the master of this ambiguous ceremony. He has access to both worlds through his New York past and the Lahore present. The American listener, who remains equivocal to the reader as his voice is left out of Changez's narrative, is passive and for most part appears as the weaker link. His fearful reactions are reported by Changez, who often makes use of his advantage over his listener. He is surprisingly open to his listener and from the very beginning talks openly about private and intimate matters concerning his relationship with Erica or his first feelings about 9/11. He gives the impression of a man who has no fear of losing anything.

Birgit Däwes points to the frequency of "self-reflexive statements and addresses of the narratee" (*Ground Zero Fiction* 332), and the use of italics and exclamation marks that according to her indicate a strong emotional involvement. Italics indicate an emphasis on a given word or expression used by Changez and often give his statements a radical touch. Changez positions himself as a chronicler, as a witness writing history by telling his own story on that particular evening in Lahore. His advantage over the American is clearly marked by his latent usage of irony which appears throughout the novel. Changez agrees with the American and grants him a feeling of understanding, only later to do the exact opposite or to show his slightly different position on a given matter, thereby radicalizing his listener. When a beggar appears at their table Changez says:

> Will you give him something? No? Very wise; one ought not to encourage beggars, and yes, you are right, it is far better to donate to charities that address the causes of poverty rather than to him, a creature who is merely its symptom. What am I doing? I am handing him a few rupees—misguidedly, of course, and out of habit [45].

Changez also comments, not without sarcasm, on his listener's choice of words which then seem so out of place in the context of Lahore:

> Observe, sir: bats have begun to appear in the air above this square. Creepy, you say? What a delightfully American expression—one I have not heard in many years! I do not find them creepy; indeed, I quite like them [71].

In this case also Changez reacts at first positively, only to then immediately contradict and indirectly criticize the American. Looking at bats acts as a cultural test: the reaction provides information about the character's views towards the given city and culture. The same happens with the beggar: the reaction to him is location-sensitive and shows cultural knowledge connected to the place but also the attitude towards it. To ignore the beggar and to call the bats "creepy" are signs of weakness and ignorance in regard to Lahore—the other crucial place in the spatial axis that defines the setting of the novel.

In Between Lahore and New York

As in Joseph O'Neill's *Netherland*, the actual events of September 11 are mentioned only briefly in Hamid's novel. However, they mark a crucial shift in the story and their consequences, which often function as catalysts, lead to a metamorphosis of the protagonist. The terrorist attacks remain in the background but they throw a shadow over Changez's life, which no longer appears fulfilled, happy or sensible to him. 9/11 and its military and political consequences are also the ultimate reason for the types of behavior the two characters of this one-sided conversation come to represent and the gap of ambiguity between them. The main character of a novel so focused on two cities and the relationship between them is not in either of them on September 11, 2001. Instead, Changez is in Manila in the Philippines and watches the Towers fall on a TV screen. It makes him feel "remarkably pleased" (83). The way the tragedy is broadcast live makes it impossible for Changez to think about the victims and identify with them as individuals or as symbolic Americans. He rather has the impression of watching a staged, planned and accordingly fulfilled, highly symbolic act of performance that does not seem to be real at first, since real tragedies are not supposed to be *acted*:

> I realized that it was not fiction but news.… At the moment my thoughts were not with the victims of the attack—death on television moves me most when it is fictitious and happens to characters with whom I have built up relationships over multiple episodes—no, I was caught up in the symbolism of it all, the fact that someone had so visibly brought America to her knees [83].

Flying back to the U.S. shortly after 9/11 he is exposed to discrimination and humiliation by security controls at the airport. The New York he returns to is a different place with different social coding and norms. He observes radical changes in American democracy and questions its foundations: "Pakistani cabdrivers were being beaten to within an inch of their lives; the FBI was raiding mosques, shops, and even people's houses; Muslim men were disappearing perhaps into shadowy detention centers for questioning or worse" (107). Changez is shocked by the mental state of the metropolis:

> Living in New York was suddenly like living in a film about the Second World War; I, a foreigner, found myself staring out at a set that ought to be viewed not in Technicolor but in grainy black and white. What your fellow countrymen longed for was unclear to me—a time of unquestioned dominance? of safety? of moral certainty? I did not know—but that they were scrambling to don the costumes of another era was apparent. I felt treacherous for wondering whether that era was fictitious, and whether—if it could indeed be animated—it contained a part written for someone like me [131].

New York City becomes a strange and foreign place, dangerous and unfriendly, moody and aggressive. A "final catalyst" (170) for Changez arrives as his encounter with Juan Bautista, a publisher whose Chilean company, based in Valparaiso, is being consulted by Underwood Samson. Indirectly but forcibly, he compares Changez to the medieval janissaries in the Ottoman Empire who, taken from their families in a very young age, were schooled to fight against their own societies and nations. Changez, devoted to the U.S., his "adopted empire" (172) and disappointed by its radical shift after 9/11 feels like a modern janissary and his pride at being employed by Underwood Samson is rapidly replaced by embarrassment.

Valparaiso is, like Manila, another significant city in this novel—it is the locus of mental awakening which influences the perception of both New York and Lahore:

> Valparaiso was itself a distraction: the city was powerfully atmospheric; a sense of melancholy pervaded its boulevards and hillsides.... In this—Valparaiso's former aspirations to grandeur—I was reminded of Lahore and of that saying, so evocative in our language: *the ruins proclaim the building was beautiful* [163, emphasis original].

In Hamid's novel, leaving and returning to the cities generates new meanings and understanding of them. A geographical transition, a movement connected with change of setting, is necessary to gain perspective, to see New York and Lahore from outside through the lens of another urban reality, with people and lifestyles often so different from the well-known one: "Juan-Bautista wore a hat and carried a walking stick, and he ambled at a pace so slow that it would likely have been illegal for him to cross at an intersection in New York" (171). The city provides unique reference points that, attached to memories and experience, influence the way Changez perceives reality. He will never be able to entirely detach himself from New York, as it will always be a part of his emotional vocabulary and worldview. It is the other places that he visits for Underwood Samson that provide him with new lenses through which his perspective on New York changes; in other words, what is supposed to be the Universal Nowhere becomes a sense-generating spatial experience that makes Changez more and more skeptical of the company and pulls him away from its "fundamentals."

Throughout his monologue, Changez celebrates, explains, mystifies and threatens with Lahore that he opposes and at the same time relates to New York City. His account points to the long and complicated history of reciprocal influence and struggle for power between the two cultural spheres embodied by the cities. They are marked by many similarities, and elements of New York can be easily found in Lahore, just as Jim could recognize parts of himself in

Changez. Providing a reflection of the self, the "other" (city) becomes intriguing, unpredictable, dangerous, and surprisingly well-known, all at the same time. The power of the Other derives from this combination and ambiguity, no matter from which perspective its nature is addressed. When disregarding, fearing or opposing the Other, one also threatens the self. *The Reluctant Fundamentalist* thereby addresses the concept of the Other through the dimension and category of space.

"Hardcore homeboys": Post–9/11 New York in Husain M. Naqvi's *Home Boy*

The protagonists and first person narrators of both novels analyzed in this chapter share many similarities. Hamid's Changez and Naqvi's Chuck both come from Pakistan, from Lahore and Karachi respectively. Both study at prestigious American universities, Princeton and NYU and both end up working on Wall Street either fulfilling a dream (Changez) or following a mother's advice (Chuck). Like Underwood Samson, the bank that Chuck works for creates value and makes markets "more efficient," (36) and more comparable with one another. By promoting this attitude, it aims to make global utilities and work forces easily exchangeable and replaceable. Both stories, told as first-person accounts, feature flashbacks and chronological ruptures. Both narrators are young, live in New York and are conscious lovers and explorers of the metropolis. Their metropolitan experience in both cases is overshadowed and highly influenced by the events of September 11, which change their urban and social status and which make them perceive the city differently.

In *Home Boy* moving through the city makes the reminiscences of 9/11 visible, a mechanism similar to that used in Teju Cole's *Open City*—the city reveals its past to the stroller. The more he or she walks the more open the city becomes, like a newly acquainted person willing to tell their story, sentence by sentence. September 11 is called the "eerie, odd bank holiday or Judgment Day" (120). Chuck sees New York's wounds through the lens of his immigrant existence and the radically changing fearful attitude of his American co-urbanites. After 9/11 Chuck loses his job on Wall Street and after weeks of loneliness and depression he decides, like Chanu, the Bangladeshi character in Monica Ali's *Brick Lane*, to become a taxi driver. That way he fulfills the stereotype of a profession typical for New York and London immigrants from this part of the world. He is ashamed of becoming a "cabbie" and does not tell his mother about it, just as Chanu keeps his decision within the city and does not let it "leak" home. At the same time this new experience connects him more intensely to the city than his previous job did, and exposes him to a new group of people. Enrolling in the Taxi Drivers Academy marks a beginning of a process of becoming a professional urban dweller, a certified city cartographer, a map connoisseur and a crucial and visible urban presence. The temporal transition between those two jobs is what Chuck calls his "blue period" (39) during which the city becomes his only companion, similarly to when Changez is abandoned by Erica and "mourns" his loss in and with New York. Chuck takes his depression on walks, following always the same route. The routine derived from the repeated pattern replaces the missing work routine and is soothing and stimulating:

> On afternoons that I actually made it off the futon and out of my apartment (on average, four days out of seven), I moved from refuge to respite. I had developed a routine, a tour of the Upper West Side, really, commencing at the Moroccan-run newsstand down the street, where I purchased the Times and made small talk with the proprietor, pausing at Gray's Papaya for a Recession Special (two hot dogs and a Tropical Breeze for $2.99), and ending up at Central Park [38].

Manhattan absorbs his lethargy and provides a comforting repetition. These walks also, as in O'Neill's *Netherland*, Cole's *Open City* and Hamid's *The Reluctant Fundamentalist*, bring back memories of the past, of different places and people. Chuck recalls his first visit to New York, when he has moved to NYU's university dorm and suffers the loneliness and confusion of being in a new and foreign environment. In order to cope with this situation, he tries to "get lost" in the city, a process Hamid's Changez calls "diving." Long and exhausting walks bring inner peace, reassurance and strength. Overwhelmed by the size and speed of the city, but most of all, disgusted with his dorm and scared of the unknown, he calls Mini Auntie, his mother's friend who has lived in New York for many years. He ends up talking to a stranger who has picked up the phone. The anonymous voice tells him to go outside and walk until his feet hurt. After the phone call Chuck goes for a long walk, which is the beginning of a process of taming and making sense of the metropolis, and hence of mapping it for the first time and adjusting to it. This is what becomes Chuck's medicine; his antidote to problems and sorrows. The movement through the crowds and the reassuring grid structure of Manhattan streets calm him down and at the same time fascinate him. Discovering the richness of options, possibilities and choices that New York offers, he starts experiencing the feeling of constantly missing out, a sensation that he associates with New York only and that becomes an inseparable part of his urban know-how:

> [I] had lost myself in the city many, many times, and on occasion, I'd even rolled the famous New York nightlife (armed with a fake state ID, furnished by AC, that claimed I was born '74 and christened Papadopoulus).... At certain juncture in New York, after you have discovered the city's like a grid, and that the best god-

dam falafel joint in the city is Mamum's in the West Village, and after you have forged relationships with the local newspaper vendor and the good folks at the twenty-four-hour Duane Reade, you get this feeling that the inner life of the city still eludes. You feel that you're missing out, that at any given moment, day or night, there's an epic party taking place to which you have not been invited [204].

This sensation of partial exclusion is inscribed in the existence of an urbanite and connected to the feeling of being an outsider, which to some extent affects all metropolitan residents. Hana Wirth-Nesher refers in this context to the modern urban life as to a "landscape of partial visibilities and manifold possibilities that excludes in the very act of inviting" (Wirth-Nesher 9).

Returning to mapping the city through walking in times of personal crises is what many characters in the novels analyzed in this study do. For Hans in *Netherland*, Changez in *The Reluctant Fundamentalist* and Chuck in Naqvi's novel, the city remains when everything else disappoints or vanishes. Therefore, all of these characters take the 9/11 attacks personally, as Jimbo in *Home Boy* puts it:

I DON'T CARE ABOUT THE FUCKING COLOR SPECTRUM, CHUM!.... I care about this city.... Those bastards, they've fucked up *my city*! THEY'VE FUCKED UP EVERYTHING! [29].

Exploring the city in a cab, first as a passenger and later as a taxi driver, acts as an extension of the process of "getting lost" in the city on foot. "Cruising" the city makes Chuck contemplate its relation to his own past:

Hailing a cab, I cruised down the West Side Highway with the window half open, taking in the night. The air was warm and fishy, and the moon, brilliant and low, was torn to shreds by the jagged waves of the Hudson. Downtown seemed festive, lit up with floodlights, but the buildings obscured the mayhem, the mountains of rubble behind them. Three months earlier I'd worked on the forty-first floor of the WTC, the third building that went down. My colleagues escaped with cuts and bruises but brushed against the spectacle that would scar their lives [8].

City traffic can also be unbearable—lack of movement in congested Manhattan and thick air overwhelms the individual whose only option for action is walking, which depending on the distance and number of other strollers can be problematic: "At such time the city got to you. Everyday, straight-forward things like getting from point A to point B became epic struggles, [like] playing chess with the Devil" (120). Congestion in the cardio-vascular urban system has an impact on its other parts. It is shown as a disease, a paralyzing illness, but at the same time the city's power over the individual becomes visible. The metropolis strikes back with man's own weaponry—there are too many people and cars, too much pollution. The addiction to speed is a common urban malaise. Chuck, who, like Changez in *The Reluctant Fundamentalist*, provides a cultural context from Pakistan, points to similarities and brings the realities of the two cities and symbolically the two societies closer to one another. He compares Manhattan traffic to that in Karachi, which "requires skill and testosterone" (75) to navigate. Trying to arrive on time for a job interview, Chuck quite literally fights with the city and with time—a battle impossible to win and yet he manages to be punctual. His feet bring him there, and walking in this case again proves the most reliable way of opposing the congested metropolis. Throughout the novel, East-West urban analogies and comparisons address people's behavior in relation to the city, for example: "'Ooay!' AC called, as if hailing a rickshaw in Karachi Traffic" (14).

Later in the novel Chuck admits, similarly to Changez, that some of his "fondest memories reside in the city" (200) as do his friends, AC and Jimbo, young Pakistani New Yorkers, "hardcore homeboys" with whom Chuck explores the city. They all walk a fine line between the freedom and permissiveness of New York City and the rules of their conservative Pakistani immigrant families. They consider themselves New Yorkers, "boulevardiers, raconteurs, renaissance men … self-invented and self-made" (1). They know New York like the backs of their hands; they go to parties, and they rap about the reality that surrounds them. During his post–9/11 "blue" period of unemployment Chuck isolates himself from the other men and turns into a lonely walker who does not comment on reality, but rather observes it, linking him to other flâneur figures of post–9/11 fiction who, in reaction to September 11, find new reasons to move through the city on foot in search for solace.

The isolation from his friends and walking the same streets everyday mark a feeling of claustrophobia that Chuck starts to explore after 9/11, and which also requires a renegotiation of space. The city he has perceived as liberating, especially by comparison with Karachi or Jersey City, becomes stifling and oppressive. Manhattan's urban grid, at first considered friendly and easily approachable, leaves no space to hide. Its spatial predictability makes it impossible for Chuck to get lost, to "dive," to feel anonymous. Brooklyn, on the other hand, is empty in places that once were crowded; Chuck feels uncomfortable in Little Pakistan. The feeling of claustrophobia in a huge metropolis starts to dominate his life. He feels observed. Walking no longer brings solace, as he is unable to free his mind in order to get lost.

Urban Dichotomies and Post–9/11 Storytelling: Both Sides of the Hudson

The novel creates an interesting urban dichotomy through its portrayal of New York City and Jersey City. They are two entirely separate cosmoses divided by the Hudson. Jersey City is the counter-society, a distorted reflection of Manhattan, an answer to the metropolitan flair and character of the "real" city on the other side: "Jersey City was like Manhattan gone awry" (54). Full of immigrants, it becomes a space of asylum, an entirely separate urban reality which often seems to be disturbed by the closeness and apparent uniqueness of New York City, in the context of which it is always perceived. The relation between the two cities acts as a binary, next to race and origin: "It doesn't matter if a person is Eastern or Western, black or white, from New York or from New Jersey. In my experiences, each human needs the same things: food, water, shelter, loving" (225). Jersey City is "uncool" and in the novel not yet gentrified. Everybody who wants a better life leaves.

In his novel *Terrorist*, John Updike chooses New Jersey as the origin of young terrorist-to-be Ahmad. Described as an industrial wasteland and not the "fanciest part of the planet [with] a share of losers" (Updike 233), it is a hopeless place whose frustration and lack of perspective can even turn against and attack New York. The characters in Naqvi's novel generally do not commute; they remain on either side of the Hudson. When Chuck goes to visit Old Man Khan, his friend's father in a Jersey City hospital, the train journey feels long and exhausting. The city is depicted as grey and forgotten. No new buildings are built; stagnation replaces the constant movement and never-ending progress assigned to Manhattan. Jersey City's skyline which constantly looks at Manhattan is described as lost in thought:

> The skyscrapers downtown were erected in the seventies and looked it: you didn't see any stucco or stonework, only steel and darkened windows. At night, the buildings seemed to brood. And despite the gentrification of Jersey City through the Great American Bull Run, there were boarded-up storefronts in the side streets, closed movie theaters [56].

The relation between the two cities on each side of the Hudson does not undergo any change after 9/11 in the novel. Jersey City remains a forgotten metropolitan "ruin" in the shadow of Manhattan; the economic rules remain ruthless and unchanged despite New York's "wound." Their relation remains unchanged, following Jacques Rancière's argument that "September 11 did not mark any rupture in the symbolic order" (Rancière 104).

In *Home Boy*, the people of Jersey City have no claim on 9/11, unlike New Yorkers. Chuck says that every New Yorker has a 9/11 story. They are the counter-narratives in a DeLillian[2] sense, expressions of desire to revisit the tragedy until it becomes nothing but a story (119). New Jersians are not mentioned in this context, as if they were not entitled to their own 9/11 stories.[3] This corresponds to the ongoing urban change and the off-side character of

New Jersey. Spaces and social groups too troublesome or too dangerous to Manhattan are moved to New Jersey, as in the case of the harbor workers of the previously industrial waterfront. As Sonja Schillings and Boris Vormann point out, "The workers, as well as their deplorable living and working conditions, have simply been relocated to Newark and Elizabeth [the ports in NJ that took over the container traffic in the late 1970s]—and, beyond the United States, to the Export Processing Zone (EPZ) of South Asia" and other remote destinations (Schillings and Vormann 156). The novel's portrait of New Jersey shows the continuation of this process. The "other" side of the Hudson, the anti–Manhattan is a stop between New York City and the more remote abstract and hence fully exchangeable nowheres that absorb unwanted social spaces within the metropolis. "Business as usual," as Peter Eisinger titled his review essay on post–9/11 New York.

Cartography of Freedom and Independence

In *Home Boy* the city depicted as a manifestation of individual liberty becomes, after 9/11, a claustrophobic space invaded by surveillance, mistrust and hostility. Chuck's perception and understanding of the city changes so radically that post–9/11 New York seems to be an entirely different place. Naqvi describes pre–9/11 New York as a space in which everyone can navigate his or her own way, literally and metaphorically. Chuck says:

> In New York you felt you were no different from anybody else; you were your own man; you were free. At any given minute you could decide to navigate your way up Fifth Avenue to regard shiny luxury watches in shop windows, eat a kosher hot dog on Central Park South, or read Intro to Sociology at an outdoor café off Christopher…. And sure, independence had its dark dimensions, its lonely frequented loci, like a scarred green bench in the north-west corner of Washington Square where nobody sought out to you [20].

Unlike many other city novels which portray New York as a place difficult to meet people and forge friendships, in Naqvi's novel the pre–9/11 city is shown as an open space where people bump into each other, party together, and share the urban experience. In *Home Boy* the whole city can turn into a feast in no time:

> The best parties in the city took place in the great outdoors, in parks, on sidewalks and boardwalks; … there's a party on the street every day. Later I would realize that I was already part of the inner life of the city. That's how things worked here. You had epiphanies and that led to other epiphanies [206].
> That's how things worked in the city. You met somebody, then somebody introduced you to somebody else, and then they would become part of your story [207].

Bumping into people accidentally and letting them become part of one's own story, so positively connoted in the above quote, after 9/11 turns into a burden that contributes to the feeling of inescapable claustrophobia. When on his subway ride back from prison Chuck craves for anonymity and avoids other passengers' gazes, he meets somebody he knows from one of the parties and feels followed and spied on, his privacy compromised.

Enrolling in the Taxi Drivers Academy, referred to as "Hunuck," marks an attempt to control the city. It triggers a shift in perceiving New York but also gives a beginning to a new community experience. The type of relationships that develop between the training taxi drivers is similar to the dynamics of the cricket team in O'Neill's *Netherland*. The "cabbies" are all men and all immigrants: "A bony Indian from Patna, a wide-eyed Bangladeshi, a square-faced Egyptian, and a small, intense Xingjiangi fellow ... an Albanian, a Haitian, and a Sikh.... The rest hailed from the Dark Continent: a Kenian, a Congolese" (46) with the instructor being the "sole Caucasian" on the team (46). Chuck spends many hours every day at the academy in Long Island City and learns about the city; its history, bridges and connections. After the exam most of the "cabbies" lose contact but start desperately calling one another again after 9/11— offering each other a form of urban reassurance, making sure the "team" is still there. In that sense the Academy has provided a bonding experience of belonging and a sense of community, endangered and "othered" after the attacks. Chuck describes his work as a taxi driver as a joy that surprises him—a mode of becoming an integral part of the city, a professional observer and a fluent speaker of the urban language, the city's street names and connections between places:

> Cruising into the city on I-95 at night, for instance, or from Hoboken, across the George Washington, was thrilling each and every goddam time. It was like discovering Manhattan anew. Each turn promised something else: you would see crazy bastard fistfights in Yonkers, crazy bastard wedding parties in Chinatown. You would meet the great celebrities of our age, raise your thumb to that naked cowboy guitarist in Times Square ... and the beautiful women who would chase after a cab in stilettos and states of dishabille at four, five in the morning [78].

Being a "cabbie" is a crucial urban experience for Chuck. He never seems closer to the city; he rediscovers Manhattan in order to then carefully and consciously return to Karachi to finally break free from the overwhelming feeling of post–9/11 urban claustrophobia.

Emergence of the Other in the Urban Context After 9/11

When at their favorite bar "homeboys" are confronted with politics and the intrusion of the outside world into their party routine, they notice that "things were changing" (31). Eventually they are expelled from the bar after their involvement in a minor fight. While this is only an indication of the changing sentiments after 9/11, the day itself is referred to through the lens and language of media reactions, as in other texts which refer to 9/11 through its media coverage, for instance David Hare's *Stuff Happens*, Michael Moore's *Fahrenheit 911* or Oliver Stone's *WTC* (otherwise a feature film but 9/11 is "told" using original footage). In *Home Boy* news can be found in the streets and therefore form an important part of the textual structure of the city. Chuck provides a press round-up when studying the titles at a local newsstand. Interestingly, the novel focuses on the link to Pearl Harbor. The press commentaries in Naqvi's novel are aggressive and the context in which they are put together makes it a socially critical statement (52). Chuck quotes from *The Post*: "The response to this unimaginable 21st-century Pearl Harbor should be simple and quick—kill the bastards.... As for the cities or countries that host these worms, bomb them to basketball courts," *The Time*: "The cage of Rage and Retribution.... For once let's have no 'grief counselors' standing by with banal consolations ... no fatuous rhetoric about 'healing'; ... what we need is a unified, unifying Pearl Harbor sort of purple American fury—a ruthless indignation that doesn't leak away in a week or two, wandering into Prozac-induced forgetfulness ... or into corruptly thoughtful relativism " (52).

While the story progresses, different parts of the city reveal themselves as wounded, stricken, offended and suffering after 9/11. The normally busy Tribeca is empty. Emptiness of the usually crowded places creates a sense of insecurity and panic and symbolizes disaster. It also seems unreal, nightmarish. The incongruous emptiness of usually busy public spaces designed for masses is a motif employed in many pre– and post–9/11 representations of New York (e.g., *Vanilla Sky* directed by Cameron Crowe or the already mentioned *The Reluctant Fundamentalist*). In *Home Boy* it is combined with an individual's personal relation to the city; empty streets seem longer than usual and Chuck's memory begins to acquire a metropolitan urban structure:

> The doors closed on vulgar music, distant drums. Tribeca, stricken, was deathly quiet, a ghost town. The streets were empty and strewn with the usual garbage. I hurried past closed doors and shuttered entrances, farther and farther away from disaster, thinking *this is what it feels like to be the last man on earth*. Turning into West Broadway, there was the suggestion of civilization in the porters loitering outside the Soho Grand.... The blocks between Canal and Houston seemed longer than usual, probably because there was a certain urgency in my stride, as if I already knew that years later, in retrospect, that night would stand out in the skyline of my memory [17–18].

Here the city and the individual blur; the architecture and the extraordinarily complex character of the metropolis influence the way it is memorized and remembered—it becomes a crucial part of perceiving the world and one's own existence within it. In this context Chuck comments on the repetitiveness of broadcasted and streamed violence and death, and relates it to pornography, "in vivid color, charred bodies among concrete ruins" (71).

After 9/11 the Pakistani community in New York tightens. In the face of danger, oppression and insecurity, the disaster puts an end to previously established boundaries, and people contact each another to make sure they are fine but primarily, to reassure themselves: "After 9/11 we heard not only from family and friends but from distant relatives, colleagues, ex-colleagues, one-night stands, neighbors, childhood friends, and acquaintances, and in turn we made our own inquires, phone calls, dispatched e-mails" (27–28). It is in this spirit that one day, AC, Jimbo and Chuck take Chuck's cab (which technically is not his but his partner's Abdul Karim's who helped him with the job transition) and decide to visit Shaman, their friend in Connecticut whom they have not heard from for a long time. Arriving at their friend's empty place, the three characters decide to stay at the house and wait for him. Anxious neighbors inform the FBI about "suspicious activity" going on in the house.

It is the culmination point of the novel—when Chuck, AC and Jimbo are arrested and brought over to the Metropolitan Detention Center, a place with the ill-famed reputation of being Brooklyn's Abu Ghraib.[4] The narrative of the arrest is interrupted by presidential speeches quoted verbatim issuing from a TV at Shaman's house. This narrative hybrid provides a touch of absurdity to the entire arrest scene and manifests the novel's overall social criticism.

By depicting fear as a means of political and social manipulation that all U.S. citizens have been exposed to, Naqvi contributes to the picture that Hamid's novel draws of a changed and paranoid (Am)Erica that needs to be saved from herself. The Shaman is yet another Gatsby figure in post–9/11 fiction, next to Chuck Ramkissoon in O'Neill's *Netherland* and Jim in *The Reluctant Fundamentalist*: a "drifter, a grafter, an American success story, a Pakistani Gatsby" (27) but also a loner, who, as it turns out at the end of the novel, happened to have a business meeting in one of the World Trade Center towers on September 11. The reason for his absence at the house, revealed at the end renders the arrest, the paranoid neighbors and George W. Bush's speeches ridiculous.

In prison, Chuck is tortured and humiliated before being eventually released. The events of 9/11 are shown as a momentous shift in what it means to be an immigrant and a Muslim in the United States: "In prison, I finally got it. I understood that just like three black men were gangbangers, and three Jews a conspiracy, three Muslims had become a sleeper cell" (153). After his jail experience Chuck falls into what he calls a culture-bound psychosomatic psychosis, like the hysteria in fin-de-siècle Vienna that had inspired the Great Quack, or brain for in West Africa that periodically turned men and women into zombies, or anorexia and bulimia that ravaged prep-school and party girls in Manhattan. The authorities gave me existential heebie-jeebies [250].

Treated as a criminal during interrogations, he begins to feel like one, a phenomenon that seems natural to him but which he cannot explain. After his release, Chuck feels on one hand claustrophobic in the city and on the other finds being surrounded by buildings reassuring. The continuous presence of the city, its sounds, smells, and speed, comfort him, an idea echoed by Masha Hamilton's novel *31 Hours,* in which the constant noise of the outside urban world of New York offers solace and consolation and functions as a reference of everyday normalcy.

Chuck's subway ride from prison results in paranoia: he feels scared to look people in the eyes. The crowd on the train is multicultural and represents all ages and classes—this carriage is a New York in miniature that confronts Chuck and scares him by making him feel like a suspect, a criminal. For the first time he tries to avoid people; he lacks air to breathe and feels that his freedom is limited by the city. While still on the train Chuck sees a "Poetry in Motion"[5] poster. In this way the city makes itself readable and becomes poetized for the character within the text of the novel. Chuck feels personally addressed by the verses:

You ask me about that country whose details now escape me, / I don't remember its geography, nothing of its history. / And should I visit it in memory, it would be as I would a past lover, / After years, for a night, no longer restless with passion, with no fear of regret. / I have reached that age ... when one visits the heart merely as a courtesy [158].

City becomes text and as such is incorporated into the novel. In the process it becomes not only readable but also, and most importantly approachable. The poem provides yet another way of seeing memories and feelings through space and addresses the hybrid existence of an immigrant for whom "home" is a space frozen only in memory.

The trope of "reading" the city plays an important role in Naqvi's novel. Manhattan is "like a grid" and can be read as such: streets have numbers and distances are measured in blocks—the primary unit of the grid structure. It is easily understandable and accommodating:

You could as Mini Auntie told me once, spend ten years in Britain and not feel British, but after spending ten months in New York, you were a New Yorker, an original settler, and in no time you would be zipping uptown, downtown, crosstown, wherever, strutting, jaywalking, dispensing directions to tourists like a mandarin. "You see," you'd say, "it's quite simple: the city's like a grid" [19].

Brooklyn and Queens are different; it is in Little Pakistan in Queens (without which and the "famous Pakistanis New York wouldn't be New York" [23]) that Chuck has the impression that the streets are longer and out of control. A sentence describing Chuck's friend Jimbo addresses the diversity of New York's neighborhoods. Jimbo, said to ethnically "fit" into different parts, is thereby viewed through the lens of the city and characterized by the internal urban coding, from south Brooklyn, through Queens to North Manhattan:

> He passed for Italian in Bensonhurst, Greek in Astoria, Russian in Brighton, Jewish on the Upper West Side (or the old Lower East Side) and was always told that he did not look Pakistani, which of course meant nothing [60].

Chuck's American adventure in Naqvi's *Home Boy* concludes, as do Monica Ali's *Brick Lane*, Amy Waldman's *The Submission*, Mohsin Hamid's *The Reluctant Fundamentalist* and also O'Neill's *Netherland*, with the protagonist leaving the country. Chuck reflects on his decision to return to Karachi and describes escape "not so much a destination as a frame of mind" (252), just as the city itself can be perceived as a state of mind (Park 1): changeable, adjustable but also incomprehensible and unpredictable. Birgit Däwes calls these return-patterns in novels in the context of 9/11 "interruptions of an experiment in cultural mobility" (*Ground Zero Fiction* 214). Chuck flees the process of "othering," of becoming "marked" in the post–9/11 system of racial and ethnic dichotomies:

> What do you want me tell you, Ma? That life's changed? The city's changed? That there's sadness around every corner? That there are cops everywhere? You know, there was a time when a police presence was reassuring, like at a parade or late at night, on the street, in the subway, but now I'm afraid of them. I'm afraid all the time. I feel like a marked man. I feel like an animal. It's no way to live. Maybe it's just a phase, maybe it'll pass, and things will return to normal, or maybe, I don't know, history will keep repeating itself [262].

Cities as Social and Political Seismographs

Both of the novels analyzed in this chapter are structured around the sense of place. Cities from each side of the East-West dichotomy serve as synecdoches of the respective cultures and perpetually reflect one another. The young male Pakistani narrators recognize parts of themselves in each of the cities in question and try to identify accordingly, a process that poses a great challenge post 9/11. Space and place in both novels are attached to ideology and politics. The cities are irreplaceable and unmovable, whereas characters claiming to carry parts of the cities in themselves can transport them and mediate between the ideologies and world-views. 9/11 changes the perception of space and the lens through which the characters are viewed and judged. In both novels the impact of 9/11 stretches much further than New York City or the U.S. Both Changez and Chuck are constantly in between of the cosmoses. 9/11 makes them abandon New York City, a change that creates a sense of displacement and presents a severe identity problem. The city remains emotionally close but at the same time is geographically and symbolically as remote as ever. It cannot be revisited without becoming a new space, incompatible with the memory of it. This discrepancy results in incompleteness, a missing cultural context, a broken link.

Both novels use cities to address the multifaceted post–9/11 dichotomy on different levels. The city acts as the key to understanding the complexity of the scope of that dichotomy and its consequences. The ambiguity of the Other is also addressed through place, as the process of "othering" is location-sensitive. In Hamid's novel the mute white American in Lahore is "othered" and thereby latently infantilized and patronized by Changez. In this way Changez reverses the relationship he had with Jim, his mentor at Underwood Samson, and on a more abstract level the relationship of power between the East and the West. In *Home Boy*, Chuck decides to return to Karachi, to confront his memory of home with the real city, so that he does not have to embrace being marked as the Other in post–9/11 New York. He also escapes the feeling of claustrophobia evoked by post–9/11 New York City. The metropolis becomes oppressive and Chuck no longer feels free in it. He is scared and his spatial interventions within the city are marked and influenced by fear. Getting lost in its urban grid is no longer possible; the cartography of Manhattan, at first considered approachable and welcoming, becomes overwhelming in its predictability and its inability to grant anonymity. Chuck feels constantly observed, as if his steps visibly marked the streets and made him easily traceable. He continues walking according to always the same pattern, which makes his actions redundant and turns them to an eventless routine.

In both novels the cities change with political tensions and post–9/11 sentiments. They reflect shifts in the lives of singular characters and as such cannot be revisited; in both novels they turn into memories and seismographs of moods, both individually and collectively. These different memories of places also deserve different names, as according to Italo Calvino:

> For those who pass it without entering, the city is one thing; it is another for those who are trapped by it and never leave. There is the city where you arrive for the first time; and there is another city which you leave never to return. Each deserves a different name [*Invisible Cities* 132].

In Hamid's and Naqvi's novels 9/11 functions as a caesura in perceiving, living, walking and writing the city. In both texts post–9/11 New York is a space changed by the attacks, and, following Calvino's argument, deserves a different name, as the space from before can be revisited only in memory and this fades with time.

IV

The Plurality of Voices and Urban Paths in Amy Waldman's *The Submission*: The Metaphors of Submission

Amy Waldman's novel *The Submission* is another study of the process of "othering" and discrimination against Muslims in the specific urban context of post–9/11 New York City. Written in 2011 and set in 2003, it reimagines the aftermath of September 11 and, on a fictional ground, provides a very critical and bitter portrait of the American society. The plot revolves around a fictitious competition for a 9/11 memorial to be built at Ground Zero. The prejudice-driven conflicts around the future of this new space within the city and the media discourse of paranoia, fear and smear campaigns reflected in the novel symbolically stand for the condition and general confusion of the American society at the time. Also in this novel, just like in Hamid's *The Reluctant Fundamentalist* the city is the key in understanding and approaching the phenomenon of the post–9/11 Other.

After the decision has been made and the winning project chosen by the competition jury, the winner's name turns out to be Mohammad Khan, "a goddam Muslim" (16), and the conflict that the text addresses begins to escalate. The ambiguous title of the novel addresses not only Mo's (Mohammad's) "oppression" by the post–9/11 American society, but also the connection between text, (urban) space and the process of "othering." In so doing, the narrative set around the navigation of the city, addresses the important angles of the discourse applied in this study.

"Submission" refers on one hand to Mo's competition entry with which he wants to participate in remapping the metropolis after 9/11. On the other hand, "submission" is the process of Mo's capitulation/giving up when exposed to the massively practiced discrimination directed at him as the embodiment of the Muslim Other. Finally, all of the characters that the narrative voice follows submit to the city while walking and otherwise moving through it; while adjusting to its logic and rules. "Submission" on a meta level of writing the city also refers to the entire novel which is Waldman's submission to the body of city texts that contribute to (re)creating, shaping and (re)appropriating New York. Interestingly, Waldman's text proposes a new scenario for an unchangeable but reimaginable past and in doing so offers an alternative history which involves changing the city's architecture.

The city in the novel becomes a language through which the atmosphere, fears, hopes and feelings are being communicated and manifested. New York City speaks and is being articulated and communicated by people who live, read and create it. The 9/11 memorial in the novel is a very important part of the city's language since it is meant to protect the site from wild capitalism and from the desire to build bigger and higher that has always been present in New York. It is meant to speak for the dead (their names forming an essential part of the memorial), preserve the memory of that day and make the space reclaimble for cultural attention of future generations. Most importantly, though, it is meant to fill an empty space and provide a counter narrative, a response to terrorism:

> [T]he developer who controlled the site wanted to remonetize it and needed a memorial to do so, since Americans seemed unlikely to accept the maximization of office space as the most eloquent rejoinder to terrorism.... The longer that space stayed clear, the more it became a symbol of defeat, of surrender, something for "them" whoever they were, to mock [8].

Interestingly, the real recreation or rewriting of that space in Manhattan combined the two ideas: a memorial next to the new World Trade Center as the "maximization of office space."

The novel features an array of characters that are connected to particular parts of New York City and their individual and public lives, partly joined with one another, form a network of stories and a plurality of voices through which the city is told. One of the characters, Claire, says, "Sometimes I feel I've got one leg in New York and one in America" (200), stressing the extraordinary microcosmic character of the metropolis and at the same time the fact that its people are a minority on the scale of the whole country. Everything that happens in this novel up to the epilogue happens in New York with the exception of Mohammed's journey to London and Kabul, which are important but mentioned only briefly. All addressed social processes are accompanied and co-told by various media, the discourse of which is shown as biased, powerful and dangerous. They play an important role in shaping the plot of the novel, and the public opinion of New Yorkers in the text. What happens outside of New York is, if at all, summed up through press headlines or announcements. This is the only way in which the outside world enters the city in the setting of this book.

The featured characters all move through New York and in the process are given equal attention. The third person narrator, atypical for post–9/11 fiction, accompanies each of them and the perspective keeps shifting as the narrator "walks" with one character at a time. This narrative mechanism has the effect of reflecting a plurality of voices which all contribute to writing or telling the city. The lens of the novel's narration "jumps" from one mind to another and also from one place within New York City to the next, as each of the characters represents a different urban microcosm within the metropolis, symbolizing the social diversity and antagonisms of the city.

The seemingly fragmented lives and stories are being connected as the narration progresses. The opening shows the competition jury debating on their choice of the winner behind closed doors. The group recalls the War Cabinet as portrayed by David Hare in his 2004 play *Stuff Happens*, gathered in Camp David and arguing over the future of the United States and the war in Iraq. Similarly in *The Submission*, the surreal reality of this microcosm is being confronted with the world outside, resulting often with shocking or ridiculous effects: the jury members seem helpless and nonadjustable to the urban reality and also partly incapable of maintaining contact with one another outside of the isolated safe zone; once they leave their meeting room, they are "scattering like loose petals" (23). The jury as an institutional and official body is portrayed as completely out of place in the metropolis; the members feel insecure and long for the peace environment of their (often suburban) homes, another metaphor through which the novel criticizes the distribution of power within social structures.

During their long meetings, just like in Camp David in Hare's cosmos, comforting food is being served that, despite the intentions, does not provide much comfort; constant severe disagreements prolong the decision making process. Eating as a cultural construct itself is being ridiculed when a ginger bread replica of the World Trade Center towers is being served, "chandelier light glinted off the poured-sugar windows" (7). The result of this morbid humor is confusion among the characters, deadly serious in their roles, unable to laugh, calculating every step and move. When one of the members leaks the news to the press, a social crisis, created and constantly heated up by the media, begins. The Garden is being called a "paradise for martyrs." Mohammad Khan (Mo) becomes the quintessence and the universal personification of the post–9/11 Other and *the* Muslim for the media.

Portraying the stereotypical post–9/11 Other in the urban context as an American born architect, i.e., a knowledgeable and experienced creator of urban structures and artist, is a powerful way of approaching social processes that emerged in the U.S. after 9/11. It also provides ground for a strong social criticism. Mohammad, born in Virginia, considers himself a New Yorker. Buildings are his religion (212). He is an urbanite, conscious about his emotional attitude toward the city and buildings and enters the competition to actively participate in the shaping of the city:

> He had been indifferent to the buildings [the World Trade Center towers] when they stood, preferring more fluid forms to their stark brutality, their self-conscious monumentalism. But he had never felt violent toward them, as he sometimes had toward that awful Verizon building in Pearl Street. Now he wanted to fix their image, their worth, their place. They were living rebukes to nostalgia, these Goliaths that had crushed small businesses, vibrant streetscapes, generational continuities [29].

Mo's victory exposes him to the process of "othering" and confuses his sense of belonging and identity. Throughout the novel Mo keeps repeating, "I am an American, just like you," but the fear-driven public is deaf to his argument and treats him like an outsider, a traitor. As a result, he does not believe himself anymore and subjected to the continuously escalating process of submission to the venomous system and society, he eventually leaves the country.

The fictitious memorial competition and the political and social fight over the project are "located" at the very center of a very real city and surrounded by its post–9/11 circumstances. In Waldman's novel this scenery is continuously entered by "real" people who appear in the plot to take part in the discussion; Susan Sarandon and Tim Robbins show their support for Mo's project. On a party organized by his supporters at the Dakota, Mo meets Robert De Niro and Sean Penn who is very briefly characterized as "drunk." At the same party Mariam Said, Rosie O'Donnell and others discuss the situation in Palestine. The president of the U.S. in this novel is an ex-baseball coach who prefers to stay away from the memorial competition and generally avoids public appearances. At times the fictional characters reflect on the fictionality of other fictional characters, for instance Alyssa Spier talks about Carry Bradshaw and Paul sees a boy who wears Harry Potter glasses (150).

Waldman uses meta-fiction in creating the urban cosmos of her protagonists and in that way positions them within the social and political structures of "real" New York City. All of the characters on all levels of fiction and reality have first and surnames and seem very "real" in their newspaper-like depictions.

Mapping the City through the Characters: The City as a Body

The featured characters that the narrative voice follows are Mohammad (Mo), the winner of the competition who lives in China Town in Lower Manhattan, which Paul Rubin, the head of the jury, finds bizarre. Paul also lives in

Manhattan although it is not specified where exactly. "Despite all efforts" (13) he is relieved when his Muslim driver quits the job three months after the attacks. Paul employs a Russian instead.

Claire Burwell, a member of the jury who lost her husband in the attacks and who is supposed to represent the families of the victims united in grief, lives in Chappaqua, Upstate New York in a huge house with her two little children.

Sean Gallagher, founder of the Memorial Support Committee and a wannabe activist, lives with his parents in Brooklyn (Ditmas Park) and so does Asma Anwar, an illegal immigrant from Bangladesh who has not left Little Dhaka/Kensington since she first arrived in the U.S. These two worlds, so close geographically, hardly ever interfere. They coexist without having the slightest interest for one another. Asma's husband used to work illegally in one of the towers and died on September 11.

Alyssa Spier, a reporter and journalist for *The Post* who sees the memorial competition as a chance in her career and disregards all moral rules when it comes to tracing a story she could sell, lives in an East Side Manhattan neighborhood referred to as "Curry Hill" (the area around Lexington Avenue and 28th Street) which she prefers to call "Curry Hell"—naming as a place-making practice. Mostly lonely and unhappy ("sexiness must come easily when your topic is sex and the single woman. Pondering terrorism—or 'The Muslim problem' … didn't exactly make for a seductive scribe" [105]) she imagines herself as the newspaper columnist Carrie Bradshaw, a character from the sitcom *Sex and the City* who in the series lives in the Upper East Side, not far from Alyssa's place:

> Staring down at her first column, Alyssa Spier had imagined herself as Carrie Brad-shaw: golden hair tousled, cigarette in hand, petite, tank-top-clad frame perched on the bed, pitchy comments filling the laptop screen. But Alyssa's one-bedroom smelled, as it always did, of the farted exhaust of the Indian restaurants around her building. Curry Hill, they called her neighborhood; she called it Curry Hell [104].

The presence of these two characters representing two levels of fictionality and positioned in Waldman's novel within New York in 2003, suggests that the events of 9/11 did not only change the actual city and the way it is being reflected in fiction but also that already existing fictional representations change after 9/11 in the way they are being incorporated into the altered body of the city through other fictional texts. In referencing Carrie Bradhsaw, Alyssa Spier locates her in post–9/11 New York and on a meta-fictional level inscribes her into that specific urban environment.

Lives of all of the characters in the novel change after 9/11 and all of them are to some extent involved in the process of creating the new urban place in question—the memorial. In taking positions in the conflict, they interfere with the city and try to claim it as their own. In this space-based struggle they have to position themselves on either of the sides of the conflict emerged around Mohammad Khan. They all have to support or to be against him—the novel draws a strong parallel to the either-or dialectics of George W. Bush's administration at the time.

For Sean Gallagher, 9/11 is a sense-generating event which he "uses" together with the death of his estranged brother, to re-establish himself. He is a clearly negative, selfish and weak character, described as primitive and arousing aversion. Yet, in the dynamics of the political post–9/11 dichotomous rhetoric which the novel references, he can easily make it as the iconic white American patriot. His moral advantage over Mo is unquestioned by the brain-washed society, the novel is suggesting. When Sean's anti-memorial movement starts an alliance with the "SAFIs" ("Save America from Islam") and his authoritarian leadership position is in danger, his frustration grows and makes him even more angry and aggressive. The SAFIs—mostly women and mostly from Staten Island, Queens and Long Island—so from outside of the quintessential metropolitan center of Manhattan, see the discussion about radical Islam as their "freelance obsession" (139). Patronized by their female leader, Sean develops a frustration deep enough to influence his perception of the city—all of a sudden New York seems to be hostile and full of enemies. As a literary motif it becomes even more prominent when Paul Rubin agrees to have breakfast with Sean in an expensive coffee shop on Madison Avenue in which the scale of the economic gap that lies between these two men becomes visible. The "weaker" character immediately blames the metropolis for social inequalities and his position within the turbo-capitalistic society. Manhattan as its quintessence with its exorbitant rents and coffee prices, and at this point also gendered, since Sean's frustration generally has a lot to do with being unsuccessful with women, becomes an unreachable object of desire:

> He felt himself in the camp of the enemy—not Muslims but the people born with silver sticks up their asses, the people who had made Manhattan a woman too good to give Sean her phone number [127–128].

The unreachability does not result in fascination or growing interest but evokes an even stronger frustration and aggression, and brings back the feeling of displacement, the presence of which has strongly marked Sean's pre–9/11 past. When he moves out of his parents' house, Debbie, the SAFIs leader, offers him to stay at her place on the Upper East Side. This experience only confirms his feeling of being out of place in Manhattan, of not being good enough for it:

> It was his first time living in Manhattan, and his days were his…. He walked the blocks around Debbie's apartment trying to look like he belonged. But he didn't; he was the only man not in a hurry [164–165].

Manhattan in the novel does not have the capacity to accept behavior that does not inscribe into its metropolitan norms. Sean, on the other hand, does not have the capacities to become a silent observer of the crowds, a stroller against the grain. Unable to stand the pressure and speed of Manhattan, he feels entirely displaced and excluded. Manhattan makes him angry because it makes him feel weak and overwhelms him with its possibilities, expectations and urban ambitions.

Later on in the novel Sean becomes known as "the headscarf-puller" after he publically tries to pull a headscarf off a Muslim woman's head, provoked by a banner she is holding. His act starts a country-wide chain of similar racist and hostile episodes directed at Muslim women. As a motif in post–9/11 fiction it also crosses the ocean, together with the "New York dust" and reappears in Monica Ali's *Brick Lane*, where in post–9/11 East London women are being harassed in exactly the same way.[1] In both novels, the result is fear and rage among Muslims as well as spatial cultural condensation within the given community in each of the cities. The tendency to remain within the safety zone of a district or borough leads to social changes in the city, creates ethnically specific enclaves and triggers geographical discontinuities within the urban system.

Also in other parts of the novel and from the perspective of other characters, the city is personified; no longer referred to as a "woman too good to give her phone number" but as a wounded, crying body whose pain reaches over to the people. Its appetites are "quelled" (28) and its structure changes: printed faces of the missing people cover the suffering urban body and form a blanket, a protective quilt over its streets and fences. The novel portrays the shared collective pain as unifying and equalizing at first; people identify with New York more and suffering brings them closer to one another and to the city:

> The city reeled—the air ashy, the people ashen, the attack site a suppurating wound you felt even when you didn't see it.... The eternal lights were off in the nearby office towers, as if the city's animal appetites had been quelled. A quilt of the missing—bright portraits of tuxedoed men and lipsticked women—had been pasted on fences and construction plywood, but the streets were empty, and for the first time in memory, he [Mo] heard his own footsteps in New York City [28–29].

Wounded New York becomes silent and this is what makes it frightening and uncanny; silence symbolizing lack of life, mourning and potentially preceding an approaching disaster.

In *The Submission* the city is portrayed as a breathing giant, Prospect Park in Brooklyn forming its lungs (97), that overshadows an individual and his/her intentions. When Claire takes her kids to the city to start a tour of building cairns—heaps of stones that are meant to show their father the way back home—

her son feels overwhelmed by the city's scale in which the pile of stones becomes invisible. "The hapless pile did look meager—disappointing—against the city's vertical thrust. So did the three of them, for that matter" (84). The piles are their little "easily missed interventions in the city" (84). New York is not only overwhelming but also moody: on humid miserable gray days it is "surly" (272) and the weather only reflects its bad temper.

New York in Waldman's novel, similarly to Naqvi's *Home Boy* can enter the characters' minds and shape their lives. Similarly to Chuck in Naqvi's novel, who talks about the skyline of memory, Claire feels the influence of the dark Hudson on her thoughts while driving over it. The river enters her thoughts and becomes her state of mind: "Claire drove up Manhattan in the dark. The wind roughed facets into the black river, its foreboding look coloring Claire's thoughts" (90). When Paul imagines the garden on the map of Manhattan, the first green spot in the grid since Central Park a century earlier, he imagines it like a pulse, like a life: "he imagined a spot of green flashing on the subway map, then vanishing, flashing, then vanishing. A pulse" (273). New York is also an omnipresent, natural and hence inescapable reference: the head of Thomas Kroll, Mo's friend, colleague and partner is compared to the map of Manhattan: "The bald spot lurking within the full hair reminded her [Alyssa] of the blank spot in Manhattan, its aerial view, and a fleeting urge to reach out and touch his head came over her" (95).

Amy Waldman, herself a journalist, explores the nature of information production and the power of the media in shaping the post–9/11 social and political reality. The novel talks about the hierarchy of newspapers and the ruthlessness of journalists; Alyssa Spier is even being called a "bulldog" (37) by the editor of *Daily News*. Here, similarly to Naqvi's *Home Boy*, one way of telling the story is to quote a number of (fictitious) newspaper accounts or TV reports in order to present an overview of the general media atmosphere as it physically invades the city. News enters the most private spheres; its methods are ruthless, *The Post* "screams" at Claire (116). One of the main messages of the novel is that historical events and the way collective memory of these events is shaped are a product of different and hardly ever genuine collaborating forces since "historical events, as much as skylines, are collaborations" (277). The news which invades the city and looks at its people from newsstands and billboards interferes with the city's traffic and directly influences everything that happens. Just like in Cleave's *Incendiary* in the case of London, here New York becomes readable and the power of headlines and words is so strong that it is impossible to escape it. When Mo sees the headline of *The New York Post* opening an article about him, he buys the paper and starts read-walking which is, like sleep-walking would be, dangerous and almost suicidal in the human traffic of New

York City: "Mo read as he walked, heedless of the sidewalk's jostle and cuss" (52).

Just like in, for instance, DeLillo's *Falling Man*, in *The Submission*, 9/11, through the conflicts emerging around the memorial competition, serves as a bonding experience which brings people together who would have otherwise most probably never met. Mo starts a relationship with Laila, a lawyer and a member of the Muslim Committee which is involved in Mo's case. Parallel to the post–9/11 love affair in DeLillo's novel, the new relationship surprises the characters themselves but has a deeper meaning in relation to perceiving and remapping the city. Laila is not Mo's "type" and clearly it is the circumstances that make her appear attractive to him. She lives in a studio on Murray Hill, so very close to Alyssa Spier, although the characters do not know about it and generally lack interest for one another. Laila's apartment which becomes a new isolated from others cosmos within the city once Mo moves in, has a view on the Chrysler Building. Only when experiencing the city from her place, Mo discovers a whole new set of memories attached to this particular view; connections he was not aware of. It is the city and the circumstances of 9/11 that bring these two characters together. Their at first seemingly random acquaintance triggers a new understanding and contributes to a remapping of the city: "The first thing he saw out her window was the Chrysler Building, which he had loved as a child, and a circle he hadn't known to be incomplete closed" (124). In other words, the relationship is rooted in the urbanity of New York and leads to different interpretations of particular places within it.

Monstrous Mohammad Threatening Manhattan: A Hysterical Portrait of the Post–9/11 Urban Other

Immediately after the results of the memorial competition are revealed, the profiling machinery of "othering" sets into motion and divides New Yorkers in Waldman's novel. The novel makes it to a point that the post–9/11 Other in the U.S. is no longer black; he/she is now Muslim with potential Islamic fundamentalist inclinations: "The police used to stop African Americans solely for 'driving while black.' Now it's acceptable to single us out for 'flying while Muslim'?" (41), provocatively asks a character called Malik, the executive director of the Muslim American Coordinating Council (both Malik and the Council are fictional) in a debate on Fox News introduced in the novel.

The Islamic Other emerges out of the urban crowd and "finally" has a face: it is Mohammad Khan, the architect. This sudden physical emergence of the Other evokes the need of self-reflection and self-positioning in the post–9/11 social dynamics. Paul Rubin reflects, more generally, on the changing nature of being American after 9/11. One of the criteria is, in his understanding, participation in the continuously repeated footage of the towers collapsing:

> You couldn't call yourself an American if you hadn't, in solidarity, watched your fellow Americans being pulverized, yet what kind of American did watching create? A traumatized victim? A charged-up avenger? A queasy voyeur? [13].

All of these types of Americans seem to be represented in the jury that as a peculiar body randomly put together resembles the whole nation and is related to it: "How can we ask this country to come to healing if this jury can't?" (11).

Just like other Muslim protagonists in the analyzed novels, Mo goes through a continuous struggle with the U.S. authorities after 9/11. Just like Chuck in Naqvi's *Home Boy*, he feels like a criminal because he is being treated like one. He notices that even in his trusted work environment that he considers natural, he starts behaving and feeling differently as a result of the omnipresent paranoia and aggression floating around him. Quite suddenly he feels marked as a potential enemy, a racist assumption made on the basis of his looks. He realizes that

> the difference wasn't in how he was being treated but in how he was behaving. Customarily brusque on work sites, he had become gingerly, polite, careful to give no cause for alarm or criticism. He didn't like this new more cautious avatar, whose efforts at accommodation hinted at some feeling of guilt, yet he couldn't quite shake him [25].

The power of the mass reaction is hence so strong that it disrupts the integrity of Mo's own judgments and awareness of himself. Mo distances himself more and more from the medial image originally based on himself but reused and recreated in such a way that he finds it impossible to identify with. His persona is used to fulfill a mass expectation regarding the looks and profile of the universal Other and disregarding his factual identity (an American, an architect, etc.). The Other constructed in such a way becomes a universal, potentially exportable enemy and a threat. Debbie's daughters when they do not get their way, threaten her with marrying a Muslim (164). Laila in a conversation with Mo about this very radical form of racism legitimized by the vague concept of national security and self-defense offers a parallel to the Holocaust and anti–Semitism in Nazi Germany: "The Jews thought they were German, until they weren't. Here they're already talking about us as less American" (175). She also recalls her parents coming over to the U.S. from Iran and points to the fact that post–9/11 discrimination of Muslims is in fact nothing new and has only become vivid again, "digged" out from an already existing repertoire of schemes.

Quite amusingly, under these circumstances Mo is being sent to London to participate in a counter-terrorism seminar for architects. From there he flies

with a group of architects to Kabul where his company is entering a competition
to design the new U.S. embassy. Kabul is described as a "minotaur of a city"
(45), an urban beast whose body consists of contradictory parts and whose age
and character are impossible to determine unambiguously:

> [a] vigorous, erect young man above, where billboards advertised Internet cafés
> and hideous office buildings of blue-and-green glass sprouted; old, flaccid, depleted
> below, where raw meat hung exposed in sagging wooden stalls and bent, haggard
> grandfathers lugged handcarts [45].

In Kabul Mo decides to grow a beard, out of principle but also in order
to check its allegedly provocative power—a reactionary motif deriving from
rage which also appears in Hamid's *The Reluctant Fundamentalist* where it is
also connected to travelling outside of the U.S. and then returning with different
looks, in other words a form of metamorphosis linked to the geographical and
cultural remoteness. After Mo's return Laila compares a man's beard to a
woman's headscarf and decides she would never want to check the public reaction to her wearing the latter:

> He had grown a beard on his return from Kabul merely to assert his right to wear
> a beard, to play with the assumptions about his religiosity it might create. She
> would never adopt a headscarf for the same reason. He imagined himself as indif-
> ferent to the opinions of others. She really was [114].

The above quote and Laila's position within it pin down the gender aspect of
post–9/11 "othering" and its gender-specific attributes. In this stereotyping
practice described in the novel a beard is perceived as a political manifesto, a
conscious confirmation of one's identity which can potentially generate comfort
and power. A headscarf in the mainstream, elegant, legal world in which Laila
lives and works, would be an obstacle potentially weakening her position and
threatening her professional image, independence and credibility.

The competition winning garden with its geometric structure is meant to
be inscribed in the Manhattan grid and become part of the organized urban
body. Mo defends it in front of Paul saying that it is his response and his
counter-narrative that could become a part of the city's map:

> The Garden has order, which its geometry manifests, for a reason, which is that
> it's an answer to the disorder that was inflicted on us. It's not meant to look like
> nature. Or like confusion, which is what the attack left behind. If anything, it's
> meant to evoke the layout of the city it will sit in [139].

Since disqualifying Mo just on the base of his creeds and/or skin color
would be against "everything America stands for," the media and public opinion

seek excuses that would justify such a decision. The argument against the garden is that supposedly it is inspired by Islamic motives and that "gardens aren't our vernacular. We have parks. Formal gardens aren't our lineage" (5). The public blindly accepts it, without questioning the dichotomous character of "our vernacular," the project is rejected and Mohammad Khan eventually leaves the country to become famous in the Middle East and have his projects exhibited in American galleries without living there. Mo consciously becomes a foreigner and as a consequence gains an entirely new take on the country and society that made him feel expelled to only then appreciate his work.

The fictitious medial, social and political scandal set around the memorial and the architect is created to address and mirror processes which to some extend happened in New York and other Western cities after September 11. Some of the addressed aspects and reactions, however, are presented in an exaggerated form and form a caricaturized picture of New Yorkers. Manhattanites are shown in the novel as neurotics famous for their inclinations to psychotherapy and city-related disaster fantasies:

> Manhattanites who had always prided themselves on their liberalism confessed that they were talking to their therapists about their discomfort with Mohammad Khan as the memorial's designer. "It's awful," a thirty-two-year-old music executive who declined to give her name told *The New York Observer*, which accompanied the article with a color drawing showing an ominous-looking Mo looming over a shrunken Manhattan. "There's this primal feeling in my gut saying 'No' to it, even though my brain is saying 'Yes'—sort of like when you think you want to have sex with someone and your body won't cooperate; or you think you don't and your body cooperates *too much*" [125–126, emphasis original].

The image of oversized Mo over a small fragile Manhattan recalls catastrophic visions from different decades of pop culture which featured humongous monsters posing threat to the metropolis, such as King Kong or Godzilla. By analogy, although the novel does not make it any more explicit than in the above quote, the post–9/11 Other is demonized and monsterized, and the potential threat blown into ominous size and in this way made ridiculous. Collages of real 9/11 footage *spiced up* with fictional catastrophic visions of "tsunami of smoke" (168) in New York are also the basis of the anti–Garden and anti–Khan TV spots that the novel features parodying the style of sensational journalism.

After he is forced to withdraw his submission, Mo decides to leave the country. He takes the same journey his parents made once but backwards: he is leaving America, the land of the free. He unwinds the immigration pattern in order to escape the U.S. and what after 9/11 turned to an American nightmare and tries to start a free and anonymous life somewhere else. He also develops interest for Islamic architecture and starts working abroad:

America had offered his immigrant parents the freedom to reinvent themselves. Mo had found himself reinvented by others, so distorted he couldn't recognize himself. His imagination was made suspect. And so he has traced his parents' journey in reverse: back to India, which seemed a more promising land [293].

Similarity to other characters who leave the post–9/11 metropolis, Changez in Hamid's *The Reluctant Fundamentalist*, Chuck in Naqvi's *Home Boy* and Chanu in Monica Ali's *Brick Lane*, Mo cannot quite accommodate elsewhere, misses New York and develops the feeling of displacement. He feels foreign everywhere he goes and when visiting New York he also feels like a stranger since once revisited, the place changes its character.

Kensington (Little Dhaka) in Brooklyn as an Example of a Cultural Vacuum

The whole medial quarrel over the memorial design is silently observed by Asma Anwar whose husband Inam worked in the World Trade Center and died on 9/11. They are both illegally in the U.S. and after Inam's death Asma is left with their little American-born son Abdul. For her, Manhattan seems to be "another country" (71) but her faith is to her "an indestructible building" (74). Without any knowledge of the English language, closed in the vacuum bubble of Little Dhaka and restricted from any interaction with the outside world, she is dependent on the community but finds it, just like the news in the local newspaper "like local life ... blander" (99). She misses a wider perspective that she has only had once, when Inam took her on a trip with the Circle Line Ferry. She recalls this trip as an initiation into the city that turns out to be only a short encounter. In her story, this experience makes her and her husband look at the city as a whole and for the first time they truly perceive it:

> They held hands and looked down at the water and studied the city, as if from this distance they could finally understand it.... Each thought about, and knew the other was thinking about, ferry travel back home.... From the boat Manhattan had no sound, like a television turned to mute.... Inam took her picture with a disposable camera and asked a Swede to take their picture together, then a Japanese man asked Inam to take a picture of him and his wife, and so easily they became a part of everything, New Yorkers. They had no worries that day, money and jobs, language and family, all as insignificant at that moment as a bucket of water poured into the harbor [145].

The trip brings back memories of home and is a symbolic farewell to it as it metaphorically offers a whole new set of impressions; an entirely new world opens to these two characters on that very boat. They become a part of New

York, something between tourists and immigrants: New Yorkers, like everybody else on the boat. An important identity shaping process takes place during this trip: people who look at the city's skyline from a distance and take each other's photos with it in the background are connected with one another and with the city in the moment of the collective experience.

The skyline is a natural part of the city and embodies its history, diversity and moods. It reflects the sun and stretches out to the world, embracing the rest of the urban grid "hidden" behind it. It is an intergenerational "collaboration ... seeming no less natural than a mountain range that had shuddered up from the earth" (29). The sudden absence of the towers, the newly emerged "gap in space" (29) moves back time. The effect is similar to the one Julius in Cole's *Open City* witnesses: the characters see their lives contextualized through the history of the city and it appears to them as continuity inscribed in the history of a nation of immigrants. For Asma and Inam, it is also an entirely new view on a city they have been living in, isolated it their community of a hermetic microcosmic character. It is a similar experience to the one Nazneen, Chanu and their two daughters in *Brick Lane* have when after over a decade in London, they leave the east London borough of Tower Hamlets and go to see the Buckingham Palace. Both of the cities are gigantic creatures, tamable and approachable only locally for the immigrants portrayed in these two novels.

After Inam's death and the memorial scandal two years later, Asma's microcosm very slowly expands beyond her neighborhood in Brooklyn and similarly to Nazneen, the main character of Ali's *Brick Lane*, 9/11 functions as a trigger to look for the self in the city, unchained from marriage and disregarding obligations imposed by the radical religious community. For both women, 9/11 is indirectly liberating in terms of spatial perception of the city. New spaces become accessible and shape their new urban life. Leaving Kensington is not easy at all though, as she is being followed by men from the Bangladeshi community who want to "protect" her. Kensington is "sealed" and Asma realizes that the compulsory belonging her community imposes on her, makes her feel imprisoned (171). Especially after the head-scarf pulling episode and the wave of hostile acts against Muslim women, the community of Little Dhaka tightens. When she eventually manages to leave it to go to the City Hall for the public hearing about Khan's memorial design, she observes other women on the subway and comments on the remarkably private character of this public space that becomes the extension of each and individual home:

> She [Asma] relished the way private lives were conducted in these public cars, as if they were just extra rooms in a house. Women put on their makeup and took off their heels, ate their lunches and cooled their coffee. They had no shyness about sharing the lines of their underwear or the color of their bras, the veins in

their calves or the moles on their arms. They chewed, read, spoke, sang, and prayed [227].

The subway in the post–9/11 context is an important space within the city's body: an extension of home, an underground parallel universe of arteries. It is an equalizer, a place of random encounters and exchanges but also a potential target, so a subject to catastrophic visions. Masha Hamilton's dystopian post–9/11 novel *31 Hours* for instance uses the subway system as a center of its plot and as a target of a fictitious terrorist attack.

Asma is fully aware of the hermetic aspects of her community and the previously imagined life in America remains a remote concept, unreachable despite the geographical proximity. During the public hearing Asma speaks up as the only Muslim woman in the "camp" of the victims' families. Few days later Alyssa Spier writes an article about her entitled "Illegal" and Asma faces a deportation. Preparing for her journey back to Bangladesh, she tries to grasp the essence of the imaginary attached to the country of her dreams and fills her suitcase with what she would like to become her American memories:

> Nike shoes; T-shirts with Disneyland and the White House and all the places she had never been; glossy magazines and American flags; history books she could not read.... As Bangladeshis had created a Little Bangladesh here, she would create for herself and Abdul a Little America back home [250].

The symbols Asma chooses for her son to associate with the U.S. bring to light her feeling of displacement and cultural confusion. Despite living a life within the symbolic borders of Little Dhaka, she keeps idealizing America. Her memories of the ferry trip in form of photos are "flat and mute" (252), miserable and unsatisfactory. Living in the city, she remains outside and keeps dreaming about belonging to the other, imaginary and inaccessible reality. Asma is stabbed on her last day in the U.S., outside of her house, when leaving for the airport. Journalists, portrayed again as a flock of vultures, are all around her ready to document her departure and not unhappy about the scoop that her death turns to be.

One of the many masks of the city this novel portrays is the one of a beast; untamable, aggressive and evil. Asma is the victim-figure in this story that falls into the clutches of New York and does not manage to escape.

The Future of the City: A Literary Vision

The novel provides an epilogue in which all the characters are shown again. The setting, quite atypically for post–9/11 fiction, moves into the future and puts everything, including 9/11 into perspective: twenty years after the memorial competition, in year 2023 Claire's son William and his girlfriend make a documentary about the selection process and interview people involved. The film within the novel features an interview with Claire whose skin is gray and unhealthy, "devastated like the ruins of Kabul" (294). She regrets withdrawing her initial support for Khan. Mo lives a jetsetter's life, lonely but full of privileges. He co-owns an architecture company based in New York but hardly ever visits the city, stigmatized by the events of the reimagined year 2003. His designs are famous, mostly built in the Middle East and only exposed as showpieces-models in galleries in the U.S. Asma's son Abdul is back with his grandparents in Bangladesh, filmed surrounded by his mother's memories of the U.S. that he has never unpacked or used. They form a museum, a private memorial for his mother that replaces Abdul's own missing memories of her.

Waldman shows New York as a city that fears the urban ruin and that wants to have all superfluous elements removed. It also fears the memory of the ruin, a process Liam Kennedy refers to as the "willed amnesia" (36). The conflict over the creation of a new space within Manhattan that is meant to preserve the memory of the towers, looked at from a time perspective seems superficial and serving only the satisfaction of frustrated individuals. New York in this novel has lost a great architect and a design that could literarily grow into the city and partly change its character. Mohammad Kahn, the media-creation and the universal Other has been deprived of his identity for the purposes of mass satisfaction. He became successful elsewhere, shifting the idea of the American Dream and moving with it outside of the U.S., after he was forced to submit to its post–9/11 discriminatory politics and practices. Waldman's novel in its fable-like character tries to provide a bitter lesson and a thorough criticism of the hypocrisy and bigotry of the U.S. society. She does so through assigning her characters to different parts of the city which serves as a structure for the novel and the conflict.

Thinking of the city as text and consequently as a language, Waldman and other writers who, as Sebastian Groes points out in his study of the city novel are "interpreters and translators of the various, often conflicting discourses the city offers ... take their city right inside our minds to construct profoundly real, imaginary" (16) New Yorks and Londons. Waldman's reappropriation of New York through this novel is her submission to writing the city after 9/11. Choosing "The Submission" as a title, she provides a frame of space, text and "othering" within which the plot of the novel, centered on navigating the city, is set.

Part Two

London

V

Unpredictable and Insane: London as a Body, London as Brain

Personifications and anthropomorphisms of London play a prominent role in post–9/11 fiction and in each of the novels chosen for this study. In Cleave's *Incendiary* the nameless narrator of a letter addressed to Osama bin Laden, the post–9/11 enemy number one, can be read as an embodiment of London. Her letter functions as an attempt at self-defense and auto-therapy which the city desperately needs. In Ali's novel the street Brick Lane swallows demonstrating marchers entering its neck (Ali 468). In McEwan's *Saturday* the city is portrayed as a brain—smart and independent but damaged and fully unpredictable.

The metaphor of London as a wounded body which experiences pain and must be healed, stems from a long tradition of imagining cities as systems belonging to the human organism. It also contributes to the post–9/11 urban discourse that portrays cities as ill bodies and individuals living in them as a collectively wounded organism requiring communal healing—an urban therapy and joint storytelling. Many novels and theoretical philosophical texts refer to the post–9/11 urban space in organic terms (Däwes *Ground Zero Fiction* 290) and the notion of a collective contagious disease is present in many fictional responses, and directly or symbolically appears in all of the novels analyzed in this study. The fact that the threat, the aggressive *virus* can actually be coming from within one's own (American, British) organism (Žižek, Borradori and Derrida) establishes a whole new rhetoric and perspective marked by distrust, paranoia and helplessness with regard to one's own symbolic body. These sentiments find reflection in literature; there are a wide range of post–9/11 "medically symbolic approaches" (Däwes 295) which focus on physical and emotional healing processes. In many of them the threshold between therapists or doctors and patients becomes blurred as they all seem to require a cure and often appear equally helpless in their respective roles. Bodies are shown as rebellious and immune to treatments; able to develop suicidal tendencies–a notion derived from an enemy whose power over the Western logic is marked by a readiness to sacrifice its own life. Jacques Derrida talks about symptoms of "suicidal autoimmunity" in the context of the terrorist attacks but also in the context of the hijackers as individual bodies: "these hijackers incorporate, so to speak, two suicides in one: their own (and one will remain forever defenseless in the face of a suicidal, autoimmunitary aggression—and that is what terrorizes most) but also the suicide of those who welcomed, armed and trained them" (Borradori 95).

Richard Sennett's study *Flesh and Stone* provides a thorough analysis of the history of the concept of portraying cities as bodies, from ancient Athens to multicultural 20th century New York. According to him, the body system stands for completeness, wholeness, coherence and unity with the environment it dominates. What Sennett calls "master images" of the body have been used frequently in the history of urban development to define what a building or a whole city should look like. However, the body metaphor has always been limited to ideal bodies: young males in ancient Greece, Christians in Renaissance Venice (Sennett *Flesh and Stone* 24). Chris Cleave's novel chooses the anemic form of a hysterical white uneducated woman to embody the powerful capital; the resulting incongruity is purposefully humorous. His narrative in this context is set against the power practiced by body politics that repress by exclusion (Sennett *Flesh and Stone* 24) and indicates that the post–9/11 (urban) body stands for unpredictability and chaos rather than wholeness and harmony.

According to Sennett, the city has always had to accommodate the changing needs of the civic body and the metaphor of city as a body developed and changed with new medical discoveries. A tremendous shift in perception of both body and city was marked by William Harvey's discoveries about blood circulation. His 1628 *De motu cordis* was "a scientific revolution in the understanding of the body" (Sennett *Flesh and Stone* 255). Harvey claimed that the circulation heats blood and causes its movement rather than the reverse. This occurs mechanically—through the heart that works nonstop. Pain, like blood, circulates through the body. According to Cleave's *Incendiary*, so does fear. When 18th century medical research showed that human skin must breathe in order to keep the whole body healthy, not only fashion changed, but also the city's skin became more exposed and transparent and European cities became cleaner. Cities were intended to function as healthy bodies (Sennett *Flesh and Stone* 263).

Alexis de Tocqueville called the 19th century the Age of Individualism (*Democracy in America*) and, according to Richard Sennett, London became the 19th century's world capital in terms of its exemplary individualism (Sennett *Flesh and Stone* 323). The modern city was highly influenced by the lonely and ever faster moving individual. It was meant to adjust to the desire of a constant, free and independent speed. Harvey's revolutionary concept influenced urban planners. The city was intended to become an organism with veins and arteries of constantly moving individuals, circulating freely. However, these individual bodies became restless and atomized in this fast operating urban cardiovascular system, as "circulation as a value in medicine and in economics has created an ethics of indifference" (Sennett 1994: 257). Constant movement at individually adjusted paces makes the modern individual lose connection to other constantly moving bodies.

A movement-based system fragmentizes society. The 19th century produced urban spaces adjusted to individuals in motion (rather than to moving groups or crowds). Together with the terrorist attack in Cleave's novel, the freedom of movement stops, as does the modern circulation of the city. London is being fortified, which stops its development and essentially moves back time, bringing the city back to the Middle Ages, or to the Great Fire as the textual framing of the novel suggests, making a multicultural coexistence practically impossible. In Cleave's novel this almost totalitarian redevelopment of city space is being justified by national security. People, acting now as a mass, feel threatened and comply. This exaggerated caricature links the dystopian portrait of London to post–9/11 New York and to the process of "securitization" (Schilling and Vormann) of the urban space. The exposure to London provided in this text by an emotionally instable and possibly insane woman makes the link between city and human brain especially prominent. The society invaded by fear and "brainwashed" by the security discourse acts inconsistently and dogmatically as a mass. A post-traumatic brain disease can also metaphorically be seen in the city's structure in which basic connections are being blocked or removed. As a result closed bridges do not connect anymore and the urban hemispheres of Cleave's London do not function as an entity, causing a communicational collapse and social immobility, effectively paralyzing the metropolis.

The link between the human brain and the metropolis is present most prominently in McEwan's *Saturday* and Cole's *Open City*. Both feature characters who *work* with brains and take their neurological knowledge with them when walking through the city. In Cole's *Open City* the post–9/11 flâneur Julius is a psychiatrist who seeks emotional rest from his work by mapping the city. The motif is even more explicit in McEwan's *Saturday*, which focuses on one day of a neurosurgeon whose work interferes with the text of the novel on a semantic and linguistic level: his professional neuro-cognitive vocabulary enters the narration and the city on several occasions and so do the functions of specific parts of the human brain. Brains and brain surgeries influence the way he sees and perceives the world around him; accordingly a part of his patient's brain is a "familiar territory, a kind of homeland" to him (McEwan 254) and parts of it are to be avoided just like "bad neighborhoods in an American city" (254) and the surface of the scull resembles a "paving" (256).

Such metaphorical imagery has been consistently employed throughout the centuries and remains a highly exploited motif. Among the most remarkable examples of visual urban references to the human brain is the map of Hamburg from 1853 (Figure 2) printed in Steven Johnson's *Emergence* next to a photograph of a side view of the human brain; the more contemporary subway map of a 'brain-city' which appeared on HSBC advertisement billboards or the 2010 illustration by an artist called Mr. Sutu (Figure 3) which combines the human brain with, in the post–9/11 context, fear-generating skyscrapers.

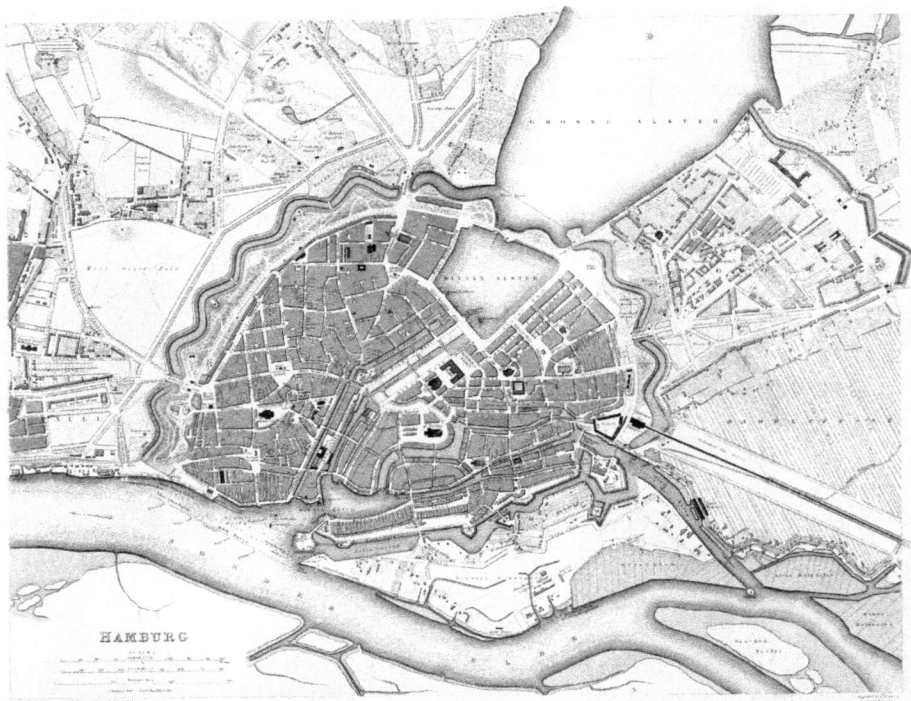

Figure 2. Map of Hamburg, Germany, 1853. Drawn in 1853 under the direction of William Lindley, Esq. C.E. April 1841; engraved by B.R. Davies. London: George Cox, 1853. Courtesy Harvard Map Collection.

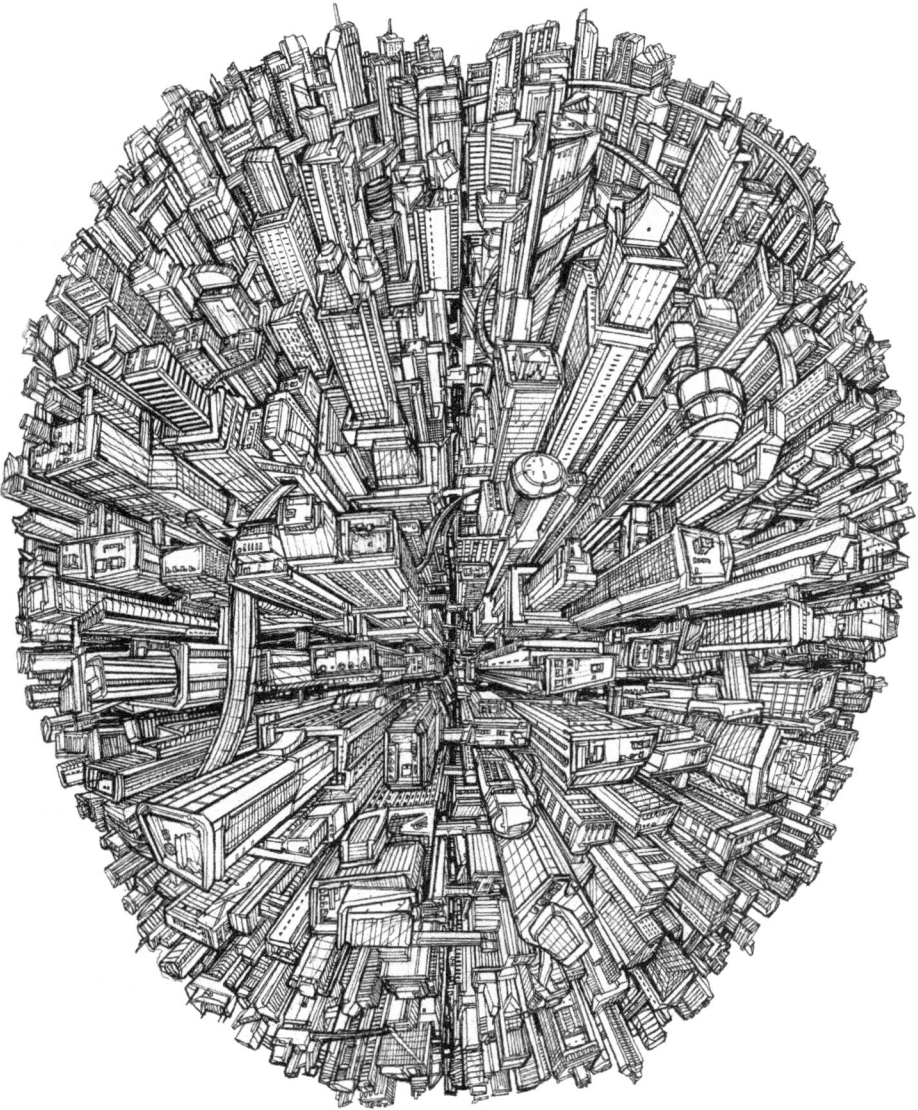

Figure 3. City brain full of fear-generating skyscrapers. Corresponds with what the main character in Naqvi's *Home Boy* calls "the skyline of memory." Sutu. Online interactive comic, Nawlz. www.nawlz.com.

VI

Hemisphere 1: London East End

Two novels analyzed here are set in the East London Borough Tower Hamlets, described in the 2011 Census as a place "of continued increasing diversity, with sizable Bangladeshi (32 percent) and white British communities (31 percent) but also an increasing number of smaller ethnic groups in the resident population re-affirming the hyper diverse nature of the Borough" (Census 1). While Monica Ali's *Brick Lane* focuses on the Bengali community, Chris Cleave's *Incendiary* is set among the white working class living next door. On the ground of these two novels, these worlds are aware of one another but hardly ever interfere. In *Brick Lane*, despite the lack of actual contact or exchange, demographical changes in the borough trigger an abstract dichotomous relationship between the Bengali community and the white population.

The process of gentrification and its consequences feature in both of the narratives. Ali's novel shows life in Tower Hamlets from mid–1980s up to 2002. *Incendiary* covers the period of one year marked by changing seasons and is set after 9/11 but without a specific time frame. It creates a catastrophic vision of a wounded and suffering London after an imaginary terrorist attack. Both novels feature female characters and narrators, Nazneen—a Bangladeshi woman who lives in London because "this is what happened to her" (Ali 72) when her father arranged her marriage (*Brick Lane*)—and a nameless narrator in Cleave's *Incendiary* whose family comes from this area and has always been London's "back rotten teeth" as opposed to the "decadent" (5) West End.

In both of the novels the main characters write letters that connect them to an imaginary world outside of the microcosmic borough. The process of writing within the novels is a liberating practice which offers escape to a different set of images. *Incendiary* is one seemingly never-ending letter in which the narrator describes the reality around her to such a degree that it seems remote and unreal. *Brick Lane* features regular epistolary intervals consisting mostly of letters that Nazneen receives from her sister Hasina from Dhaka. These letters do interfere with Nazneen's London life, but the clash between the world described in the letters and the one behind her kitchen window is dramatic. Hasina's letters form a linguistic rupture in the narrative, as they are written in broken English, a narrative decision highly criticized by some scholars.[1] It is through the correspondence Nazneen receives that the content of her own letters can be anticipated. Through her sister's accounts, the reality of life in Dhaka enters the gloomy setting of Nazneen's residence on London's Dogwood Estates, establishing a trans-metropolitan connection of almost magic quality. In both novels letter-writing is a mode of storytelling that connects the characters with East London and with their pasts, spatially or symbolically attached to remote elsewheres.

In *Brick Lane* the events of 9/11 reach Tower Hamlets in the form of "New York dust" (Ali 368) blown over through the wind across the ocean. This dust sets on the buildings, streets and the everyday life of the metropolis and, most importantly, it marks Muslim inhabitants of London as Others. In *Incendiary* the events of 9/11 are embodied by the evil Other, to whom the 340-page letter is addressed. The detailed account of London's multifaceted reactions to the imaginary terrorist attack links the city in the novel to post–9/11 New York and anticipates a threat that floats over London. In both novels the metaphor of city as body is prominent and forms a key concept in the relation between the female protagonists and the imaginary bodies of London they are continuously confronted with.

The events of 9/11, though geographically remote, enter in all three novels the body and cartography of London and fill it with fear, a fear difficult to connect to anything from the city's past, although attempts are made; Cleave refers his disastrous vision to the Great Fire of London and McEwan tries to connect his main character with someone of his profession in Edwardian England a century earlier. The fear that enters London has to be analyzed spatially. The city is tense and nervous, as are the characters. The influence is reciprocal and the urban fear causes chaos. One way of escaping it is to remain within the comfort zone of one's own neighborhood. The female narrators in *Incendiary* and *Brick Lane* write and reappropriate London after it has been covered with the "New York dust" but they do it differently to the narrators in post–9/11 New York novels.

Writing the City Out of Chaos: Chris Cleave's *Incendiary*

Chris Cleave's *Incendiary*, published on the day of the terrorist attacks in London on July 7, 2005, takes the form of a dramatic monologue, like Hamid's *The Reluctant Fundamentalist*. It is written as a long letter addressed to Osama bin Laden from an anonymous English woman. This chapter discusses how the narrative voice stands for both a wounded individual and the wounded metropolis, bringing together the concepts of cities as bodies and of contextualizing human bodies through urban space. It points to the specificity of London-related references and dark British humor as ways of localizing, retelling and processing a fictitious disaster in an urban environment. Following H.V. Savitch's[2] writing on urban terror, I propose to establish a link between the fictitious act of urban terror and chaos and to look at writing performed within the texts as a therapeutic way out of it, within the metaphorical frame of a metropolis. The chapter also focuses on the process of "othering" in post–9/11 London, as mirrored in Cleave's novel.

The narrator begins to write after the death of her husband and son in a fictional terrorist attack on a football stadium in London on the 1st of May. In this disaster fantasy that becomes known as "May Day," Arsenal is playing Chelsea at home, which, quite significantly and ironically considering the plot is in the Emirates Stadium in Islington in North London. It is a sunny bank holiday in the multicultural capital of a country where football is a sport of national importance. The stadium is full of people, a joyful crowd that becomes exposed, a vulnerable mass deprived of individualism—similar to the marchers in *Brick Lane* who are exposed to incontrollable violence. The attack is conducted by eleven suicide bombers, six wearing fragmentation bombs and five wearing incendiaries underneath their Arsenal kits. One thousand and three people die in this imaginary act of city terror. H.V. Savitch links the phenomenon of urban terror to chaos perceived and spread through space. Central and crowded urban spaces are especially vulnerable and therefore become targets because of the chaos which their destruction causes:

> From the standpoint of territory, urban terror is directed against bounded areas characterised by high-density, continuous development, diversified activities and interdependent environments that are central to the larger society. Centrality is important and urban terror is designed to challenge control over these key areas in order to demonstrate their propensity for disruption and vulnerability to attack. Certain concentrated spaces are targeted because hitting them will optimize damage and precipitate chaos [Savitch 362].

Accordingly, London in this catastrophic vision turns into urban chaos: it becomes an overwhelming, incoherent, unpredictable and furious body impossible to control. Described by a traumatized character in a letter to an enemy that she herself has to recreate and reimagine in order to address, the city's wounds melt with her own ones. This female narrator is a bizarre hybrid who, it becomes clear as the story progresses, embodies the city and personifies its distortion and chaos. The motif is similar to that used by Mohsin Hamid in *The Reluctant Fundamentalist* where a woman named Erica and America become indistinguishable, both on the level of language and text. In Cleave's novel the anonymous woman becomes the voice and the body of London. She rewrites the city out of chaos. The traumatized individual writes the traumatized city and in this process they start to emulate each another. The imagined chaos which over-shadows London and changes its structure and character is a dystopian urban answer to the events of 9/11. In this novel the British capital mirrors many aspects of post–9/11 urban reality of New York City. *Incendiary* is a response to 9/11 from the other side of the Atlantic; it is a projection that represents deepest fears restrained by morbid humor. Despite the irony intended to ease the apocalyptic vision, the novel is a dark and fearful anticipation of the attacks of July 7 2005.

Incendiary begins and ends with inscriptions taken from the monument to the Great Fire of London of 1666, which marks a continuity of disasters and stresses the strength of the city that will always recover, it seems, after even the most terrible catastrophe. An inscription from the north side of the monument opens the novel:"A most terrible fire broke out, which not only wasted the adjacent parts, but also places very remote, with incredible noise and fury." The ending frame is taken from the south side:"The work was carried on with diligence, and London is restored; but whether with greater speed or beauty, may be made a question." The letter is placed within the mentioned historical frames; writing it serves as "work carried on with diligence" and is meant to restore the city, to cure it from commotion. The chaos that overwhelmed New York City on 9/11 hatched between the two plane-hits: the time frame—after the North Tower was hit and before the South one became a target—was enough for the media to start transmission and "spread" terror. Fictional "May Day" is framed in the city's real history, embedded in its past and inscribed in its presence. In this way Cleave creates a continuity of urban disasters.

As a city much older than New York, London has a longer history of disasters of all kinds. Further, its medial image more completely incorporates its past to the present; its history and legacy are important elements of the city's current everyday life; they are inseparable from the here and now, which Cleave points to through a number of historical references. In his novel London is built around gaps that stand for the past and connect the city with its history. In Cleave's novel, just as in McEwan's *Saturday*, London is defined through its history but it is not protected by it. In the face of terrorism it becomes vulnerable and "lies wide open, impossible to defend, waiting for its bomb, like a hundred other cities" (McEwan *Saturday* 276).

The narrator of *Incendiary* writes through the period of one year. She establishes a one-sided relationship with the addressee of her letter who from the collective evil Other becomes her secret companion and imaginary therapist. First she addresses him with hatred and aggression, later on with humor and trust. She writes retrospectively, recalling the events that followed the "May

Day" attacks, and presents herself as a completely unreliable narrator. She keeps seeing her dead son and describes herself as being often in "quite of a state." This marks further similarities with Hamid's novel, whose narrator Changez describes himself as an "emotional madman." Through questioning the relevance and accuracy of his own statements, he confuses the addressee of the dramatic monologue. Both Changez and the author of the letter in *Incendiary* address their own unreliability, and make themselves unpredictable. This paradoxically gives them power over the mute narratees. The endings of both novels are left open. At the end of *Incendiary* the narrator kills a woman and awaiting consequences continues writing the letter:

> The coppers will find me here soon and they'll take me away and have me banged up. I don't blame them I mean you can't have people like me strolling around with petrol cans [337].

Writing becomes the ultimate reason to live; it brings continuity to her life and to the life of the city. It also connects her to the city and places her own insanity within a larger urban context. Writing is the only form of narrating and controlling her life and her identity; it is addictive and necessary to survive. Once she stops, her life and the novel are over.

Humor as a Cure

The narrator finds out about the attack on the stadium through live media coverage, which again links "May Day" to the attacks of 9/11 and comments on the role of mass media and the production of images which spread terror and transform the attacks into a collective experience. The narrator of *Incendiary* watches the live coverage of the football game on her "telly," while cheating on her husband with another man in her living room. When the explosion happens, cameras keep showing the stadium and the horror of the attacks. Only afterwards the transmission is being interrupted, just like the sexual act on the sofa. A commercial panel is displayed on the screen—"WHY NOT UPGRADE TO SKY DIGITAL?"—to which the narrator thinks/answers, "Yes ... why not?" (58). This satirical take on an internal monologue is one of the first indications of many tragic-humorous effects that Cleave makes use of throughout the novel.

Humor is an important therapeutic tool in writing the trauma and chaos of the city. In the text it is achieved through bringing together incongruous elements which as an entity appear ridiculous. Another example of this is that the narrator's husband works in bomb disposal, the stress of which causes her to seek physical attention from other men, as sex and "G&Ts" are her way to deal with stress. This is how she meets Jasper Black—her lover and witness of the news delivered by British Sky Broadcasting. He drives her to the stadium where she is injured while looking for her husband and her boy, as she refers to them throughout. Only characters from outside of the broken family microcosm have names; these are always referred to with both first and surname. This way of referring to people universalizes the concept of family and makes her particular one symbolic of many. After these tragic events the narrator wakes up in a hospital where she is told that her husband and son died. Lying there, she has a view on London from above and observes the way the city changes after the attack on its urban body:

> London and me healed slowly. They worked on the city to make it stronger and they worked on me too.... I had 4 operations and then that was that. There was nothing to do except lie there and wait for myself to get better. For 6 weeks I just stared out of the window watching them fortify London [86].

The above quote is the first textual reference that appears in the novel that indicates the link between the city and the human body. The text works with this motif intensely and uses it to both make London more approachable and degrade it to a vulnerable creature with inclination to addictions.

Gentrification and the Urban Other

The narrator comes from and represents the poor white East London—the now highly gentrified area around Shoredich, Hackney and Bethnal Green where cultures coexist but do not really interact. This is the area, the borough of Tower Hamlets, where Nazneen in Ali's *Brick Lane* lives. Its large Bangladeshi community together with the 'indigenous' white Eastenders is slowly pushed away as the borough becomes more and more popular among investors and white middle-class newcomers. The 2011 Census noted a decrease of the Bangladeshi population of the borough by 1.4 percent comparing to 2001.[3] Cleave's narrator refers to the ongoing process of gentrification in her typically sarcastic way:

> One thing you start to hate when you live in London is the way rich people live right next to you. They'll suddenly plonk themselves right next door and the next thing you know your old street is An Upcoming Bohemian Pot With Excellent Transport Links which means there are posh motors boxing in your Vauxhall Astra every morning [38–39].

Her well-off lover Jasper Black symbolically represents the process of gentrification. He has a good job at a newspaper and lives in an expensive new apartment just opposite the run down Wellington Estates where the narrator lives. He takes cocaine, a luxury drug, and is bored with the hermetic world in which he works and lives. This boredom of privilege makes him perceive the area and the no-name narrator as exotically attractive, an experience in its nature similar to the colonial gaze.

In the context of New York City, gentrification can be addressed through the scope of the frontier narrative (Schillings and Vormann): previously unpopular areas in the city are being "conquered" by wealthier people. In changing the character of these areas, also the people involved in the process change. The gentrifiers undergo a transformation along with the "conquered" area, just as European settlers moving west on the American continent established new identities through the newly conquered places, a parallel suggested by Sonja Schillings and Boris Vormann in their article *The Vanishing Poor*. Following this argument in regard to New York, Jasper, the embodiment of London gentrification becomes somebody new and changes with the "conquered" area of East London. His presence is linked to the colonial legacy of East London and its large Bangladeshi population. Gentrification as a force imposing itself on particular culturally and socially defined urban spaces is hence compared to colonialism on a scale of a metropolis.

In Cleave's parody, the narrator is granted a developed sense of humor and distance from herself and the world around her. Combining trauma with humor within the protagonist links the Freudian understanding of humor as the highest defense mechanism with Critchley's notion of laughter as the power of turning the world awry. According to him, laughter has a certain "redemptive or messianic power" (Critchley 65). The narrator reflects on her writing and admits she is doing it for the first time; her response to trauma is subconsciously to turn towards a new activity. Michelle Balaev's study of traumatic behaviors defines trauma as "a person's emotional response to an overwhelming event that disrupts previous ideas of an individual's sense of self and the standards by which one evaluates society" (150).

> The last thing I wrote was N/A on an income support form that wanted NAME OF SPOUSE OR PARTNER. So you see I'll do my best but you'll have to bear with me because I'm not a big writer [4].

In the same way, disruptive processes caused by urban trauma become visible in the city: after 9/11 garbage cans disappear from the streets of London, which unsurprisingly become covered with waste. Racial profiling and discrimination in the urban public becomes accepted and justified by security measures. The traumatized city also reacts emotionally and impulsively.

Long before 9/11, Jane Jacobs wrote about the urban Other in the context of New York City. When a person or a group is "othered" in the urban context (because of being poor, immigrant or different), they are excluded not only socially but spatially. Forced out of the city center through rising prices and racial discrimination, they have to move to the outskirts. Jane Jacobs calls this process "the self-destruction of diversity" which causes downtowns to shift their centers and move (256), a force that creates "has-been districts" and is responsible for the inner city stagnation. The Muslim Other in the context of post–911 social changes in *Incendiary* is created by the mass media after the fictitious "May Day," similarly to the image created through media in Waldman's *The Submission* after the identity of the main character Mohammad is revealed. The omnipresent fear that quickly infiltrates the entire city body evokes racism and discrimination against foreigners, particularly Muslims. At the hospital the narrator befriends a Muslim nurse Mena. One day she is replaced by a white nurse:

> Hello. What happened to Mena?—They stopped her working didn't they? ...—Come again?—Muslim wasn't she? said the new nurse. Security risk. They suspended all of them from working as of midnight. This country's finally starting to get it. Don't get me wrong. I'm sure 99 percent of the Muslims are fine but if you can't trust some of them you can't trust any of them can you? [91].

Everyone in *Incendiary*, including the authorities, acts as if under a bad spell, making them appear ridiculous. Cleave shows this absurd behavior by using common stereotypes, again with a humorous effect, as in the episode when the police arrest Japanese tourists for taking photos on a bridge. Cleave's novel ridicules the absurd paranoia post–9/11 that weakens the entire urban system instead of protecting it. The text suggests that there is a new, very limited post–9/11 "image repertoire" to use Roland Barthes' phrasing (*A Lover's Discourse*) in which intuition, cultural knowledge and experience are made irrelevant and are replaced by blind paranoia and basic instinct. According to Richard Sennett, the classifying powers of this kind of prototyping are so strong that "people shut out further stimulation" (*Flesh and Stone* 365) and become passive, which is very much the case in *Incendiary*. Additionally, Cleave's projection anticipates the events in London after the 7/7 attacks, when police killed innocent Jean Charles de Menezes because he was classified as a threat.

Although the narration in *Incendiary* is set specifically in East London, other parts of the city and their historical and cultural contexts also play an important role; they are also parts of the whole body—elegant and expensive South Kensington, the river Thames dividing south from north, the postcolonial legacy of places dominated by the immigrant population. All spatial and cultural references that the narrator makes are London-related. It is not the country that is important or relevant; it is London that is being described as a microcosm, as an independent space, an island, a world in itself. The rest of the United Kingdom or the world outside are entirely secondary.

The novel describes London in a state of delirium; it is portrayed as a sick body that needs help. At the same time the letter is a form of a collective therapy and motivation to recover. Referring to the city's history puts the events of "May Day" into perspective. After all, London is a strong urban body with tough personality. The narrator notes how after the fire Londoners "got up the next day and the world hadn't ended so they rebuilt the city in three years stronger and taller." In fact "even Hitler couldn't finish us" (79). However, after "May Day" London mourns and is deeply traumatized.

Trauma is the source of writing—it motivates the narrator to describe, to process, narrate and bitterly laugh about the tragedy. Later on in the novel she also admits that she does not know much about punctuation, a fact visible in her letter. The position of commas is random, and in some sentences punctuation is entirely missing. The parts of the letter express different moods: the more stressed or nervous she gets, the less attention is paid to punctuation, reflecting the current emotional state. This corresponds to Robert Ezra Park's idea from the 1920s that the city is much more than buildings, streets and public transport networks; a city is in fact a "state of mind, a *body* of customs and traditions" (Park 1, emphasis mine) and a place that enforces specific urban behaviors (Pile 1). Steve Pile argues that a given city's irreplaceable state of mind, "its sentiments, its attitudes, its sense of self" (2), influence the way cities are imagined, perceived and written. Frustrated and paranoid London is deprived not only of garbage bins but also of punctuation, its mood inscribed in the texture of its writing. The process of writing has a soothing effect and becomes the only sense-generating aspect of the narrator's life. She performs writing for writing's sake and is trying to write herself and the city out of trauma.

"Royalty, crime, transport, weather": London's Tabloid Discourse

The letter is written in Cockney English—a slang associated with the East London working class. A cultural reference mentioned frequently is the British tabloid *The Sun*. Before expressing her own views, the narrator first mentions what has been written in the tabloid on a given subject, and then comments on that. Her thoughts seem therefore to be derivative and produced by a strong influence of the tabloid's dichotomies. However, quite remarkably, she mostly disagrees and comes to opposite conclusions which go far beyond the social and educational status that she assigns to herself. This discrepancy also makes her appear less reliable and less trustworthy as a narrator. Sometimes she writes in quotes from *The Sun*; they are marked in the text by the use of capital letters—as if one was reading the first page headlines.

> The Sun says you are an EVIL MONSTER but I don't believe in evil I know it takes two to tango. I know you're vexed at the leaders of Western imperialism. Well I'll be writing to them too [4].

This tabloid discourse and the immediacy with which it delivers the message become a part of the narrator's and London's identity. The headlines seem to be everywhere—in the narrator's mind as well an in the city—and it is impossible to escape them; they "hit" people passing by. Just like the streets of New York in Amy Waldman's *The Submission*, here the papers scream at passers-by and shape their opinions, influence their well-being, and transmit moods, often in such a way as to be unnoticed. One does not have to buy a copy of the paper to be exposed to its headlines. Iain Sinclair sees the boards outside newsagents' shops as a medium for the city to compose "its own disposable legend. Royalty, crime, transport, weather. On a daily basis. Unselfconscious surrealism" (17). This reflects the way in which tabloid discourse forms the city discourse in Cleave's novel. Just as the life of the royal family, which the narrator closely follows, crime, transport and weather play important roles. Rain and cold constitute a part of the city's image and influence *people's* lives, moods and ways of inter-human communication. The weather is a common topic in superficial metropolitan small talk but also has the power to make people aggressive and unhappy:

> Rain makes us vicious. People were bumping into each other and giving it the old lip and stepping into puddles and all the traffic was jammed and as if all that wasn't enough it was effing Monday wasn't it [251].

Bad weather combined with unreliable public transport shape London's everyday reality but also make the city great, and according to Cleave's narrator somewhat exclusive; it distinguishes people from the "Arab types" and makes them nobler:

> Everyone was late for work and complaining to people on their mobiles. Loudly so that the rest of us could all get an earful. People took it in turns. That's how the English have a good moan these days Osama. Heaven forbid we should actually grumble to our neighbors in the bus queue. We're not like you hot-blooded Arab types.... It's the climate you see. It's the rain on Bethnal Green Road that makes Britain great and I stood in it for half an hour before I gave up and walked to the Tube and the Tube was closed too so it was your typical bloody London good morning [250].

The weather is a part of what constitutes London—it is inscribed in the city's geography. Not only does it interfere with the individual bodies of passers-by, it also screams at them from the newsstand. At the same time it functions as a safe haven: it is always there and can be talked about, written about, complained about, discussed.

The narrator acknowledges the uniqueness of the language, pronunciation and the Cockney slang that she links to the city and through which she identifies with it. She is one out of many London's "teeth" in the middle of the city's extraordinary mouth:

> I saw the video you made Osama where you said the West was decadent. Maybe you meant the West End? We aren't all like that. London is a smiling liar his front teeth are very nice but you can smell his back teeth rotten and stinking. My family was never rotten poor but we were hard up there's a difference.... We were not the nice front teeth or the rotten back teeth of London and there are millions of us just like that.... If you're interested Osama just put down that Kalashnikov for a second and look up chav pikey ned or townie in Google [5].

The city's illness is a result of a long chain of disasters visible in its architecture and the urban structure. The present architecture is linked by destruction to its descendants and hence to its past. New buildings replace old destroyed ones but carry their legacy and history: "They built our tower blocks in the Fifties. They built them in the gaps where the Georgian Gems had incendiaries dropped on them by Adolf Hitler" (6).

The way in which the narrator "writes" her city allows her to share her loss, and as she believes, to heal the world with it. In other words, writing is a mission. In the process, her sorrow and grief develop to positive feelings towards Osama and in consequence she gradually starts to blame others for her loss. She shifts her reproaches away from the "evil Other"; when talking about his heart and imagining his feelings she "un-others" and befriends him: "As for you I know you'd stop the bombs in a second if I could make you see my son with all your heart for just one moment" (4). After she finds out that the police knew about "May Day," she blames them instead of Osama, who at this point has become a friend or imaginary therapist.

There is also a strong parallel to the constantly circulating conspiracy theories linking the attacks of September 11 to the U.S. government. In *Incendiary* the risk of the warning that came from a 'maul' has been underestimated by the police. When the narrator finds out about it from her boss and lover, Terence Butcher, her madness reaches an apogee. Everyone becomes a potential threat or enemy and the person whom she feels closest to is paradoxically Osama Bin Laden. As a consequence she feels so bitterly disappointed by everything that she once trusted that she is lost in her seemingly well-known reality. Feeling emotionally lost indicates displacement, also linked to the city. Obsessed with violent images she cold-bloodedly kills Jaspers' wife, the journalist Petra Sutherland, who failed to bring the narrator's story to the press and used it to make her career.

Locating trauma in a physical space is, according to Michelle Balaev, an important aspect of addressing it, as this location enables a larger cultural contextualization:

> The physical environment offers the opportunity to examine both the personal and cultural histories embedded in landscapes that define the character's identity and the meaning of the traumatic experience" … it anchors the individual experience within a larger cultural context, and in fact, organizes the memory and meaning of this trauma [150].

Chris Cleave's representation of London as a location traumatized by urban terror is very much based on the medial image and condition of New York City after 9/11. Following Max Page's argument that each era has its own concept or motif that dominates its destruction fantasies, this literary example confirms terrorism as the dominant fear in the 21st century's western imagination (*The City's End*). Types of behaviors and reactions that appear in a Western metropolis threatened by an unknown enemy appear here as a parody. The novel shows the weakness and vulnerability of individuals and masses overexposed to media's manipulative content. A society dominated by fear tends to exclude in order to protect. People are willing to give up their individual liberties for the sake of a vague concept of national security. Fear is a cause of mistrust; it is distracting, weakening and destructive, which Cleave shows in regard to an individual and entire community.

Disaster Goes Pop

The disaster's reflection through mass media is one angle offered by the novel; another angle is offered by popular culture more generally. It plays an equally important role and is also a source of humor. There are references to a fictitious song performed by Sir Elton John called "England's Heart Is Still Bleeding," a clear allusion to his song "Candle in the Wind" written after the death of Princess Diana and performed at her funeral, and also to Bruce Springsteen's post–9/11 "My City of Ruins." This symbolism goes against Georg Simmel's statement that "London has never acted as the heart of England but often as its intellect and always as its money bag" (3).

Mentioning monarchy in this humorous way portrays London as a very specific and non-replaceable urban setting. The novel shows the heart of the crown and the empire as fragile and stubbornly resistant to changing circumstances. The role of the contemporary *poet laureate* is to perform soppy songs and have them remixed according to occasion and season. The ridiculousness of this statement applies to the whole wounded city including the monarchy, unprepared for reality. "Barrage balloons" printed with the faces of "May Day" victims float over Cleave's London. They are visible from everywhere, forming a new landmark that can almost pull the city up into the sky: "London was a misty floating city with the thousand thick cables of the balloons lifting it into the sky" (90). The city becomes an isolated body, an independent island, a microcosm that can float and possibly disappear. This is a fantasy that can be linked to Foer's conception of New York's Sixth Borough in *Extremely Loud and Incredibly Close*—a part of the city that together with its people separates from the rest of New York and floats away to never return.

Although the novel is full of strictly British connotations and references, it addresses universal urban behaviors in a time of major crisis and fear. The latter brings people down to entirely predictable creatures and shapes a pattern of reactions ruled by fear and basic instincts which lies very close to a (simple) self-defense mechanism. The narrator admits that after "May Day" everyone has become more like animals. On a rainy day a man drops his briefcase while crossing a street and everything falls out of it. As he tries to collect his belongings, people keep walking and step on his things:

> OH FOR FUCK'S SAKE the man was shouting. CAN'T YOU FUCKING ROBOTS GIVE ME A CHANCE HERE? HAVEN'T YOU HEARD THIS IS MEANT TO BE A CIVILISED FUCKING COUNTRY? [251].

The public is portrayed as a brainwashed herd. It is hysterical, naïve and fed with dichotomous discourse that wants to divide good from evil. The narrator sarcastically comments on the distinction between "us" and "them" in one sentence: "There were no rubbish bins anymore and no Muslims with jobs. We were all much safer" (116). She seems to be the only one who in her insanity paradoxically has kept traces of common sense—nobody listens to her though, a metaphor for not respecting the city's social structures in times of collective paranoia.

The novel has a very pessimistic ending: it suggests the only chance to move on, to get out of trauma, is to "blow the world back together," to turn back the time.

> You've hurt London Osama but you haven't finished it you never will. London's like me it's too piss poor and ignorant to know when it's finished ... I am too stupid to know better I am a woman built on the wreckage of myself [115].

Incendiary ends, similarly to Foer's *Extremely Loud and Incredibly Close,*[4] with an attempt to bring things back to normal by erasing the attack from city's history: "Come to me Osama. Come to me and we will blow the world back together WITH INCREDIBLE NOISE AND FURY" (338). The inscription from the south side of the Monument to the Great Fire of London follows.

Cleave's novel is a catastrophic vision of a disaster that never happened, but the fact of its publication on July 7, 2005, makes the relationship between fiction and reality starkly prominent. The human body of the narrator and the urban body of London are so strongly interlinked and the wound affects both so deep, that it spreads over the entire world and London is everything that remains: "Everywhere is London…. For us. Don't you see? We are London. Anywhere we could go you'd always be grieving and I'd always be" (305).

London through the Kitchen Window: Monica Ali's *Brick Lane*

Monica Ali's 2003 novel *Brick Lane* was strongly criticized by male members of the Bangladeshi community of the East London borough Tower Hamlets, which the novel uses as its setting. Seen through the lens of the statistics[5] quoted by the character Chanu, Tower Hamlets is the place within London where there are "three point five Bangladeshis to one room…. All crammed together. They can't stop having children, or they bring over all their relatives and pack them in like little fish in a tin" (49).

In his analysis of critical media responses, Dominic Head mentions the aspects of representation and belonging as main arguments against Ali coming from within the community. It is again Chanu, who in the novel pronounces anti–Sylhetti prejudices, when in fact the majority of Bangladeshi population living in the borough is from the district of Sylhet. Ali was criticized for misrepresenting the borough—neither her nor her characters are from Sylhett (Head *Britain and Beyond* 76–77). A second wave of protests against the picture of the community drawn by the novel emerged during shootings for the film adaptation in 2006. It was perceived as an "despicable insult" for the Bangladeshi community which in the novel was portrayed as "backward, uneducated and unsophisticated" (Richard Lea for the *Guardian*, as quoted by Head in *Britain and Beyond* 77). Additionally, Brick Lane itself became at once "an icon of multicultural exotica and an incipient threat posed by cultural and religious difference" (Alexander 203), a culturally ambiguous and simultaneously highly gentrified space.

The title of the novel, which literally locates the plot by linking it to a specific London street, provides a spatial reference to writing and imagining the city. Narrowed down to one street and observed through a Brick Lane kitchen window, London becomes an abstract and mysterious cosmos which has to be imagined and written. At the same time, the novel constitutes an attempt to locate the inaccessible and provides a cartography of the invisible "locked" parts of the city; a map of a parallel reality.

The plot spans a period of thirty-five years, the longest of all the novels analyzed in this study. *Brick Lane* starts in 1967 with the birth of the main character Nazneen in Mymensingh District in East Pakistan (territory that four years later became part of the independent Bangladesh), continues in 1985 when she arrives in London's Tower Hamlets to be married to Chanu, a man twice her age with a frog-face (17), and "rolls of fat hanging low from his stomach" (23), chosen for her by her father. The narrative continues with a larger interruption between 1996 and 2001 through to the year 2002 and is set almost entirely in Tower Hamlets. It hence covers important shifts in the main character's life and the arranged marriage, and simultaneously spans essential political changes in the UK, the effects of which are visible in the otherwise hermetic community of the borough.

Chanu, who works at the local Council, comments on the political changes when describing the altering atmosphere in his office: "This Mrs. Thatcher is making more cuts. Spending cuts, spending cuts, that's all we hear. The council is being squeezed dry. Now we have to pay if we want biscuits with our tea. It's ridiculous" (42). Sebastian Groes sees *Brick Lane* primarily in this political context, as a politically critical piece of fiction set within the frames of Thatcher's and Blair's visions of society, none of which seem to include the Bengali community of the East London's borough (Groes 235).

Later, as a consequence of political change, Chanu loses the job and becomes a cab driver. This downgrades his intellectual aspirations but turns him more towards the city, an experience shared by Chuck in Naqvi's *Home Boy*. I argue that for both of the characters the new job is a way of controlling the city, which after 9/11 in both cases becomes overwhelming and dangerous.

UK Politics and Tower Hamlets: London through the Lens of the Other

According to Groes, Ali's novel is a "response to New Labour's attempts to translate their ideas about Britishness into reality" (235) and a proof of a "lack of genuine interest" (237) for certain areas and aspects of British society. In the novel it is 9/11 that eventually brings attention, interest, social concern—

embodied by social workers and news reporters—to the community. The borough, already highly gentrified in 2001, becomes subject to post–9/11 urban securitization, blown over the Atlantic together with the "New York dust" (Ali 368). The wave of false interest in the Bengali community of the borough, which in the novel serves mainly as evidence for the incompatibility of cultures and religions, results in a deepening of the process of "othering." This form of post–9/11 discrimination takes place on different levels but is symbolically addressed, just like in Waldman's *The Submission*, through hostile street acts of headscarf pulling.

The novel focuses on Nazneen and enters the isolated, inaccessible reality of the houses on Brick Lane, in which Muslim women, often "imprisoned" by their husbands, lead lonely and displaced lives. Locked in the flat, Nazneen has very little access to the actual city and its geography. Viewed from this angle, places lose their "materiality and substantiality" (Kral 66); they are disconnected and appear as different worlds, as islands. Bangladesh is a memory, London is a mystery: physically, linguistically, and culturally inaccessible. Banned by her husband from learning English, she holds on to every single word she can catch and memorize, since for her the language is one of the missing links to the world outside and to what she believes to be a better life.

The physical isolation in the flat in the high-rise Dogwood Estate transports Nazneen to a universal vacuum, an urban nowhere, an input-free and culture-proof place with thick walls and a broken toilet. Groes points to the language of realism that the novel uses in order to embrace this nowhere. Her cultural imprisonment is linked to the linguistic one, as in the case of Asma Anwar in Waldman's *The Submission*. Consequently, Nazneen is "forced to contextualize the urban and domestic world by means of her rural Bengali frame of reference" (Groes 238) and she compares the television glowing in the corner of the room to a fire place.

The description of the hermetic community of Brooklyn's Kensington in *The Submission* resembles London's Tower Hamlets in Ali's novel. Both Nazneen and Asma are entirely dependent on men and isolated, both literally and symbolically, from the rest of the city. Groes sees Nazneen as the "multiple Other: female, married off, semi-literate financially dependent, Muslim" (239), which suggests a debatable gradualism of otherness and touches on the fragmented migrant identities marked by a dislocated sense of home and belonging. Remarkably and paradoxically, the gendered cultural isolation within a migrant community in both novels is portrayed as a phenomenon that emerges in and is attached to the Western metropolis: inaccessible from outside, but perfectly localizable on the city map.

Leaving the mother country and the mother tongue, even if it is possible to return and to maintain contact, means losing the most instinctive sense of home and replacing it with adopted aspects of foreign "elsewheres." Nowhere at home and nowhere quite foreign, or everywhere a little bit at home and equally foreign: forms of an unbounded identity. According to Zygmunt Bauman, "leaving options open" in terms of identity is one of the challenges of postmodernity. While modernity was "built in steel and concrete; postmodernity, in biodegradable plastic" (Bauman "From Pilgrim to Tourist" 18), which encourages avoiding clear and unambiguous commitments. Ali's novel explores this identity struggle and negotiates the concept of belonging in London pre– and post–9/11. Its point of departure is the hermetic space at once precisely localizable on the London map and culturally sealed.

In the vacuum of the apartment, Nazneen feels trapped, not only by the physical space framed by walls and sounds from the neighbors' flats, but also by her own body. Both apartment and body seem inescapable: "She saw that she was trapped inside this body, inside this room, inside this flat, inside this concrete slab of entombed humanity" (76). As a consequence she becomes disassociated from her body and reacts with surprise at the sight of her own legs that catch her eye in the bathroom one day.

Nazneen observes the outside world through the apartment window and sees Brick Lane. This is how she finds out about the rules and structure of her community. She observes Bangladeshi men who seem to hang around with no particular purpose. Later on, she realizes, they are controlling the neighborhood.

> It was dark, and cosy with lamp-posts. The people were tucked into big coats, and steamed as they walked. Headlights and red rear lights turned the road into a crawling carnival. The bus bumped along. The shops were lit up still. Leather shops, dress shops, sari shops, shops that sold fish and chips and samosas and pizzas and a little bit of everything from around the world. Newsagents, hardware shops, grocers, shops that sold alcohol, shops whose windows were stacked with stools and slippers and cassette tapes and seemed to sell nothing but were always full of men in panjabi-pyjama, smoking and stroking their beards [100].

What she cannot see through the window has to be imagined. People entering the frame bring parts of the city closer to her and make her realize how much there is to see and explore but at the same time confirm the misery of her situation. The patches of sky between the blocks of flats are so small as to be measured by her spread fingers, whereas in Gouripur, Nazneen's home village, "the sky reached to the very ends of the earth" (423). Tower Hamlets is portrayed as a grey, gloomy area that mirrors the mood and resignation of people seen on the streets:

> Nazneen looked up at the grey towers, the blown-by forgotten strands of sky between them. She watched the traffic. There were more cars than people out here, a roaring metal army tearing up the town.... The people who passed walked

quickly, looked ahead at nothing or looked down at the pavement to negotiate puddles, litter and excrement [43].

Eventually London makes Nazneen break through the gender limitations of her community but for a long time the world outside, beyond the window view, remains inaccessible, as with Manhattan in Waldman's novel, which Asma Anwar in the Brooklyn Bangladeshi community of Kensington sees as a different country, entirely disconnected from her life. When Nazneen's friend Razia leaves Tower Hamlets on a bus, she goes to "distant lands" (481) which turn out to be other boroughs in West and South London: Tooting, Ealing, Southall, Wembley. The world outside of Tower Hamlets is therefore equally remote and it takes decades for Nazneen to discover the city and explore its richness. Imagined distances tend to be enormous and so from the perspective of the hermetic community, London appears as a giant.

The traces of the London outside of Tower Hamlets enter the community through legends and rumors which often come across as cultural jokes, as in the case of the following quote about Mrs. Islam's sons:

> There was a rumour that they owned a pub in Stepney. There was another rumour that on Sunday mornings a woman danced in the pub and took all her clothes off. It was said that this was an English tradition. That the men went to the pub on Sunday morning, sent by their wives who wanted to cook and clean while their husbands were out of the way, looking at another woman's breasts [443].

Mrs. Islam is a curious figure, a permanent and uninvited inquisitive guest who knows a lot about Bangladeshis in Tower Hamlets but whose observations also reach outside of the closed community. Although the setting is different, Mrs. Islam resembles the hypochondriac pawnbroker in Dostoyevsky's *Crime and Punishment*: an unsympathetic, ugly, dangerous and parasitic character often accompanied by her two sons. Together they control and blackmail the community. Remaining hermetic, the community is easy to manipulate and regulate. She sees the position of the community within London and comments on its economic and financial weakness that results in lack of respect from "white people." She situates the community within the city and its financial milieu, which she refers to with street names, which signify the whole area in question. In the following quote Adler Street, a short street between Whitechapel and Commercial Roads stands for the entire borough and heralds gentrification-driven changes:

> "Now, if we had money ... then you would see the difference. The block off Adler Street, the council sold it off. Do you know how many flats inside there now? Eight! Each one size of a cricket pitch. Only one or two people living in each flat. How are they going to respect us, living ten to one room?... If they want us out of here, they can buy us out" [442].

The "white people" and their "English traditions" which also include, according to Nazneen's friend Razia, falling in love, are so exotic to the Bangladeshi community in Ali's novel that they too become subjects to all kinds of stories and legends. "White people" are seen as curious with strange desires and longing for authenticity. Nazneen is surprised when she notices a Buddha in a restaurant window on Brick Lane. Chanu comments on its selling factor: "'Not Hindus. Marketing.'... The white people liked to see the gods.'For authenticity'" (446).

The picture of the English created by dubious tales with no traceable source turns the view of British society upside down. The narration twists power dynamics and offers a perspective from the areas of London neglected by politics. It also offers a reversed colonial gaze, directed at the exotic white colonizer. 9/11 breaks the recurrent lack of interest in Ali's novel. All of a sudden all eyes are on Brick Lane and as a reaction to the attacks, plumbers come to repair the toilet in Nazneen's apartment that has been broken for years. The incongruity of this setting ridicules the authorities.

The window is not only a screen on which a tiny fragment of the city is displayed, but also a medium through which Nazneen tries to communicate with the world outside, for instance with Karim, who later on becomes her lover. As the years go by, the view through the window changes:

> She began to spend time at the window, as she had in those first few months in London, when it was still possible to look out across the dead grass and concrete and see nothing but jade-green fields, unable to imagine that the years would rub them away. Now she saw only the flats, piles of people loaded one on top of the other, a vast dump of people rotting away under a mean strip of sky, too small to reflect all those souls [364].

As Tower Hamlets becomes more and more gentrified, the interested gaze directed at the exotic Other becomes mutual. Restaurants serving curry on Brick Lane gain popularity among young white Brits and international tourists, and once Nazneen is photographed by a curious young white girl with an impressive camera who has "dispensed with a shirt" (254) and is wearing underwear only. The curiosity and fascination with difference works in both ways: Nazneen finds the woman photographing her equally exotic. Gentrification in the novel triggers mutual interest but is also the reason for radicalized antagonism between the social and ethnic groups living in Tower Hamlets. It provokes identity questions and triggers an immediate need to confront them. A dichotomy of "us" (Muslim Bengalis) versus "them" ("the white people" or "the English") emerges and adds to this antagonism. Chanu's attitude shifts from idealization and admiration to contempt:"And what is *their* culture? Television, pub, throwing darts, kicking a ball. ... in *their* minds *they* have become an oppressed minority" (254, emphasis mine).

Clothes as Cultural Signifier

Gentrification is linked to the concept of London as body, moving and rapidly changing, not always predictably. In Karim's words: "this area started going up. And the City started *coming out* towards Brick Lane. You got grant money coming in, regeneration money. Property prices going up, new people moving in, businesses and that" (311, emphasis mine).

The demographic changes feature mutual cultural exposure, which is at once eye opening and contributes to the radicalized self-defense of ethnic and religious identities. Nazneen, inspired by women she sees on the streets in her borough, fantasizes about wearing trousers and swinging her hips while walking. At the same time she observes two young women "upgrading" from hijabs to burkhas (279) in reaction to the same pictures of femininity. She sees clothes as an important identity-shaping factor which she links to the city and its social moves.

Nazneen becomes aware of her urban identity which seems to her to be determined by clothing and not by fate (278). She realizes that wearing a sari, she is contextualized within the cloths of the western metropolis, as it appears in front of her window:

> Suddenly she was gripped by the idea that if she changed her clothes her entire life would change as well. If she wore a skirt and a jacket and a pair of high heels then what else would she do but walk around the glass palaces of Bishopsgate, and talk into a slim phone and eat lunch out of a paper bag? If she wore trousers and underwear, like the girl with the big camera on Brick Lane, then she would roam the streets fearless and proud. And if she had a tiny tiny skirt with knickers to match and a tight bright top, then she would—how could she not?—skate through life with a sparkling smile and a handsome man who took her hand and made her spin, spin, spin [277–278].

Clothes are signifiers for social status and cultural identity. They locate the characters within the city's structure and assign them to its particular parts. Clothes are a way of identity manifestation and provocation against the post–9/11 "othering."

Tower Hamlets, 9/11 and the Notion of Belonging

"The English next door" also have positive qualities and a "peculiarity" Nazneen is thankful for: they mind their own business (304), and being entirely uninterested they do not produce rumors. When Nazneen tries to get lost in the city once, she recalls Razia's advice to never go shopping on her own to Bengali shops in order to avoid gossip: "If you go out to shop, go to Sainsbury's. English people don't look at you twice. But if you go to our shops, the Bengali men will make things up about you" (59). In this context becoming invisible offers protection from the patriarchal community but does not provide an alternative way to live outside of it. The cultural reality of Tower Hamlets is interlaced: it is a Bengali space within the English capital but the Western influences and identity of the metropolis interfere with its cultural specificities. The chain Sainsbury's symbolically stands for capitalism and consumerism that enters the seemingly sealed community and grants its women anonymity, so paradoxically a certain form of asylum. Becoming invisible is a form of freedom granted by a metropolitan environment and absent in (territorially) small communities.

Karim is a character somewhere between the world of Bengali men and the English next door. He has never been to Bangladesh and Nazneen notices that he stutters in Bengali (she later on finds out he stutters in English also). He is torn between the expectations of the traditional Muslim community and the everyday life of modern London. These worlds are not compatible but to choose one and give up the other is also impossible. Karim's hybrid existence is full of contradictions and challenges. One day he reveals to Nazneen his guide to women which, absurd in its very existence, is evidence of his general confusion and sense of cultural conflict:

> "Well, basically you've got two types. Make your choice. There's your westernized girl, wears what she likes, all the make-up going on, short skirts and that soon as she's out of her father's sight. She's into going out, getting good jobs, having a laugh. Then there's your religious girl, wears the scarf or even the burkha. You'd think, right, they'd be good wife material. But they ain't. Because all they want to do is *argue*. And they always think they know best because they've been off to all these summer camps for Muslim sisters" [384–385, emphasis original].

In this context, Nazneen sees herself as an embodiment of home for Karim, who was born with no sense of one. "She was his real thing. A Bengali wife. A Bengali mother. An idea of home. An idea of himself that he found in her" (454).

After 9/11 Karim radicalizes and undergoes a metamorphosis; he starts wearing a panjabi-pyjama and grows a beard. He takes the process of "othering" going on in London as a personal provocation and responds to it, as does Changez in Hamid's *The Reluctant Fundamentalist* or Mo in Waldman's *The Submission*. All three characters take the social changes personally and try to fight against the Western metropolis and its new prejudices. All of them eventually leave, full of anger and disappointment. While Changez returns to Lahore, Mo and Karim, whose parents immigrated to the U.S. and the UK, respectively, leave for a place they do not know. They do not return, they escape, with different expectations. In pursuit of an idealized vision of his parents' home, Karim becomes radical and vulnerable to more disappointments.

Before leaving, Karim becomes active in the local Muslim community and helps organize a march. The march, intended as a peaceful demonstration, turns violent and overwhelms the individual participants who can no longer control their moves and are "used" to form the new collective and extremely violent body.

New York's Dust Over Tower Hamlets: Reclaiming the Space of the Borough After 9/11

After 9/11 Brick Lane and Tower Hamlets become a different place and hence the perception of people who live there and are linked to it also changes. Identities defined through the space and community need to be renegotiated and the space itself has to be either reclaimed or abandoned. Very fast the "dust" from New York City reaches Tower Hamlets, with all the consequences:

> A pinch of New York dust blew across the ocean and settled on the Dogwood Estate. Sorupa's daughter was the first, but not the only one. Walking in the street, on her way to college, she had her hijab pulled off. Razia wore her Union Jack sweatshirt and it was spat on. "Now you see what will happen," said Chanu. "Backlash." … Nazneen went to buy ghee and chapatti flour. Four men leaned over the counter, studying a paper so closely that when they looked up she almost expected their eyeballs to be smudged with newsprint [368].

There is a rupture in the everyday life of the borough and the Muslim population becomes not only visible but also subjected to "othering," and although this happens in the last fifth of the novel, it clearly marks a beginning of a new post–9/11 era in writing London. According to Kumarini Silva, "while the act [9/11] itself was temporal (it happened on a particular date at a particular time), the post-moment was, and continues to be, a spatially grounded discourse about belonging" (Silva 179). In Ali's novel the post–9/11 discourse is grounded in Tower Hamlets, which in spatial terms becomes London's post-moment and the condensation of the symbolic "New York dust." Silva elaborates further on the specific turn the identity which she calls "brown" took after 9/11 and observes a "shift of brown from identity to identification" (Silva 167), so to a social marker linked to the emergence of the picture of the Muslim Other.

In Ali's novel 9/11 brings death, violence and deep insecurity to Tower Hamlets; it makes Chanu awaken from his monotonous life and see his position in light of the criticism directed at Muslims and dominating British public opinion. He no longer idealizes the UK, he feels threatened and displaced: "'It's time to go,' he told no one in particular and hitched up his stomach, girding himself for action.'Any day, any moment, life can end. There's been enough planning'" (369). Similarly to Karim, Chanu sees the smear campaign against Muslims as a personal provocation. His admiration for England gives way to disappointment expressed by a historical analysis of colonialism shared with his daughters in one of his speeches. He takes the famine of 1942 in Bangladesh as a starting point. This "lesson" that he gives the girls is his first open criticism of the UK, the country he has so much been in love with. 9/11 makes him lose his faith in London:

> Three million people died because of starvation. Can you imagine that? You cannot. Can you imagine something else? While the crows and vultures stripped our bones, the British, our rulers, exported grain from the country. This is something that you cannot imagine, but now that you know it, you will never forget [370].

9/11 is introduced as a family experience, at first uniting and enthralling. The images of the burning towers enter the cosmos of the Tower Hamlets apartment and break the daily routine. The events enter the flat along with Chanu, whose first reaction, so surprising to Nazneen, comes across as almost humorous:

> Chanu slammed through the door as if he would take it off its hinges. This man, who would not sit if he could lie, would not stand if he could lean, moved faster than Nazneen had ever before witnessed. "Quick. Be quick!" he shouts. "Put on the television." ... "Oh God," he says. "The world has gone mad" [365].

He then freezes in a squatting position which is "part reverence part subjugation" (367). Nazneen thinks "she has understood but she also thinks she must be mistaken" (366). "It is hard to look at the television and it is impossible to look away" (367). When she sees the "jumpers" she thinks that "hope and despair are nothing against the world and what it holds and what it holds for you" (368). At night she dreams of her home village Gouripur. Chanu's long-term reaction is somatic: his whole body suffers, his ulcer grows and he loses weight. Nazneen stops cooking, they no longer eat together as a family—the unifying and bonding experience leads to a rupture in the family routine. After some time Nazneen has the impression that life in the borough has returned to normal and that it is only her husband and Karim who are thinking "all the time about New York and the terrorists and bombs" while everybody else is "just living their lives" (382). Both men eventually decide to leave the city while Nazneen stays with her daughters and feels liberated at last.

Responses to Post–9/11 "Othering" in Tower Hamlets

Already pre–9/11, the world from the perspective of the Bengali community in Tower Hamlets is divided into white people and brown people, "to a white person, we are all the same: dirty little monkeys all in the same monkey clan" (28), says Chanu. Karim, when talking to Nazneen about the drug problem in the community states bitterly that the government is "more scared of Islam than heroin" (311). He further comments on the images of Islam produced by the media after the attacks:

> A devout Muslim, right, willing to sacrifice himself for his religion. Does he go to bars and watch naked girls and drink alcohol? What kind of Muslim takes his Qur'an into a bar? And *leaves* it there? These stories are made up by idiots. People who don't know nothing about Islam. Maybe a Christian carries his Bible round like a pack of cigarettes. He don't know how a Qur'an is treated.... They're saying another Qur'an got left behind in a rental car by these so-called Islamic terrorists.... All these devout men throwing away the Word of God like sweet papers [382].

The Muslim Other is presented as a product of the white media, here by the imaginary local paper *Tower Hamlets Bugle*. Through "othering" the image of the dangerous and violent Muslim men replaces the black Other from before the attacks:

> There were no gangs at all. The white press had made them up to give Bangladeshis a bad name. The *Tower Hamlets Bugle* was the worst offender (but all white newspapers were culprits); if you read that rubbish you'd think that our boys were getting as bad as the blacks [388].

> "They should get their facts straight.... Islamic terrorists. Islamic terrosrists. That's all you hear. You never hear Catholic terrorist, do you? Or Hindu terrorist? What about Jewish terrorist?... All of these people going around talking about gangs, all they're doing is feeding the racists. The newspapers love it. But the truth is there are no gangs" [407].

Organizing the Bengali community is an answer to the provocation of racial or ethnic "othering." The march of the Mullahs is intended to show the strength of the Muslim community in Tower Hamlets. Its mission is to show the white community that "Islam is peace" (413). The march turns into a violent street riot and hence counterproductive. The Bengali Tigers, a group organized by Karim, who is no longer interested in the sewing business he was in before and instead directs all his energy to leading the community, consists of men only. Women are in charge of preparing the banners. The organization is exclusive and shows the community as a male domain with women remaining in the shadows.

In the epilogue of the novel in March 2002, the borough becomes interesting to the media and reporters come to film the dilapidated Tower Hamlets estates. They search for sensation and organized crime but they are not sure in what form. The novel pictures them as completely ignorant and overwhelmed. Their assumed superiority is pictured as stupidity when confronted with the

Bengali community: "'Where are the gangs? Are you a member?' 'No,' he [Tariq] said. 'There are no gangs here.' 'Fundamentalists then. Are you one of those?'" (485)

The Maps of Home: Between Gouripur and London

Regular flashbacks from Nazneen and her sister Hasina's childhood in Gouripur interrupt the chronologically narrated plot. Stories, legends and myths constitute an important part of Nazneen's London life. The more she thinks about them, the more mystical they become. Also sensually perceived elements connect these two places on a level that is resistant to the time passing: the taste and scents of cardamom, cumin and other spices bring memories of Gouripur to London.

The process of cooking sets memories in motion and is soothing. On multiple occasions in the novel it is cooking and the cooked food that Nazneen finds comfort in. Food complements the magic repertoire of stories and legends from "home" that Nazneen passes on to her daughters, for example the story of Nazneen's mother possessed by a Jinni in which Jinni stands for untreated depression. Dreams are important as they contribute pictures of the village and the past that are not always desired but still inescapable. In her dreams, Nazneen is often visited by her deceased mother, who blames Nazneen for the death of her first-born baby son. Her presence in the nightmares signifies guilt, and she embodies Nazneen's fears and insecurities. In one of the dreams her mother reminds her that when she was born, she did not want to be fed, "caused troubles from the very beginning" (432). With this refusal in the back of her mind, Nazneen turns to food in moments of desperations. Food becomes a magic quality itself and eating, alone and at nights is Nazneen's obsession and asylum. Food, as alcohol does in Cleave's novel, suppresses fear and insecurity:

> Sometimes she [Nazneen] fell into a state of bottomless anxiety. She spent the night eating leftovers in the kitchen as if layer on layer of food inside her would push out the anxiety, displace it like water from a bath. And at the end of these sessions she felt nauseous and tired, too tired to care what would happen and certain that in any case nothing could be helped [300–301].

In memories of home, senses become confused; the pictures of Gouripur that "come" to Nazneen are sometimes "so strong she could smell" (217) but could not see them. These magic elements and sense perceptions constitute her memory of the past and build a bridge between her childhood in Bangladesh and her adult life in an arranged marriage in London. The longer she lives in London, the more blurred and unreal her memories of home become: "As the years passed the layers of netting multiplied and she began to rely on a different kind of memory. The memory of things she knew but no longer saw" (217).

Letters from and to her sister Hasina are another regular intervention of Bangladesh (Dhaka) in the London life. Her broken life in Dhaka, translated into disturbing broken English, enters Nazneen's London life and is a testimony of the brutality of life in Bangladesh. Uneducated and pushed to the margin of society, Hasina's life is a mere survival. She is abused, beaten by men and forced to prostitution. Nazneen's memories of Bangladesh, blurred into imaginary idealizations, are confronted by the tough reality described by Hasina. The more London enters Nazneen's life, the less she idealizes her brutally interrupted childhood. The notion of "home" is disturbed and dislocated as Nazneen cannot negotiate it anyway—it is imposed on her by her husband and detached from all memories she herself has of Bangladesh.

Nazneen's decision to stay in London despite her husband's determination to go "back" means appropriating the city as her home, the place in which she finally becomes herself, rooted and contextualized by Tower Hamlets rather than through her father or husband. The affair with Karim is an important step on her way to an emotional and spatial independence; it gives her power and strength she needs in order to choose London over both men and let Chanu, who suffers from the "Going Home Syndrome, the special Tower Hamlets disease" (456), go to Dhaka. The time in the novel is divided between before Nazneen knew what she could do (486) and after she has realized it. The process of discovering herself is linked to discovering the city. Nazneen chooses London, and through finally discovering the city, she discovers herself. The city gives her a context, a space in which she can inscribe her life and live it independently. London gives Nazneen independence, but only when she consciously makes the decision to stay.

It is not only that the letter exchange between the sisters in Dhaka and London connects the cities with one another, but also that the city functions like a magic bridge connecting the sisters. London brings Nazneen closer to Hasina, and when the latter is symbolically "lost" in Dhaka, leading a life of a "fallen woman," Nazneen gets lost in the streets of London to be closer to her:

> Nazneen walked. She walked to the end of Brick Lane and turned right. Four blocks down she crossed the road (she waited next to a woman and stepped out with her, like a calf with its mother) and took a side street. She turned down the first right, and then went left. From there she took every second right every second left until she realized she was leaving herself a trail. Then she turned off at random, began to run, limped for a while to save her ankle, and thought she had come in a circle. The buildings seemed familiar. She sensed rather than saw, because she had taken care not to notice.... She had got herself lost because Hasina was lost [55–58].

While trying to get lost in the city Nazneen subconsciously applies a pattern to her route. Getting lost cannot evolve according to any plan; it requires recklessness which Nazneen enforces upon herself. When she finally does not know where she is or how to get back home, she feels for a moment united with her sister, both of them "lost in cities that would not pause even to shrug" (59). A magic trans-metropolitan connection is established but it disappears quickly and gives way to self-criticism and disgust: "Nazneen wept and as the tears started to come she knew that she was weeping more for her own stupidity than for her sister" (59).

She also starts feeling aware of herself and of her body, surrounded by other bodies walking, eating and rushing through the streets of London: "Without a coat, without a suit, without a face, without a destination. A leafshake of fear—or was it excitement?—passed through her legs" (56). On her mission to get lost she encounters people who walk and eat at the same time (60), the city is in a constant hurry, its buildings are proud (60) and Nazneen feels invisible. Nobody seems to notice her; she feels anonymous and frightened. On another occasion, walking with her husband years later, she thinks of angels and connects them to the streets of London:

> It struck her then—and the force of it made her gasp—that this street was filled with angels. For every one person there were two more angels and the air was thick with them. She walked with her face turned down to her feet and she felt her head pushing through a density of wings. She was seized with a fear of inhaling a spirit, and pulled cloth over her mouth and nose. For the first time then, she heard the beating of a thousand angel wings and her legs would take her no further [254–255].

Overwhelmed and scared by the invisible crowd of city angels, she nearly faints and her nervous breakdown begins. The sudden appearance of the city's past symbolized by the angels and their breaths stuns the main character but also brings her closer to London which in this reveals itself to her. Similarly to Julius in Cole's *Open City*, Nazneen through walking discovers different layers of the city's hidden past. This urban past flashes back at her with a strength that makes her confront it with her own story and experiences.

Masks and the Escapism of Tourism in the Urban Environment

Another way losing oneself in the city and finding reasons to leave the borough is to wear a mask. "Playing" and pretending makes the city a different place and opens up possibilities for new, better identities. It is a way of claiming new spaces. When Chanu decides to play tourist one day and takes his family for a sightseeing tour in London, Nazneen is disappointed with the plainness of Buckingham Palace:

> Nazneen looked at the building. It was big and white and as far as she could see, extraordinary only in its size. The railings she found impressive but the house was only big. Its face was very plain.... If she were the Queen she would tear it down and build a new house, not this flat-roofed block but something elegant and spirited, with minarets and spires, domes and mosaics, a beautiful garden instead of this bare forecourt. Something like the Taj Mahal [291–292].

In bringing Taj Mahal to London and imagining the Queen living in it, Ali's main character performs an imaginary act of reversed colonialism. She orientalizes London while simultaneously inscribing herself to it as a colonized subject.

This family expedition is one of the most absurd and funny pictures that the novel offers. It is also bitter proof of London's unspoken isolation and segregation within the city's social structure. Chanu, shown throughout the novel as a big child with ambitions and a self-esteem that have little to do with reality, approaches the trip as a game, and buys himself special equipment: a pair of shorts, binoculars, maps and two disposable cameras (289). It is the first time he and his family leave Tower Hamlets. Chanu explains: "All this time I have been struggling and struggling and I barely had time to lift my head and look around" (289).

Dressed like a tourist, Chanu enters a different role and for one day becomes somebody else. Through the new self-assigned identity, combining two of the postmodern strategies defined by Bauman—the tourist and the player—Chanu's position in the city changes and so does his perception of it. Appropriating the new gaze of a tourist-player, he becomes a visitor, an observer, a non-belonging "Other" who enters London from outside and can only temporarily hold this status. At the same time the family becomes an attraction, an aesthetic and cultural revelation, and other people want to photograph them.

Zygmunt Bauman emphasizes the fact that both of the masks/strategies "favour and promote a distance between the individual and the Other and cast the Other primarily as the object of aesthetic, not moral, evaluation" (Bauman 33). Turning into a tourist is refreshing, as it enables a new aesthetic otherness, free of cultural or social responsibility. Unlike in Tower Hamlets, in front of the Buckingham Palace it is possible to enter a very different perspective, that of a tourist, associated more with privilege and open-mindedness than with cultural or linguistic estrangement. This new identity, temporary in its very foundations, requires a second spatial reference: the notion of home. When the stranger whom they ask to take the photo enquires where they are from, Chanu's answer is Bangladesh. His daughter Shahana who does not understand the purpose of the family theater and refuses to play a part in it, breaks the rules and with one sentence brings the family back to reality. She says, rolling her eyes, "I'm from London" (296).

Shahana represents the second generation untouched directly by the experience of immigration. She has never been outside London and lacks the ultimate link to the culture and language that her parents impose on her. She corrects her father's English and criticizes the institution of arranged marriage in front of her mother. She does not only lack interest in Bangladeshi culture or language but she also entirely refuses and negates it. Her defiance is programmatic and consistently directed at her parents. Their life in London, spatially and culturally detached from its past and context, strikes her as unhappy and ridiculous.

> Shahana did not want to listen to Bengali classical music. Her written Bengali was shocking. She wanted to wear jeans. She hated her kameez and spoiled her entire wardrobe by pouring paint on them. If she could choose between baked beans and dal it was no contest. When Bangladesh was mentioned she pulled a face. She did not know and would not learn that Tagore was more than poet and Nobel laureate, and no less than the true father of her nation. Shahana did not care [180].

It seems that lacking the immigration experience, Shahana does not need to hide behind any masks. She is a part of the city, an insider who can change roles and access different parts of the city as she pleases. She does not have to pretend she is somebody else because she is shaped by the city; she is a child of the postcolonial London.

Brick Lane as a Body

Brick Lane itself is an organism; it has a mouth, neck (468) and a main artery (470) that when blocked by the march causes a disease in the whole area: "Something coursed down the artery, like a bubble in the bloodstream" (470). Buildings are also personified: when Shahaha runs away from home, Nazneen is in a trance, obsessively looking for her in the city. It is dark and the borough is alert because of the march. The well-known reality she faces while running through the streets recalls a chamber of horrors or a bad dream as the march turns violent. She runs through the streets of Tower Hamlets and sees the "jaws" of a butcher shop (468). She then passes the Berner Estate whose lower rises appear to her as crippled monsters, windows look at her as "gouged-out eyes," a lamppost produces a "sick orange light," the block of flats are "pale-faced," the glass counter in a sandwich shop is "naked" and at the end, when she finally reaches Brick Lane, its "mouth" is covered by a row of police vans (468). From there she can look into its "neck," which is dark and reveals nothing. There, at the blocked mouth of the street Nazneen is confronted with "white people" and their white problems. She is looking for her run-away teenage daughter, while they are looking for a curry restaurant and are disappointed when a police officer advises them to have dinner elsewhere (470).

The city appears to Nazneen as an angry body, impossible to embrace. Houses form little veins that lead to Brick Lane—the main artery (470). The senses melt into one: noise becomes vision and vision blurs and fails due to the overwhelming darkness. Accordingly, "noise licks around Brick Lane like a flame, crackling from every corner" (470), the blue eye of an ambulance sends a "terrible, keening lament" (473), a siren "wails," smacks the sky and showers Nazneen's head. The gangs play a "sinister hide-and-seek," and chase one another where there are no white people. After the march, which was a reaction against post–9/11 racial profiling and which originally was supposed to show that Islam is peaceful, Brick Lane is "wounded" and has scars which have to be healed: "On Brick Lane scabs formed quickly over the wounds. Plasters were applied. There was nothing that would not heal and after a few weeks, when the wooden boards and the plasters came off, it was as if nothing happened. There were no visible scars" (485).

There is a certain magic in the portrayal of London in Ali's novel. The city is written on the edge of magic realism, portrayed as an organism that looks at Nazneen through the window and chases her through the streets. The novel also portrays the city as wounded, covered with New York dust, and at times taken over angels occupying too much space and taking the air away. The city is a silent companion, a witness to people's lives, and a part of them, even if they do not realize it. When Nazneen's and Chanu's baby-son falls ill and eventually dies, the city witnessing their tragedy mourns with them:

> The city shattered. Everything was in pieces. She knew it straight away, glimpsed it from the painful-white insides of the ambulance. Frantic neon signs. Headlights chasing the dark. An office block, cracked with light. These shards of the broken city [117].

In her imagination the city breaks into pieces as a reaction to what happens in her life—in the text the city is at this point mediated through her point of view. In the same way, Nazneen's internal topography falls apart and nothing seems to make any sense.

Mapping Imaginary Spaces

While packing Nazneen finds a mug on Shahana's desk, "bearing a picture of a thatch-roofed cottage and a mouse in trousers leaning on the gatepost. It was a picture of England. Roses around the door. Nazneen had never seen this England bit now, idly, the idea formed that she would visit it" (438). There is a similarity between the entirely foreign picture of England on the mug and all the attributes that Asma in Waldman's novel collects to take over to Bangladesh. Both the mug and the objects symbolize a dream country, prosperity and happiness that neither of the women had the chance to experience. These images, although physically much closer to their location within the city, remain symbolically as remote as they were before arriving in London or New York.

Nazneen chooses the city over Chanu and, more generally, over the masculinity that prevented her from exploring the city for decades. London, observed through a kitchen window for many years and eventually mapped and reclaimed, is where she sees the sense of belonging and where her independent life cartography is inscribed in the streets. She chooses London over Karim and his distorted, displaced "in-betweenness" that turns into an even more confused radicalism after 9/11. She decides to stay in the city which marks her as the Muslim Other according to the post–9/11 "image repertoire" (Barthes), the city which both of the men escape.

The streets of Nazneen's London remain covered with the "New York dust" and walking through them means constant confrontation with the attack and its consequences. But the "dust" brings Nazneen closer to London, a space she now wants to be a part of, in which she feels more comfortable and which she wants to protect. The imaginary homeland, blurred and remote, from which she was sent away remains closed, a distant land to which she does not seek access. Indirectly, 9/11 liberates Nazneen from her previous passive existence forced upon her by men. It also brings her closer to the frightened city which she starts to feel a part of. Just as in O'Neill's *Netherland*, whose main character feels more American after 9/11, Nazneen moves closer to London despite the fear that pervades the city.

VII

Hemisphere 2: London West End
in Ian McEwan's *Saturday*

Ian McEwan's *Saturday*, the 2005 "allegorical thriller" (Head *Britain and Beyond* 124), is set in the geographical center of London—the West End, part of the London borough of the City of Westminster. The description of this location suggests that it could be a completely different city from the one written in Cleave's and Ali's novels. The house of the main character where the narration begins and ends is in the area between Tottenham Court Road and Euston Square, around Charlotte, Gower and Warren Streets, west from Tower Hamlets. The narration, which in its temporal framework draws on the literature of modernism (Woolf's *Mrs. Dalloway*, Joyce's *Ulysses*[1]) embraces a single day in the life of neurosurgeon Henry Perowne and is framed by a window from his bedroom. His "day," which begins and ends in the middle of the night, is inscribed in the life of a city which never sleeps; a city which creates and celebrates insomniacs (17). His movements through the streets of London are spatial interventions that contribute to the chaos of this particular Saturday on February 15, 2003—the day of the demonstrations against the Iraq war that Tony Blair's government is about to support.

As other characters of post–9/11 fiction, Henry Perowne walks and drives through (mostly "his" part of) the city and links its particular places to memories through various associations. As a part of his digressions on the city's history and future, he analyzes his own life and tries to see it through a larger perspective offered by the metropolis. His thoughts move constantly between euphoric admiration for London and awareness of its vulnerability in the face of the threat of international terrorism, especially as the capital of a country ready to go to war. He considers the latter a part of a "new order" in which fear is the driving force that narrows down mental freedom (180). The perception and judgment of the city's condition are strongly dependent on Perowne's own shifting moods.

The spatial experience of the city interferes with his work as a neurosurgeon, with the structure of the human brain and its unpredictability. For Perowne the city is a brain itself, with functioning connections but also with many broken houses that can be healed only through destruction, as with dementia, for which there is no cure. This metaphor makes Henry see the city as organic but also as something to be protected from injuries. While walking he has the impression of "striding along a natural surface" (71). While performing a surgery, he thinks of parts of the brain as city districts. This chapter links the metaphor of city as brain to post–9/11 sentiments in London—a city that does not want to go to war. It also links it to writing, recreating and to influencing the city's mind in spatial terms (through movement, stories evoked by memories of particular places, mass demonstration).

In this novel, London is very much connected to New York City—it is the capital of the main ally, risking its peace and "waiting for its bomb" (276), and the plot features transatlantic references on various levels. Perowne's day is filled with preparations for a family dinner, as in Woolf's *Mrs. Dalloway,* in which the day is also supposed to end with a party. But the private matters are surrounded by public issues and world affairs. Hans Blix, the Iraq war, and the anxious visions of the future float against the background of this seemingly peaceful Saturday. Each occurrence is described with great precision so that the day extends in time and embraces not only the present but also the past and the future which Henry imagines in the city.

Twenty-Four Hours of Henry Perowne and London

The novel starts with a terrorist attack—which turns out to be a figment of Henry Perowne's imagination. He wakes up before dawn and sees a burning plane approaching Heathrow. His first association seems to him to be the most "natural" considering the entirely new set of images and metonymies introduced by 9/11.

> It's already almost eighteen months since half the planet watched, and watched again the unseen captives driven through the sky to the slaughter, at which time there gathered round the innocent silhouette of any jet plane a novel association. Everyone agrees, airliners look different in the sky these days, predatory or doomed [16].

When it turns out to be a Russian cargo plane with an engine problem, the significance and relevance of Perowne's eye-witness experience fades immediately.

Along with new images and shifting meanings, new vocabulary enters the everyday life of a Western metropolis. Some words and expressions lose their original significance due to constant repetition, as did the terrifying imagery of

9/11. "Words like 'catastrophe' and 'mass fatalities,' 'chemical and biological war-fare' and 'major attack' have recently become bland through repetition" (12). Perowne provides a compact analysis of what he assumes to be a disaster and of his behavior while witnessing it in the middle of the night. He feels that the appropriateness of his reactions is measured in relation to others, by what is expected from an individual in the post–9/11 mode. While seeing the burning plane he imagines his account delivered *post-factum* and contributing to world history. He is going to be judged for his inability to act, for the phone call he should have made. This new challenge that falls on an individual in the era of terrorism feels overwhelming and, remarkably, makes him feel like a criminal. "His crime was to stand in the safety of his bedroom, wrapped in a woolen dressing gown, without moving or making sound, half dreaming as he watched people die" (22). Kristiaan Versluys identifies the sight of the burning plane as first "intrusion of something horrible and incomprehensible into the banal of everyday life" (189) that the novel offers, a gloomy forecast of something hor-rifying that is yet to happen, an invisible presence that overshadows the plot. This notion of unease—abstract and imprecise—mirrors the sentiments of Londoners after 9/11, largely horrified by the pro-war decisions of the Blair government.

On the way to his car in the morning, Henry contemplates the city and underestimates the Iraq-war crisis assuring himself that the political instability is only temporal. The city appears to him as healthy and happy, mirroring his own contentment and relief: "The street is fine, and the city, grand achievement of the living and all the dead who've ever lived here, is fine too, and robust. It won't easily allow itself to be destroyed. It's too good to let go" (77). The city in his understanding is the future which will "look back on us ... as lucky gods blessed by supermarket cornucopias, torrents of accessible information ..., won-drous machines" (77).

Saturday's depiction of London in its wholeness and diversity accommo-dates and connects other cities, becoming the urban *lingua franca* that joins the past and the present of other metropolises; Charlotte Street, for instance, at its very beginning when it becomes the extension of Fitzroy, resembles com-munist Warsaw (78). Letting his thoughts jump freely from one association to another, Perowne analyzes his mood, interlinked with the condition of London. This happens when he approaches Tottenham Court Road which brings him back to this "familiar routine" (79) of auto-analysis. His thoughts and the loose chain of digressions that the third-person narrator follows and delivers, are strongly linked to particular places in London. Henry's life is rooted in Lon-don—this is where he grew up; the city is full of his traces and memories. And yet, it "lies wide open" like a patient trusting Perowne's ability to heal it.

Brain: A Familiar Territory with Neighborhoods to Avoid

The structure of the brain and the functions of its particular areas, essentially the daily bread of a neurosurgeon, interfere with the city and influence Henry's perception of it. He is lost in thought while walking through London and the two worlds (the one of his work, centered in a hospital and the one outside of it) interfere with and mutually complement one another. Henry can never fully detach from his work, a passion that determines his self-perception. Work and human brains are a filter through which he sees the world. Everyone and everything appears as distorted by it. "Perowne leaves the square and heads east, crosses the Tottenham Court Road and walks towards Gower Street. If only the mayor was right, that penetrating the skull brings into view not the brain but the mind" (243). Brains are to Perowne a "familiar territory, a kind of homeland" (254) mapped and described as a surface one could move through, walk on, a "crazy paving" (256):

> With its low hills and enfolded valleys of the sulci, each with a name and imputed function, as known to him as his house. Just to the left of the midline, running laterally away out of sight under the bone, is the motor strip. Behind it, running parallel, is the sensory strip. So easy to damage, with such terrible, lifelong consequences. How much time he has spent making routes to avoid these areas, like bad neighbourhoods in an American city [254].

In fact brain as territory becomes so common and trivial that even its mysteries turn out to be demystified and at times it resembles an object, a product that can or cannot be repaired. Henry has chosen brains because "they were more interesting than bladders or knee joints" (45). To him, after decades of professional experience the human brain is like an expensive car: "There are so many ways a brain can let you down. Like an expensive car, it's intricate, but mass-produced nevertheless, with more than six billion in circulation" (98). One instance of this is his mother's dementia, a disease impossible to cure, a permanent damage whose cause is largely unknown. Perowne visits his mother in the afternoon—he confronts her condition which separated her from the city, placed her in the outskirts, which she does not mind because she has lost the sense and any memories of space. The visit to her new home, full of other disturbed individuals, makes Henry think of his own future, the unpredictability of human brain and its ability to paralyze the entire system, similar to a mass demonstration in a city. His mother calls him "Auntie" and seems to him so fragile, though physically stable and fit, a "perfectly looking 77-year-old with amazing legs for her age" (164). She had to be moved out of the city because she could no longer cope with it, the missing fragments of her memories had made the metropolis dangerous for her.

When Perowne thinks of his mother's illness, he does so in spatial terms. The illness is locked in a small room outside of the city. Her (impossible) recovery would mean taking her back to the "heart of the city" (164). The literary motif is similar to the one featured in Don DeLillo's novel *Falling Man*, where Lianne witnesses her mother's progressive dementia and at the same time coaches a creative writing group for people with Alzheimer's. Perowne, "a man who attempts to ease the miseries of failing minds by repairing brains" (67), cannot do anything to stop his mother's dementia, and his position as a neurosurgeon makes him feel helpless and useless in this situation which partly influences his moods when walking through the city.

Hospitals and Urban Emergencies

Perowne's life is strongly linked not only to the city and to brains but also to the hospital as a space. His work is an addiction, a passion beyond comprehension, a love. It is not sensual, but almost like a sexual encounter, as cricket is in the life of Hans in O'Neill's *Netherland*:

> For the past two hours he's been in a dream of absorption that has dissolved all sense of time, and all awareness of the other parts of his life. Even his awareness of his own existence has vanished. He's been delivered into a pure present, free of the weight of the past or any anxieties about the future. In retrospect, though never at the time, it feels like profound happiness. It's a little bit like sex, in that he feels himself in another medium, but it's less obviously pleasurable, and clearly not sensual [258].

Since work is a passion deeply rooted in space, hospital is to Perowne like a city that never sleeps. It is a space in which, just like in London, time has a different meaning and forms a different dimension. It is a space that never shuts down, full of fear but at the same time offering tranquility:

> In soothing gloom he goes along the broad avenue of beds with their watchful machines and winking coloured lights. He's reminded of neon signs in a deserted street—the big room has the ephemeral tranquility of a city just before dawn [261].

There are other parallels between the city and the hospital—the latter is a place marked by struggle, pain and death, yet at the same time a place of hope, a place where people made vulnerable by sickness or an accident come. Both spaces generate chaos, an unbearable collection of influences, expectations but also objects. Perowne links the chaos of his son's bedroom to the chaos of a hospital, and any other closed space that allows people to collect objects, eventually causing an uncontrollable chaos:

Rooms full of junk, cupboards and filing cabinets that no one dares open. Ancient equipment in cream tin-plate housing, too heavy, too mysterious to eject. Sick buildings, in use for too long, that only demolition can cure. Cities and states beyond repair. The whole world resembling Theo's bedroom [122].

Both spaces also generate and cultivate insomnia and insomniacs, both are examples of "sleepless entity whose wires never stop singing; among so many millions there are bound to be people staring out of windows when normally they would be asleep" (17).

The way Henry's thoughts whirl around his head resembles the very chaos that he attempts to grasp in order to understand the world around him. While moving through the city, his thoughts are interrupted, moved onto different tracks and disciplines. The narration accompanying his brain as it produces the logical or intuitive chains of association provides a very rich set of intertextual references and interdisciplinary connotations. When driving down Charlotte Street, "a spot he's always liked, where the affairs of utility and pleasure condense to make colour and space brighter: mirrors, flowers, soaps, newspapers, electrical plugs, house paints, key cutting urbanely interleaved with expensive restaurants, wine and tapas bars, hotels" (122), he tries to recall which of the American novelists wrote about this area claiming he could be happy living on Charlotte Street. The city he confronts has already been written, and he encounters these previous accounts in different places and feels directly addressed by them.

London on that particular Saturday is controlled and dominated by the march against the Iraq war, which interferes with traffic and the general functioning of the metropolis. This is an exceptional day, a state of urban emergency, where traffic is regulated by police, many streets are blocked and masses of people occupy public spaces. The sense of unease deriving from exceptional rules of this day signals a potential dysfunction of the system and can be linked to a sickness familiar to Perowne due to his work at the hospital. When the functioning city system is deprived of its regular connections, it becomes vulnerable, as do the people who move within it. Perowne's car accident is an example of this vulnerability and of a continuity of malfunctioning particles that lead to a general collapse of the system as a whole. The accident, minor in terms of car damage, results in a violent reaction of Baxter—the driver of the other car. Provoked by Perowne with details about his brain disease (which Perowne identifies almost immediately as Huntington's disease), he feels humiliated in front of his friends and seeks revenge that evening at the surgeon's house, terrorizing his reunited family with a knife.

While still in his car, Henry sees how history and political world affairs enter the traffic of London. The immediate trigger is the march itself, but Henry's thoughts start circulating around global issues and the global malaise.

He discusses with himself the pros and contras of the war, knowing it is unavoidable:

> Or perhaps it will work out—the dictator vanquished without hundreds of thousands of deaths, and after a year or two, a democracy at last, secular or Islamic, nestling among the weary tyrannies of the Middle East. Wedged in traffic alongside the multiple faces, Henry experiences his own ambivalence as a form of vertigo, a dizzy indecision. In neurosurgery he chose a safe and simple profession [141].

The novel is framed by a window view—a cinematic effect of watching the outside world as a cut out fragment. Before going to sleep that night, Henry sees the future of his life and his family's through the city outside staring back at him. First he sees death:

> From where he stands up here there are things he can see that he knows must happen. Soon it will be his mother's time.... Yes, and then it will be the turn of John Grammaticus, one of those transfiguring illnesses that come to a drinking man, or a terminal stab to the heart or brain [273, 275].

Time passes also for the changing city, and is equally important. New generation of junkies will occupy the square beneath Henry's window. The people who will come, their lives inseparable from the political situation of their time, will change the meaning of places with their presence and expectations. Henry will outgrow this part of the city and the feeling of displacement and fear will drive him out elsewhere.

> Perhaps a bomb in the cause of jihad will drive them out with all the other faint-hearts into the suburbs, or deeper into the country, or to the chateau—their Saturday will become a Sunday [276].

Through the life kaleidoscope, Henry sees a catastrophic vision: London is a victim and there is no way to change it; the city is "impossible to defend, waiting for its bomb, like a hundred other cities" (276). The vision of urban chaos incorporates Henry's deepest fears, and involves details and assumptions that tame it by providing information, a way to replace the unknown, which seems to Henry worse than any detail. History repeats itself, just like motifs in filmic genres.

Perowne sees London's future in historical perspective—wars connected and ideologies redundant. Remarkably, he links the Iraq war that is yet to come to a sporting event, planned and arranged carefully weeks in advance:

> Rush hour will be a convenient time. It might resemble the Paddington crash—twisted rails, buckled, upraised commuter coaches, stretchers handed out through broken windows, the hospital's Emergency Plan in action. Berlin, Paris, Lisbon. The authorities agree, an attack's inevitable. He lives in different times—because

the newspapers say so doesn't mean it isn't true. But from the top of his day, this is a future that's harder to read, a horizon indistinct with possibilities.... Beware of utopianists, zealous men certain of the path to the ideal social order. Here they are again, totalitarians in different form, still scattered and weak, but growing, and angry, and thirsty for another mass killing.... The war will start next month—the precise date must already have been fixed, as though for any big outdoor sporting event [276–277].

This links Perowne's vision to the one of Chris Cleave in his novel *Incendiary* where urban terror is also transmitted under the cover of a sport event—the nature of fascination with which is being radically questioned and put in the context of individual vulnerability and mass dynamics. Perowne provides an immediate analysis of his own thoughts and feelings. He states that knowing that an attack on a Western city is inevitable; he experiences a mixture of fear, paranoia and guilty curiosity. At the same time he cannot escape a certain subconscious desire to witness a disaster. In bringing these aspects together, he addresses the voyeuristic nature of witnessing a catastrophe and the role of spectators in the 21st century: "Please don't let it happen. But let me see it all the same, as it's happening and from every angle, and let me be among the first to know" (176).

Squash and Transatlantic Relations

Squash is yet another sport that appears in post–9/11 fiction—next to cricket in O'Neill's *Netherland*, ice-skating in Ali's *Brick Lane* and soccer in Cleave's *Incendiary*—and that interferes with a character's perception of the city. The game offers isolation from the metropolis and a silence undisturbed by emergency vehicles and the city's constant rush and speed: "The silence is complete, of that hissing variety rarely heard in a city; no other players, no street sounds, not even from the march" (103).

Squash has a quality comparable to cricket in O'Neill's *Netherland*. It is shown as a male game that turns into a pure, instinctive competition between two men, Perowne and Jay, his colleague, also a neurosurgeon, an American. The game is detached in time and space from their everyday lives and its affairs. It is a vacuum in which the individual performance and the desire to win overshadow everything else. Once the game is over and they leave the room, the challenge loses its importance almost immediately.

Oblivious to their protesting hearts, they hurl themselves into every corner of the court. These are no unforced errors, every point is wrested, bludgeoned from the other. The server gasps out the score, but otherwise they don't speak. And as the score rises, neither man moves more than one point ahead. There's nothing at stake.... There's only the irreducible urge to win, as biological as thirst. And it's pure because no one's watching, no one cares, not their friends, their wives, their children. It isn't even enjoyable. It might become so in retrospect—and only to the winner [113].

Transatlantic relations overshadow the plot (and the game) in form of current politics and the planned Iraq war: before they start playing, Jay says: "They dislike your Prime Minister, but boy do they fucking loathe my President" (100). Transatlantic politics also enter the narration with music (Theo's fascination with blues, Chas's new tricks straight from New York and a song "City Square") and also as delicately applied stereotypes, "You have to be an American to want, as an adult, anything quite so sweet" (116)—says Perowne to Jay Strauss about drinking coke. The march which starts on Gower Street uses political imagery for its slogans. The faces of Perowne's Prime Minister and Strauss's President (Blair and Bush) as personifications of war are to be seen everywhere in the city. London becomes a political stage on which a protest takes place, interrupting the regular functioning of the city.

The city, despite the catastrophic visions and fear which circulate around it, appears to Henry as a masterpiece. His gaze is a euphoric one of a London lover who has his own corner in the city, his own safety zone. London is a communal project of corners claimed by individuals, which function as an entity, a mosaic of historical influences mixed with the contemporary reality. All of a sudden it appears to him incredibly fragile, facing the century of terrorism and unexpected but inevitable threat:

> Standing here, as immune to the cold as a marble statue, gazing towards Charlotte Street, towards a foreshortened jumble of facades, scaffolding and pitched roofs, Henry thinks the city is a success, a brilliant invention, a biological masterpiece— millions teeming around the accumulated and layered achievements of the centuries, as though around a coral reef, sleeping, working, entertaining themselves, harmonious for the most part, nearly everyone wanting it to work. And the Perownes' own corner, a triumph of congruent proportion; the perfect square laid out by Robert Adam enclosing a perfect circle of garden—an eighteen-century dream bathed and embraced by modernity, by street light from above, and from below by fibre-optic cables, and cool fresh water coursing down pipes, and sewage borne away in an instant of forgetting [5].

His life is inscribed in the city and is placed as well in the context of historical events. Born too early "for the Cuban missiles, or the construction of the Berlin Wall, or Kennedy's assassination, [he] remembers being tearful over Aberfan in 'sixty-six—one hundred and sixteen schoolchildren just like himself, fresh from prayers in school assembly, the day before half-term, buried under a river of mud" (32–33). The present state of Perowne's life, when seen in a larger context of international politics of his country, is marked by "international terror, security cordons, preparations for war" (32)—a post–9/11 and pre–7/7 reality that he tries to consider stable by comparing it to the weather and pretending to see it as a most daily business.

London as Theatre in Historical Context

Looking at the square outside of his window, Henry elaborates on the city structure and the extraordinary character of squares to easily turn into urban stages, something that streets cannot do. He observes how the original idea of a forum within a city can be traced in contemporary London. It becomes a theater for staged emotions. "People often drift into the square to act out their dramas. Clearly a street won't do. Passions need room, the attentive spaciousness of a theatre.... The square's public aspect grants privacy to these intimate dramas" (60–61). He then links these thoughts to an Iraqi desert, a space he has no experiences with and can only imagine. He thinks of it as a "flat and supposedly empty landscape approximating a strategist's on which fury of industrial proportions can be get loose" (60). The city square is a "private equivalent" of the endless desert, exotic within the London metropolitan context.

Saturday provides a historiographical kaleidoscope of events by linking the 21st century terrorism to the IRA, as do other post–9/11 novels which sketch a broader context for acts of terrorism, for example, DeLillo's *Falling Man* mentions the German Red Army Faction, and Hamilton's *31 Hours* features the IRA. From a temporal perspective Perowne states that "as a Londoner, you could grow nostalgic for the IRA" (34).

The world with its problems is happening outside of the microcosm of Perownes' house but it enters the rooms regularly and needs to be discussed and acknowledged. Henry discusses the current affairs, the "early-twenty-first-century menu" (34) with his son Theo at the kitchen table. This menu together with "specials" (34) is recapitulated in one sentence which puts the entire novel in a historical context and which provides a certain irony towards the easiness with which the world is being discussed and told. "Iraq of course, America and power, European distrust, Islam—its suffering and self-pity, Israel and Palestine, dictators, democracy—and then the boys' stuff: weapons of mass destruction, nuclear fuel rods, satellite photography, lasers, nanotechnology" (34). Outside, the preparations for the march begin—it starts at Gower Street and moves towards Hyde Park. The purpose of its spatial intervention within the city invades Henry's thoughts. News about Hans Blix's report, which states that there are no weapons of mass destruction in Iraq, contributes to Henry's attitude towards the demonstration. As with the march witnessed by Nazneen in *Brick Lane*, here Perowne has the impression the efforts of the masses are superfluous and shallow. Sebastian Groes wants to see Perowne's ambiguity as a "potent form of resistance to both State and dominance and to individual self-righteousness" (Groes "Ian McEwen" 101).

Urban Terror Domesticated

The city enters domestic life in a number of ways. The Victoria line trains make the furniture inside vibrate, the sound of a quarrel on the square is also audible inside. Finally Baxter, the embodiment of terror, an ill, incomprehensible and unpredictable individual, brings the horror of the outside world close to the core of the Perowne family. He comes from within London and poses a realistic and personal threat. What makes Baxter dangerous is his missing sense of the future and actions beyond the notion of responsibility or consequences. In his detachment from life he resembles a kamikaze or a suicide bomber who does not value his own existence. The only difference is that Baxter's condition can be diagnosed and Perowne, although helpless at that moment, can clearly see his future and knows there is no cure. The house, peaceful and secure, turns into a closed and claustrophobic space of inescapable terror, the city its silent witness and mute observer. Dominic Head sees the family's condition as a metaphor for all Western urban societies after 9/11; the threat to their security "parallels the broader insecurity of the West in the face of Islamic extremism" (Head *Ian McEwen* 124). To exploit this parallel further would mean linking Islamic terrorists but also dictators, like Saddam Hussein, to Baxter—the oppressor with a brain disease and the embodiment of a universal Other who may well emerge from within, but whose motives and methods remain beyond comprehension.

Perowne discusses the nature of totalitarian regimes and leaders and sees historical repetition in the utopian ideal and childish obsession with power. "Here they are again, totalitarians in different form, still scattered and weak, but growing, and angry, and thirsty for another mass killing" (276–277). The connection established between the city and the human brain, and between totalitarian rulers and terrorism and brain disease, suggests a form of a global mental malaise, a "possibility of a common psychological disorder" (Head *Ian McEwan* 181). Baxter's mood changes suddenly after he hears Matthew Arnold's poem *Dover Beach,* and he undergoes a metamorphosis from "lord of terror to amazed admirer" (223). It is striking that poetry rescues the family and tames the oppressor. McEwan's romantic vision of the power of written words and the artist-creator being in charge of world affairs comes through as a detached belief in art and at the same time, on an abstract level, as an antidote of beauty for the horrors of global terrorism. The 19th-century poem praises the world, love and nature. It seems so detached from the entire setting of the novel that it comes as a surprise. The novel proclaims that there is an antidote for every brain disease, a softener for any deviation, also on the metaphorical global level. McEwan's usage of intertextual references in the novel is seen by Groes as the main tool of writing London again (Groes "Ian McEwen" 103).

Establishing a dialogue with city writers and poets from earlier centuries, particularly the modernists, makes it possible to rewrite the city again, contextualized by its cultural and literary past and yet very different from previous written accounts. Versluys sees the poem in McEwan's novel as an "unexpected interposition of language as an agent of transcendent recognition" (192) and as an example of "the interruption of the said by the saying" (192) which he derives from Levinas's studies on the Other.

To conclude, Ian McEwan's *Saturday* shifts the focus to London's West End and provides a third-person narrator through whom a day in the life of a successful neurosurgeon is told. Despite the factual and social distance from the setting of the other two London novels analyzed in this book, Henry Perowne's house and the immediate surrounding are also covered with post–9/11 "New York dust." The uncertainty about the future of the city and Perowne's own life, so strongly attached to it, causes kaleidoscopic movements and shifts of thought. The narrator follows him as he moves through the city and a chain of his associations, often getting lost in digressions. His work at the hospital and fascination with the human brain influence the ways he perceives and maps the city in order to feel comfortable and safe in it. This is difficult, as he knows that some brain diseases are incurable—for instance the one Baxter is suffering from; his concern about the city's mental state, dominated by fear and preparations for war, leaves him helpless in the face of the potentially catastrophic future of the huge urban brain.

By perceiving the city as a brain, he makes the urban setting to a field of his expertise. He becomes the ultimate specialist, and by believing that he can change the city's future and find a cure for its dangerous moods, he gains control over London, something that all of the characters of post–9/11 city fiction try to achieve in order to master their individual lives in an altered metropolis. The question that the neurosurgeon is afraid to raise is: What if there is no cure for the disease that the city is suffering from?

VIII

New York versus London:
Joseph O'Neill's *Netherland*[1]

Joseph O'Neill's third novel *Netherland*, published in 2008, addresses the general and omnipresent sense of displacement in post–9/11 New York City. It is the only novel chosen for this study that is set in both New York City and London and thus functions as a point of synthesis in experiencing these two urban environments in post–9/11 literature. Set in cities full of immigrants, it analyzes the nature of foreignness in its capacity to connect, in the way that common catastrophes or experiences of survival do. It uses the game of cricket as a metaphorical framework to address immigrant communities, postcolonial legacies and the need for remapping of a wounded and paranoid city. The Irish author, who has lived in many places including the Netherlands and the U.S., writes about the importance and need of belonging in the contemporary globalized world and connects it with the experience of living in the suddenly altered reality of a metropolis whose freedoms have been attacked. Despite travel being much easier than ever, immigration still poses socio-cultural challenges. It widens horizons and builds tolerance and sensitivity, but it also confuses the basic sense of belonging. In *Netherland* the perception of the place originally called home, once the main character Hans leaves it, changes through the experience of new places. The memory of "home" can never again match the found reality, and Hans feels equally foreign or equally familiar in all the places he chooses to live. These memories shape and influence the understanding of new places and Hans finds traces of The Hague in which he grew up everywhere he goes. The September 11 attacks and the experience of living, redefining and remapping the city result in a stronger bond with the metropolis and its people and put a new perspective on the geography and cartography of Hans's life. Combining these elements with cricket—a sport, an art form, and ultimately a cure—makes the novel's approach on 9/11 engaging and unique. In this study it functions as a bridge between New York and London in the context of the analyzed fiction.

The destruction of the World Trade Center towers has left Hans, the first person narrator of *Netherland*, helpless, lonely and metaphorically paralyzed in a disoriented New York City. His wife Rachel, overwhelmed with the omnipresent fear and paranoia, chooses to escape the U.S. and returns to London with their little son, leaving Hans behind. This links *Netherland* to a group of novels, including Don DeLillo's *Falling Man*, Ken Kalfus's *A Disorder Peculiar to the Country* (2006) and Jay McInerney's *The Good Life* (2006), that address 9/11 through the image of a dissolving marriage, which serves as a metaphor for the surrounding events (Rothberg 9). For the quite unusual flâneur Hans, the newly and abruptly altered metropolis and lifestyle require a thorough remapping, in his case revolving around an obsession with playing cricket. He knows this sport from his childhood in The Hague and rediscovers it after many years in its U.S. version. Playing the game brings back memories and functions as a bridge between Hans's European past and his American present. It also makes him travel through the city so that eventually his geographical remapping of New York is marked by cricket fields and parks in Brooklyn, Queens and Staten Island.

Hans's life is filled with transatlantic *déjà-vus*, motifs, patterns and people that keep reappearing in different places (The Hague, London and New York), contributing to a certain coherence in his personal life cartography. Cricket has made the most significant of those reappearances and serves in the novel as a sense-generating therapeutic means. For Hans, coming to terms with American cricket and becoming a part of the team means mutual acceptance and acknowledging the U.S. as his new home. Only on the cricket field does he feel "naturalized," although paradoxically all of the players are immigrants, which makes the "American way" of playing cricket a post-national concept.

Sports can play an important role in post–9/11 fiction. They can function as a form of self-therapy and the regularity with which they are played serves as a bonding and soothing mechanism. Specifically cricket is used by literary characters to reference their countries of origin and functions as a bonding cultural element in the post–9/11 context, e.g., the already mentioned references in H.M. Naqvi's novel *Home Boy* or in Mohsin Hamid's *The Reluctant Fundamentalist*, in which both of the first-person narrators and main protagonists use cricket as a metonymy for their childhoods in Pakistan or simply as a metaphor in their everyday New York vocabulary. Cricket in *Netherland* is more than a game—it is a life concept that gradually becomes an increasingly important part of the main character's every day New York existence. It helps him acclimatize in the changed post–9/11 city and becomes his primary reference and a key to claiming back space in the wounded metropolis.

Netherland opens with the first three lines of Walt Whitman's poem *I Dream'd in a Dream*[2]:

I dream'd in a dream, I saw a city invincible to
The attacks of the whole of the rest of the earth;
I dream'd that was the new City of Friends.

Narrated retrospectively by the first person narrator Hans van den Broek, the novel shows the post–9/11 development and transformation of New York from an attacked city to a city of (potential) friends, a place possibly livable and bearable again. When Hans and his wife leave London, where she comes from, for New York, it is supposed to be just for a short time, "a year or three" (3) but it turns out to be true what Hans's boss has told him prior to the departure: once you are in New York City, it is very hard to leave it and "once you do, your life carries a taint of aftermath" (2). Hans becomes a victim of this very specific metropolitan addiction, even though he admits that New York is the place in which he has been most unhappy in his entire life. He remains in the city much longer than originally planned.

Cricket as a Transnational Bridge

When thinking about cricket in his childhood, Hans recalls his mother watching him play at the famous "HBS-Crayenhout" sports club founded at the end of the 19th century in The Hague. He then rediscovers the game after many years, as an established banker in London. He joins the South Bank Cricket Club, which he quits after a few seasons. The London cricket experience was "agreeable, English and enchanting" (57) and also strongly marked by the absence of Hans's mother watching.

Years later, alone, hurt and traumatized by the impact of the terrorist attacks on his private life, Hans rediscovers cricket, again as an immigrant and without anyone watching him play—in its modified American version. The game brings elements of Hans's geographically remote past back to his New York daily existence. In *Netherland* cricket functions as a reassuring and transnationally relevant activity, bringing a constancy and coherence to the otherwise fragmented reality. It establishes a connection between all the cities that mark the past and the seemingly closed chapters of Hans's life. Once rediscovered, cricket plays a tremendously important role in bringing back transnational memories. The game also marks differences between the cities Hans has played in and highlights the cultural clashes he is confronted with. The game has its national versions, cultural and social coding, specificities and language. In Hans's understanding it is also gendered:

> Moments of cricket scorched in my mind like sexual memories, forever available to me and capable, during those long nights alone in the hotel when I sought

refuge from the sorriest feelings, of keeping me awake as I relived them in bed and powerlessly mourned the mysterious promise they held. To reinvent myself in order to bat the American way, that baseball-like business of slugging and hoisting, involved more than the trivial abandonment of a hard-won style of hitting a ball. It meant snipping a fine white thread running, through years and years, to my mothered self [63–64].

Comprehending the local way of playing cricket and adjusting to it in order to be accepted in the team serves as a metaphor for the process of becoming accustomed to a new country as a foreigner. For Hans, coming to terms with an American cricket that is less "orthodox" (Hill "The American Dream of Chuck Ramkisoon" 226) than the Dutch means accepting the U.S. as his new home and becoming part of the society, although paradoxically all of the players are black immigrants, making the "American way" of playing cricket not only a post-national but also a post-post-colonial concept.

The relationship between cricket and nationality has always been an interesting one, as Stephen Wagg and Jon Gemmell point out. In 1720 the first agreed rules of modern cricket were written down, and this makes cricket "*the only modern sport*" to be established in a pre-nationalist age" (Wagg and Gemmell 254, emphasis mine). Hence, cricket was an identity and community shaping factor before former British colonies were recognized as nations. It was then transformed into a "national passion" through the process of spectacle, media presence and other forms of localization/vernacularization (Appadurai 106, 112). In *Netherland* it is placed above all other identification and belonging categories and has the status of a certain meta-level and superior reference.

Cricket functions as a replacement for social and family activities and is quite extraordinary to Hans because of its separateness from all other parts of his life (228). It is more than a game; it is a whole concept that Hans gradually becomes addicted to. Hans spends his lunch breaks in Bryant Park in order to smell the fresh grass, look at the sky and inhale the scent of fresh air which he now associates only with cricket (227). He also feels attached to the other players of his team and he realizes they would be the first and only people to take care of him in case of need. Cricket connects Hans not only to the other players but also, and equally importantly, to the city. It makes him explore different parts of it. The game is Hans's key to post–9/11 New York, which becomes mapped and marked in his mind by parks and cricket fields. Playing the game in the changed urban environment is on one hand something new that Hans only discovers when his family leaves him; on the other hand, it is very strongly linked to Hans's childhood, to his mother and to the Dutch language. It awakens memories of old feelings and passions. It builds a bridge between the different phases of his life and forms a strong transatlantic and transnational link that puts things into perspective and points to a certain universality of urban behaviors and reactions.

The choice of places in *Netherland* is very specific and highly signifying: the capitals of the Netherlands and England represent the old colonial empire, and the financial center of the U.S.—now New York, previously New Amsterdam—is the new world with new imperial aspirations. They are connected by the person of Hans and by the game of cricket, which since the era of colonialism has served as "a bond linking a global Empire to the mother country" (Hill "Queering the Pitch" 183) and which was "the most powerful condensation of Victorian elite values"[3] and a way of transmitting them to the colonies (Appadurai 93). The fact that in the novel the game has hardly any recognition in the U.S. and that the players feel subordinate to their baseball playing counterparts (they can only use the pitch after the baseball game is over, etc.), shows cricket as an old concept for which there is no place in modern America. At the same time it points to the difficult legacy of colonialism. It is not the colonizers who play cricket now but the new generations of the previously colonized nations who see the game as their own reference point. In *Netherland* the link to this cultural tradition is especially strong because it shows a Dutch man playing cricket with Caribbean men on U.S. soil. The confused, symbolic empire of all times "bats back," so to say. Choosing a sport that is neither popular nor prominent provides another way for Hans to escape his currently unhappy life full of privileges and superficialities. Becoming the Other contributes to the radical change that Hans's life undergoes and functions as a refreshing social shock which eventually makes him wake up from the lethargy triggered by 9/11 and its consequences.

Post–9/11 New York and the Chelsea Hotel

After 9/11 Hans and his family decide to leave, or more precisely, to abandon their TriBeCa loft and move into the Chelsea Hotel, which is further away from Ground Zero and for them a new, emotionally blank place, but one culturally and symbolically a "loaded" in the American context. They leave all their possessions in the apartment and start a very abrupt day-to-day temporary existence, which becomes so unbearable for Rachel that she eventually moves back to London. Both New York, "the city gone mad" (27), and the Chelsea Hotel, the "crappy" (27) place in which Hans feels hospitalized, form strange microcosms which he, now alone, has to rediscover and tame in order to start a new life, first to come to grips with the new situation and eventually to leave the lethargy and trauma behind.

The hotel is described as a center of weird characters and personalities, an asylum, a post-traumatic arena for an extraordinary *freak show*, an absurd theatre of neurotic actors and individuals, a cosmos in which nothing ever surprises. It is full of disturbed and random individuals, none of whom seems to be famous or successful as the history of the building would suggest or demand. It is portrayed as a shadow of its history and legends; it resembles a ruin. In addition to meeting a man dating a dog called Missie and celebrating Missie's third birthday in the hotel lobby one evening, Hans also encounters "the Angel," a Turkish man named Mehmet Taspinar. He has worn an angel costume with wings from a shop called "Religious Sex" on St. Mark's Place (44) for two years and tells Hans that New York is "the only place in the world where he could be himself—until recently" (44). He too has found asylum in the Chelsea Hotel after his landlord terminated his contract. The next time Hans and Taspinar meet is in the hotel lobby, which functions as a bizarre living room. The mostly lonely, long-term residents sit there together like a substitute family and in this strange way confront normative social patterns and expectations they know they will not be able to fulfill. Hans joins the Angel and an old lady one evening and, becoming aware of the solitude that fills the room and the hotel realizes: "He and I and the murmuring widow in the baseball cap sat in a row like three crazy old sisters who have long ago run out of things to say to one another" (47).

As a space, the lobby has a therapeutic character and is an important component of the Chelsea Hotel reality, which, as any other hotel, is marked by temporality and the constant movement of people coming and going. Hans's life at the Chelsea consists of "rhythmical miseries" (139) and pseudo-comforting routines, one of which is the habit of having long breakfasts at the Malibu Diner on weekends. There he becomes acquainted with members of the "Visionary Community"—a residence for blind people in his neighborhood. He starts calling the area "the quarter of the blind" (140), a term which metaphorically mirrors the condition of the whole of traumatized New York, full of "blind" individuals who without realizing it, have stopped seeing one another and concentrate on finding new ways to live in the altered urban reality instead.

At the Chelsea everyone seems to adjust to this concept of temporality and discontinuity. The only sexual encounter during Hans's otherwise lonely post–9/11 New York life also falls into this discourse of temporality. Danielle, who "boomeranged" in from the past (they once shared a cab in London), does not return Hans's calls and they never meet again. After this incident Hans realizes he hardly has any friends in New York. In fact, the city in the novel seems to be generally difficult for friendships. The legacy of modernity and its cult of individualism are very much present in Wall Street, where Hans's work environment is rather cold and full of superficial politeness and professional pseudo-informative exchanges. People working in his company compete with one another and do not communicate much. Even Rivera—the only colleague whom Hans considers a friend—after having lost the job never returns his calls and like Danielle, "joins those who had disappeared" from his life (138). What makes Hans's situation in New York so difficult is the fact that he does not or cannot move beyond the frame of the temporal. Nothing seems to have any particular importance because of the transitory character of his life. He reflects:

> My life had shrunk to very small proportions—too small, certainly, for New York's pickier and more plausible agents of sympathy.... I was, to anyone who could be bothered to pay attention, noticeably lost [93].

Since Hans cannot refer the attacks of 9/11 and everything that has happened since to anything from his own past, he searches for references in transnational memories in order to understand the situation which he calls "pre-apocalyptic." He wonders if his own position in post–9/11 New York resembles the one of European Jews during World War II or rather the one of citizens of Pompeii pre-lava (29). Looking for answers and understanding in his desire to find reference points in Europe rather than in the U.S., he tries to discuss it with his English father-in-law in a transatlantic call to London. But even he—a spokesman for the old and experienced continent—has no answers and the inquiry comes as a surprise that leaves Hans disappointed and even more helpless. Alfred Hornung claims that transnational memories of man-made destructions are crucial for American post–9/11 literature in general, arguing that due to the "absence of similar major catastrophic destruction in the history of the continental United States since the Civil War ... they served as the material to cope with the impact of international terrorism on the American soil at the beginning of the twenty-first century" (Hornung 172). This can be applied when talking about post–9/11 fiction that employs explicit references to World War II, the Holocaust (Foer's *Extremely Loud and Incredibly Close*, Spiegelman's *In the Shadow of No Towers* and others) or the terrorist activities of the IRA (Hamilton's *31 Hours*) or the Red Army Faction (DeLillo's *Falling Man*), but it does not work in the case of *Netherland* where none of the references seem to be appropriate or usable in coming to terms with what happened on 9/11.

Hans eventually does try to break through the set of meaningless routines in order to make his everyday life less random, to reach some internal stability and to cope with the overwhelming feeling of displacement. This process is symbolically marked by obtaining an American driving license. Taking the exam, which is connected to endless and absurd bureaucracy and requires lots of determination, is his commitment to New York, to the country and to the beginning of a new phase—the post–9/11, post-marriage life of a lonely but free cricketer-flâneur.

Walking, Recovering and Remapping Post–9/11 New York

Through cricket, Hans re-explores New York. Cricket fields, clubs and parks bring him to Staten Island, Queens and Brooklyn. To Idlewild Park, Marine Park, Monroe Cohen Ballfield, Seaview Park, Canarsie—places he has not heard of before, living and working in Manhattan. He even goes to Pough-keepsie in Upstate New York—a cricket-town maintained by a community of Jamaicans. He commutes from Manhattan to the peripheries; he leaves the island, the extraordinary metropolitan center of wealth and privilege, which centuries before carried the name of New Amsterdam, in order to turn the city's cartography upside down and to, in this way, develop a new understanding of it. Some of his cricket related journeys have the effect of moving him back in time, either through the memories they evoke or through an entirely new input and the impressions they bring. Going to one of the fields by train under-neath the Washington Bridge in Harlem has for Hans the effect of "cancelling centuries" (76). The frozen Hudson evokes transatlantic memories and brings Hans back to Holland, to the *netherland* that stands for peace and a serene childhood, abandoned for an adult life in London and then New York. All these places and memories could have been revisited and refreshed, had Hans's mother still been alive. After her death, the house he grew up in was sold and he was left with "the burden of remembering" (111), a burden which he brings back to New York. Following this loss, two years before 9/11, Hans also looks for help in the city. His aimless and excessive walking through China Town, Seward Park and the Seaport area with his baby son in a stroller is an urban farewell to his mother and to his childhood. He imagines her walking with him:

> There was a definite element of flight, and an element of capitulation, too, as if I were the one scooting along in the buggy and my mother the one steering it through the streets.... The fantasy did not consist of imagining her physically at my side but of imagining her at a long distance, as before, and me still remotely swaddled in her consideration; and in this I was abetted by the streets of New York City, which abet desire even in its strangest patterns [122–123].

New York is soothing; it offers enough space—literally and metaphorically—to recover through walking. It takes Hans some time to return to this idea after 9/11.

Hans's "new" post–9/11 city does not consist of boroughs and streets any-more, but of cricket fields which turn into new *netherlands*, extraterritorial spaces that impose their own rules and that serve as an asylum and a refreshing alternative to Wall Street, where Hans has spent most of his pre–9/11 life. Jeffrey Hill, who examines the status of the sport and its history in the U.S. and Europe, talks about cricket in America as a "nether land" of sporting, as a discipline socially and racially marginalized that has never quite made it in the U.S. (Hill "The American Dream" 221).

This specific way of individually remapping New York makes Hans an unusual cricketer-flâneur whose driving force is cricket, and what it implements is a whole new lifestyle subordinate to this game and to *chasing* new cricket fields. He, just like other protagonists of post–9/11 novels, e.g., the nine-year-old Oskar in Foer's *Extremely Loud and Incredibly Close* or the Nigerian psychiatrist Julius in Teju Cole's *Open City*, is looking for something that is difficult to grasp or describe. He looks for new meanings, similarly to the solitary Baudelaireian artist-flâneur who looks for a new quality,[4] for the "ephemeral, the fugitive, the contingent" (Baudelaire 13). Despite the traumatic circumstances, both Oskar and Hans are "lovers of life" (Baudelaire 9) who, driven by loss, try to make the whole world their family: Oskar through acquainting himself with and photographing people called Black, whose images he adds to his diary entitled "Things That Happened to Me," and Hans by seeing his team as his closest people, the ones he can rely on and feels obliged to help when in need. Teju Cole's Julius—the chronicler and hobbyist historian—rediscovers during his walks different aspects of the city's past. All three of these characters create a new dimension, a "fantastic reality of life" (Baudelaire 15) in Baudelaireian terms, which allows them to observe the world around them closely but at the same time remain hidden from it by wearing a "mask," by staying in a separate reality that has nothing to do with the everyday life they used to live before the process of personal remapping was begun.

Manhattan, Tribeca, Times Square: The Meaning of Places in Pre– and Post–9/11 New York

During their pre–9/11 time together in Manhattan, which Hans keeps recalling and analyzing after his wife is gone, Hans and Rachel have both ambitious and well-paid jobs which exhaust their days and their everyday life. Slowly but surely their marriage becomes dominated by extreme and overwhelming tiredness which is strongly linked to the city. They are too tired to cook or to go out; and they constantly fall asleep as if to escape the monotonous reality of the time left after a work day. Their daily routine comes to overwhelm them and makes them fall into a lethargy. This state is brutally interrupted by the events of September 11 which, as such, are only very briefly mentioned in the novel but which symbolically and politically "overshadow most of the plot" and provide "a crucial metaphorical framework" for the entire narration (Däwes *Ground Zero Fiction* 80) and for the process of place making that follows. The meaning and Hans's perception of places within New York change after 9/11. The atmosphere in the traumatized metropolis makes Hans develop a new nightmare connected to a place that he used to like. This nightmare is a performer dancing with a human-size dummy at Times Square underground station:

> There was something dire going on—something that went beyond the desperation, economic and artistic, discernible on the man's damp features, beyond even the sexual perverseness of his routine. The puppet had something to do with it. Her hands and feet were bound to her master's…. Crude features had been inscribed on her face, and this gave her a blank, bottomless look [25].

This nightmare develops to a phobia; Hans is eventually no longer capable of passing by the duo and chooses ways to avoid seeing it by changing his routes in the city. He realizes that his fear is irrational and yet he is incapable of controlling his reactions.

Times Square is generally an emotionally important place in *Netherland*— it is where Rachel works and fears it to become the next terrorist target. It is also one of Hans's favorite places in the city. He considers corporations vulnerable and needy and hence "entitled to their displays of vigor" (26) which finds a vent exactly there in the condensation of large format advertising, symbols of consumerism and which makes Hans feel comfortable where other people feel overwhelmed. Similarly to corporations, Manhattan skyscrapers that accommodate their large headquarters seem to Hans surprisingly vulnerable. Once he cannot see The Empire State Building through the Chelsea Hotel window because of snow:

> The magnitude of vanishing was wonderful, even to a spirit such as my own, perhaps because it preluded the seemingly miraculous re-emergence from the clouds of towers dashed from within with light. On President's day, however, the vaporous, enormously disappearing city provoked a different response. Tiring of my snowdrift vigil, I hauled myself out of the armchair and travelled to my bedroom and, in search of a fresh point of view, wandered to the window there…. I was, it will be understood, afflicted by the solitary's vulnerability to insights, so that when I peered out into the flurry and saw no sign of the Empire State Building; I was assaulted by the notion, arriving in the form of a terrifying stroke of consciousness, that substance—everything of so called concreteness—was indistinct from its unnamable opposite [124–125].

In fact, all places mentioned in the novel carry a symbolic importance and so does the time frame which is set in the "US calendar" (119). Metonymies created through references to American political and medial calendar are used to mark the time line of the otherwise fragmented narration which is often interrupted by associations and memories. Accordingly, 1998 is the year of Monica Lewinsky (119); the day on which Hans cannot recognize the Empire State Building in the above quote is referred to as the President's Day 2003. Other points in the timeline are marked through the impeachment proceedings and the power outage in the summer of 2003 that affected almost the entire East Coast.

Cricket and Identity

Names of cricket teams often match places where the game is played and hence provide a new way of identification strongly linked to the city. Players of the Staten Island Cricket Club that Hans joins refer to themselves as "We, Staten Island" (11), although the vast majority of them comes from Trinidad, Guyana, Jamaica, India, Pakistan and Sri Lanka. The fact that cricket in New York in *Netherland* is played by male black immigrants only, introduces a racial, class and gender dimension to the sport. In fact, Hans is the only white man in his team and, as he later realizes, the only white man on the cricket fields of New York (11). This puts him in the position of the Other and turns the established social structures around. It also points to a very different social status of cricket[5] that is not, as baseball, the privileged and prominent national sport in the U.S. (17). Chuck Ramkissoon, a Trinidadian whom Hans meets in the Staten Island Club says in one of his charismatic speeches, "Play cricket if you want to know what it feels to be black in this country" (18) and referring to the kits, "Put on white to feel black" (18). Chuck, whose motto is "think fantastic" and who tries to make his outsized dreams of building a cricket stadium in the city come true, is seen by critics and scholars as the Great Gatsby figure in this novel, someone who represents "a commitment to the American Dream/human possibility/narrative" (Smith "Two Paths for the Novel"; Hill "The American Dream") and is a "South-Asian Caribbean allegory of a multicultural American Dream" (Däwes 365). Hans has difficulties with thinking fantastic and his multiple confrontations with U.S. bureaucracy undermine the idea of all things being possible in America.

Once Chuck says to Hans that "people, all people, Americans, whoever, are at their most civilized when they're playing cricket" (204). Building a cricket stadium would, in Chuck's terms, mean civilizing Americans, a process that Jeffrey Hill calls "reversed colonialism" (Hill "Queering the Pitch" 2). According to Hill, there is also a strong link between the fictional character Chuck and C.L.R. James, the radical thinker and author of the first modern cricket book, in which the sport has been taken out of the pitch and used as a lens to view the American and British societies up to the 1960s. *Beyond the Boundary* depicted cricket as a path to racial liberation in the context of the Civil Rights Movement (Hill "Queering the Pitch" 187). Jeffrey Hill defines a genre of cricket writing and describes the development it went through, together with the game, from a conservative and predictable narrative to fragmented and highly allegorical texts, which through cricket, addressed socially and politically relevant issues. (Hill "Queering the Pitch"; Bateman and Hill "Introduction"). Rob Steen further claims that cricket writing can be divided, together with the development of the game on the global stage, into two ages: imperial and post-imperial. The first was dominated by "English publishers and pens for the best part of three centuries, the second by an internationalism that removed England as the center of attention" (Steen 238). It is remarkable how post–9/11 fiction uses cricket to contextualize the identity struggles of its characters, who often have to position themselves on either side of the newly emerged dichotomy and become subjects in the process of "othering." As already mentioned in Mohsin Hamid's *The Reluctant Fundamentalist* two characters who share a legacy of being the "colonized subjects" talk about cricket, which becomes a metonymy for their past: "'Hey man, do you *get* cricket?' I asked him what he meant. 'My dad's nuts about it. He's from Barbados. West Indies versus Pakistan … best damn test match I ever saw.' … 'That must have been in the eighties,' I said. 'Neither team is quite so good now'" (Hamid 43–44).

The main character in Hamid's novel, Changez, also once uses a cricket metaphor to refer to his boss's very open, friendly and honest attitude, which for him often equals a confession: "The confession that implicates its audience is—as we say in cricket—a devilishly difficult ball to play. Reject it and you slight the confessor; accept it and you admit your own guilt." (Hamid 80). Chuck, the protagonist of H.M. Naqvi's *Home Boy*, recalls playing cricket as a boy in Karachi. His father's death is in Chuck's memory, marked by moving into a new apartment and by the end of the cricket games in the garden, symbolically the end of careless childhood. In both cases, similarly to O'Neill's *Netherland*, cricket functions as an important cultural and identity-shaping and assuring reference. Each of the mentioned texts is marked with a particular place/places, and its colonial legacy is fundamental for the role of the references in the plot.

Movement, Artistic Potential and Individuality in Cricket

C.L.R. James sees a great artistic potential and value in cricket. He claims that sports in general can take up the form of artistic production, but he assigns specific and unique artistic features to cricket. It is a game that leaves space for individuality, more so than other sports (James 261). According to James, cricket is "first and foremost a dramatic spectacle" (258) based on the classical conflict deriving from Greek tragedy: two individuals, a batsman and a bowler representing different teams are pitted against one another in a conflict that reflects the nature of the game and the competition between the teams. The personal achievement and performance is equally or even more important than the victory or loss of the team. That is why the end result of a cricket game, except when "national or local pride is at stake," is not of a great importance (James 260–261). Arjun Appadurai, for whom cricket is a hard cultural form,[6] claims the opposite in the context of decolonized and indigenized cricket, stating that the game nowadays is "aggressive, spectacular, and frequently unsporting, with audiences thirsting for national victory and players and promoters out for the buck" and belongs to a different "moral and aesthetic world" (Appadurai 107). For the reading of the sport in *Netherland*, James's art-related understanding of the game applies: it is not that important which team wins a game—it is the process, the ritual and the individual performance that are so important for the players and that carry a symbolic meaning for Hans. Also the notion of nationality is left aside, at least during the game. James also underlines the importance of movement—literally and metaphorically—as a creative force that produces the artistic value of sports.

Cricket is not only a dramatic, but also a visual art (James 263). This movement is also the essential creative value in the life and impulse of the modern flâneur. Combining these features and movements (the ones on the cricket field and the ones throughout the city in order to remap it) makes Hans a 21st-century artist-flâneur *par excellence*, living in the most suitable place, at least symbolically—the New York artists' Mecca—the Chelsea Hotel. James also makes the observation that "the state of the city, the nation or the world can invest a sporting event with dramatic intensity such as is reached in few theatres" (258). It is remarkable how this comparison resonates in the post–9/11 setting of *Netherland*, which reflects the city and the traumatic reality in two forms of spectacle: cricket games and the ongoing performances of the bizarre tenants at the Chelsea.

According to Gamal Abdel-Shehid, movement is generally significant to black cultural production in the sporting world—something that Hans is confronted with through his interaction with his black team members—since it is constantly changing and is therefore "deeply contingent upon, and produced within, a historical and social milieu" (24). Abdel-Shehid also claims that, marginalized as cricket is in O'Neill's novel and in the U.S. in general, black masculinities in sports are often connected to diasporic locations where movement is the driving force and a crucial tool. This argument connects with one of the main statements in C.L.R. James's *Beyond the Boundary*, namely that sport is a foundation for Caribbean communities abroad and can function as a form of resistance, primarily in the (post) colonial context but also, as *Netherland* shows, in the process of assimilating to a different cultural and political environment. In other words, cricket as a game, as art and as a way of life is transportable, reconnectable with different cultural environments and hence becomes an important, identity-forming reference for the black diaspora. Abdel-Shehid talks in this context about "trans-border sporting communities" (115), which also in O'Neill's novel offer Hans a unique possibility of belonging.

The cricket team as a community becomes a bizarre miniature of the (immigrant) society consisting of individuals who share the fate of living abroad. In this cricket-community different languages and religions, considered equally important and as such respected, form an extraordinary hybrid: before the game starts, all religious team members, a Sikh, four Muslims and three Christians, pray together for good weather and a good game. Music and rum, sometimes also food from different parts of the world and an atmosphere "by no means rare for New York cricket" (13) accompany the game and make it into an almost mystic ritual, an extraordinary event exclusive for the players and bonding. Cricket remains a minority sport, dismissed in the U.S., which makes the position of players very difficult in this specific environment: "We're a joke ... we play out of indulgence" (18) and "we are nowhere in this country" (17), "it's like we're invisible" (18), says Chuck to his team. It also remains a very gendered, purely male, and mostly black game and social category.

After each game the players separate and head towards different directions: Hoboken, Passaic, Queens and Brooklyn. Only Hans takes the ferry to Manhattan and leaves behind the "exotic cricketing circle which made no intersection with the circumstances of ... everyday life" (22). Since these circumstances are unbearable, Hans seeks refuge on the cricket field and the original proportions between the game and his *real* life are disturbed. His obsession with the world of cricket is a way of overcoming trauma caused not by 9/11 itself but by consequences the attacks have had on Hans's (private) life. It is a way of remapping and *controlling* the city, of being in charge but also of finally belonging:

> I'd hit the ball in the air like an American cricketer; and I'd done so without injury to my sense of myself. On the contrary, I felt great. And Chuck had seen it happen and, as much as he could have, had prompted it ... and everything is suddenly clear, and I am at last naturalized [232–233].

Netherland focuses on the invisible bridges of memories and reappearing motives that link New York, London and The Hague, where Hans grew up, in order to provide a transatlantic cartography of the life of a single character. In telling a story of one family, O'Neill de-collectivizes the events of 9/11 and shows the collective experience through the particular effects and consequences it has on single characters. It addresses what Michael Rothberg calls "international relations and extraterritorial citizenship" (*Failure* 153) and does what according to him post–9/11 fiction should do: it provides "cognitive *maps* that imagine how U.S. citizenship looks and feels beyond the boundaries of the nation-state, both for Americans and for others" (158, emphasis mine) with the stress on "others" and on melting boundaries between countries and cities. In Hans's life and mind the three mentioned cities coexist, constantly interfere and strongly contribute to locating his personal identity. The borders between them are unclear since human life in *Netherland* is shown as a set of parallels, reappearing motifs and seemingly random patterns. The meaning and importance of these motifs are only visible if they remain interlinked. Birgit Däwes talks in this context about "allegorical energy" which can only be created in these fluid spaces with untraceable boundaries between them and individuals. This energy is generated "either by a person, a house, ... or by any image that redefines the domestic as a deeply political sphere" (*Ground Zero Fiction* 358). Hans sees the repetitiveness of motifs and reappearances of feelings and people that connect different stages of his life and he also reflects upon the relation between those factors and the nature of the city:

> You might say that New York City insists on memory's repetitive mower—on the sort of purposeful postmortem that has the effect, so one is told and forlornly hopes, of cutting the grassy past to manageable proportions. For it keeps growing back of course [2].

Post–9/11 London

Once the process of personal re-establishment is advanced and the driving license exam passed, Hans returns to London. After his thorough cricket-related remapping of New York, London is however no longer the same. It seems posh, exclusive and hermetic to Hans, who clearly does not belong there anymore or possibly, as he realizes, has never truly belonged. He is confronted with the British or possibly European distance towards the U.S. imperial politics and feels personally attacked and offended by it, which surprises him. This evokes an obligation to speak up:

> Not that long ago, at yet another gathering of familiars, our host, an old friend of Rachel's named Matt, makes some remarks about Tony Blair and his catastrophic association with George W. Bush, whom Matt describes as the embod-

iment of a distinctly American strain of stupidity and fear. On this side of the
Atlantic, this is a commonplace judgment, so commonplace, in fact, as to be of no
real interest; but then the conversation strays in a direction that's rare these days,
to the events synonymous with September 11 2001. "Not such a big deal," Matt
suggests, "when you think of everything that's happened since."
     He is referring to the numbers of Iraqi dead, ... I speak up nonetheless. "I think
it was a big deal" [239–240].

He is not being taken seriously since, according to the conservative and strictly
English circle of his wife's friends, as a Dutch man he is precluded by nationality
from commenting on places outside of Holland (239). This is slightly different
from his experience with New York, which encouraged a sense of nativity on
"even the most fleeting visitors" (239). Londoners whom Hans confronts appear
stiff to him; taxi prices are immense and bear no relation to the earnings. Everyone talks about their holidays since "escapism is a big issue," which is very much
unlike New York City where people never talk about their vacations (238).
     Netherland's London is portrayed as less emotional than New York, as a
healthier organism in which the spreading of the paranoia-virus is being stopped
before it reaches the masses. London symbolizes the old world, stable, experienced and down to earth, even after the attacks of 7/7, which apart from the
following quote are not mentioned in the novel:

> The rain soon becomes emblematic. The double-deckers lose their elephants'
> charm. London is what it is. In spite of a fresh emphasis on architecture and an
> influx of can-do Polish plumbers, in spite, too, of the Manhattanish importance
> lately attached to coffee and sushi and farmers' markets, in spite even of the dis-
> turbance of 7/7—a frightening but not a disorienting occurrences, it turns out—
> Londoners remain in the business of rowing their boats gently down the stream
> [236].

In other words, although voluntarily back in London and after two more
years reunited with his wife, Hans feels out of place again and misses New
York. Paradoxically, the events of 9/11 and the circumstances he has found
himself in as a consequence, have Americanized him. Once, while cleaning a
closet in their house in London, Rachel stumbles across Hans's cricket equipment, still marked by New York dirt (245), and asks whether she can get rid
of it. Hans says "no" emotionlessly. That solitary chapter of his life seems to be
closed now:

> "Are you going to play this year?"
> "I don't think so," I say, licking my finger and rubbing at the dirt, which continues
> to stick. I haven't played since my return to England. It would feel unnatural, is
> my feeling, to separate myself from my family in order to spend an afternoon with
> understated teammates and cups of tea and something essentially nostalgic at

stake; yet to throw out this odd paddle would also go against nature, even though its wood, faintly striped by a dozen grains, is now swollen with age and cannot have a sweet spot to speak of [246].

Eventually Hans considers himself a Londoner again or after all. Working in East London, he has a view on St. Paul's Cathedral and likes to walk on the south bank towards the Waterloo station. During an occasion when he is to meet Rachel and their son Jake at the London Eye, just as Oskar does in *Extremely Loud and Incredibly Close* when he visits the Empire State Building, Hans also looks at the city from above to first have a wider perspective but then to feel completely lost in the "labyrinth." London as seen from the top of the London Eye becomes just some metropolis, impossible to trace, control or even identify or locate. The view brings Hans immediately back to New York and evokes memories of his mother's visit, their trip on the Staten Island Ferry becoming vivid again:

> But the higher we go, the less recognizable the city becomes. Trafalgar Square is not where you expect it to be. Charing Cross, right under our noses, must be carefully detected.... The difficulty arises from the mishmashing of spatial dimensions, yes, but also from a quantitative attack: the English capital is huge, huge; in every direction, to distant hills—Primrose and Denmark and Lavender, our maps tell us.... Districts are compacted, in south London especially: Where on earth are Brixton and Kennington and Peckham? You wonder how anyone is able to navigate this labyrinth, which is what this crushed, squashed, everywhere-spreading city appears to be [337].

The mechanism of a very personal reconnecting of memories through places and *vice versa* sets in motion and Hans falls into a pensiveness, which he only awakens from when the Eye-journey in time and space ends and he is back in London again. London is the city in which life happens outside, "where to be in one's home is, in terms of society, more or less to be like the fellow washed up on the little island with the single palm tree" (237). For Hans this life "inside" contributes to his well-being and offers a possibility of reconnecting with his lonely New York past. During the London nights, he continues walking through the streets of Manhattan and Brooklyn while looking at cricket fields on Google Earth. He also keeps looking at the grounds that Chuck Ramkissoon, following one of his obsessive and completely unrealistic dreams, planned to transform into a cricket stadium. Hans does that even after Chuck's death, since the city somehow preserves the memory of their friendship and the time they spent in New York. Hans's flâneur-existence continues in a digitalized form, and although it does not involve actual movement, it is no less intense.

Conclusion

The city is writing. He who moves about the city, e.g., the user of the city (what we all are), is a kind of reader who, following his obligations and his movements, appropriates fragments of the utterance in order to actualize them in secret. When we move about the city, we all are in the situation of the reader of the hundred thousand billion poems of Queneau, where one can find a different poem by changing a single line; unawares, we are somewhat like this avant-garde reader when we are in a city (Barthes 95)

No matter how the official narrative of this turns out, ... these are the places we should be looking, not in newspapers or television but at the margins, graffiti, uncontrolled utterances, bad dreamers who sleep in public and scream in their sleep (Pynchon *Bleeding Edge* 322)

Post–9/11 City Fiction as a Mirror and a Seismograph of Altered Spatial Practices

The aim of this book was to show, by analyzing nine city novels, a tendency in post–9/11 fiction towards an intensified "writing" of the Western metropolis in response to its altered state after the attacks of September 11, 2001. All of the selected texts are city-centered and draw their literary energy from strictly urban sources and settings. One of the main arguments of this book is that the post–9/11 novel is preeminently a city novel, and that as such, it is written and organized to be read through the structure and concept of urban space. Consequently, all of the complex processes addressed in the following paragraphs meet in the analyzed texts in the metropolis which becomes the ultimate ground for encounters, conflicts and new social and textual formations. Movement and the feeling of being immersed in a city compel the process of storytelling, performed by the characters of post–9/11 fiction as an act that enables them to address an otherwise ungraspable reality.

Post–9/11 city fiction reflects how the September 11 attacks have influenced and transformed our spatial practices—from urban planning, memory, and architecture, to urban movement—and altered the real and imagined car-tographies of the constructed environments in which we live, work, and want to belong. My research identified New York City and London as the two most prominent metropolises in the context of transatlantic post–9/11 fiction and the changing imaginary geographies of the cities through writing. Accordingly, the book is divided spatially and attempts to embrace these two cosmoses in relation to one another. Geographic division serves as a means of comparison between the post–9/11 writing of these two metropolises, and simultaneously provides a transatlantic perspective and a reciprocal view between the two sides.

These two cities, very much distinct within their respective countries, recon-nect on various levels in the analyzed texts, which reflect social and political changes that influenced life in each metropolis. The fiction discussed here reflects and contextualizes social mechanisms that 9/11 set into motion, and which influ-ence the way cities and urbanity are perceived and understood. By reflecting con-temporary reality, this literature contributes to shaping and mapping the global post–9/11 city. The diversity of narrative voices, strategies, and literary perspec-tives within the genre of the novel, signifies the plurality and diversity of the metropolis that is constantly rewritten, retold and reshaped by literary discourse.

Most of the analyzed novels provide a first-person narration, with the exception of McEwan's *Saturday* and Waldman's *The Submission* and partly Ali's *Brick Lane*. First-person narration, generally typical of post–9/11 fiction, can be seen as a reflection of the impossibility of storytelling that is not personal and an inability to "hand over" the voice to an outsider. Accordingly, there seems to be no place for the authority of all-knowing, omniscient third-person nar-rators in writing the post–9/11 city.

This phenomenon clearly mirrors growing skepticism towards processed information and general mistrust toward, and disillusionment with political and social authorities. It also connects with the motif of seeing the city as an unpredictable body that in its constructedness reconnects with nature to over-whelm the individual. Such a body resists control of a narrator-outsider but can be observed and examined by the analytical eye of the flâneur-figure who, through walking and giving in to his stories and experiences, gradually reveals the city's subconscious. These experiences and loose associations, which connect memories and dreams, (also of other places) construct the text and inscribe it into the body of the metropolis.

Movement as a Key to Remapping: Return of the Flâneur

In all of the texts the relation between the featured characters and the metropolis undergoes a shift and requires new definitions, rules and maps. Most of the characters in the featured fiction map or remap the given urban space. In all of the novels this process evolves through movement, but the ways of moving are diverse and provide many possibilities for entering a symbolic vision of 21st century urbanity. This urbanity trespasses physical borders and the maps of the post–9/11 metropolis are formed through private and transnational memories, intertextualities and chains of sensually perceived associations.

Accordingly, some of the characters move through the city following an obsession that derives from a traumatic experience of the events of 9/11, for instance Oskar in Foer's *Extremely Loud and Incredibly Close* or Hans in O'Neill's *Netherland*. The texts feature different kinds of city strollers, who connect with and continue the modern concept of the flâneur. Teju Cole's *Open City* shows a psychiatrist and hobbyist philosopher-historian who tries to approach the urban subconscious through walking. Foer's *Extremely Loud* is narrated by a child who, as a city stroller, also wears the mask of a detective, to use Walter Benjamin's term (*Passagen-Werk* 534). Cultivating a child in oneself is a crucial element constituting every flâneur—it allows him to see the world in the "state of newness" (Baudelaire 8).

On the other side of the spectrum, characters who experience the impossibility of moving and remapping feel paralyzed in the metropolis and, as a result, choose to leave the respective city, disappointed and angry (Changez in Hamid's *The Reluctant Fundamentalist*, Mo in Waldman's *The Submission*, Chanu in Ali's *Brick Lane*), or sad and frightened (Rachel in O'Neill's novel and Chuck in Naqvi's *Home Boy*). Escaping New York or London literally does not mean escaping the post–9/11 city. London, the city to which Rachel in O'Neill's novel returns is, as Monica Ali phrases it "covered with New York dust" (Ali 368); racial profiling and "othering" become prominent though infamous social practices; the politics of Blair's government seems entirely dependent on the U.S.

Changez and Mo emotionally never leave, and remain tightly connected with New York. So does Hans, Rachel's husband in *Netherland*, who after returning to London continues "walking" through Manhattan, Brooklyn and Queens while glued to his computer screen depicting street views through Google maps. His virtual tours, just like the "real" ones, evolve around the game of cricket, a passion Hans initially developed when lonely in the traumatized metropolis.

All of these texts inscribe themselves into the cities they are set in, and through their intervention, change these cities. All of them demonstrate a move towards a broader and more abstract concept of the city: the post–9/11 metropolis is a global space, impossible to trace, follow, or narrow down to its physical limits as measured by a GPS device. The post–9/11 metropolis is a spatial concept which in its literary depictions combines influences from various cities and cultures into a wide frame of urbanity, collective thinking, living and writing. Accordingly, New York and London share many similarities when facing the post–9/11 reality. Reading them together presents them as alternatives and as answers to one another. For some of the characters, one of the featured cities (and the scope goes beyond the mentioned two) is meant to function as a geographical escape, an antidote. In each case this idea fails, as geographical escape does not guarantee mental or emotional detachment. The post–9/11 city is inescapable.

London-based fiction reacting to 9/11 reflects a latent but omnipresent fear, a vague anticipation picturing possible scenarios to describe the unknown. Characters featured in the analyzed London-based novels hardly ever leave the safety zones of their neighborhoods, very much unlike their New York counterparts, who circulate within New York City freely and curiously. All of these texts anticipate an approaching metropolitan tragedy to some extent; they attempt to "write it" in order to prevent it from happening, and to save London through this writing.

In Ali's *Brick Lane* New York dust comes straight to London and covers its people, history, traditions, making it vulnerable and exposed. In McEwan's *Saturday* London "lies wide open waiting for its bomb to drop" (McEwan 276). Chris Cleave's vision of London is a pessimistic, apocalyptic approach, and offers turning back time as the only solution. While novels based in New York try to provide a cure for the city and the characters, and feature ways of remapping and reclaiming the space, London-based texts focus on writing scenarios of the city's end.

City as Body

Cities in the analyzed fiction are often anthropomorphized and referred to as wounded bodies. There is a strong tendency towards picturing the post–9/11 urban system as a malfunctioning body (*Incendiary*, *Brick Lane*) or a confused brain (*Open City*, *Saturday*). The book shows connections between those motifs and contextualizes them in the rich sociological tradition of seeing cities as human bodies, transport networks as cardiovascular systems, and urban disasters as viruses. The motif of a malfunctioning body poses a challenge for doctors and therapists who make a strong appearance in post–9/11 city fiction.

Many of the texts connect the city with mental health and reflect concern about its urban "mind" and common sense. Strikingly, the city and in the first example to follow, the entire country, becomes gendered. The linguistic hybrid

(Am)Erica in Hamid's *The Reluctant Fundamentalist* shows the country as a depressed woman with suicidal inclinations, indicating the weakness and fragility of its mental health. Cleave's *Incendiary* provides a similar analogy—here London is embodied as a hysterical woman who finds serenity only in multiple gin & tonics. Remaining unforeseeable and beyond control, the city in Hamid's novel enters the apartment of the main character and keeps him company; in Naqvi's *Home Boy* it becomes the state of mind, the "skyline of memory" (Naqvi 17). In *Brick Lane* a street can turn into a monster swallowing marchers with its mouth (Ali 468). In all of these metaphorical depictions, the city shows its ruthlessness towards the individual—it is a powerful, often furious, unpredictable and manipulative entity. In *The Reluctant Fundamentalist* the streets in a suddenly empty Brooklyn neighborhood seem longer, almost never-ending; in *Netherland* Times Square which the main character used to like, turns into an urban nightmare after 9/11. A bizarre performance in one of its public places makes the whole square unbearable and uncanny to the narrator.

The metropolitan body is reckless and desperate; its physical and geographical limits are no longer traceable. The imagery inscribes into the history of disaster fantasies haunting New York since its very beginning (Page 202) and invading London after 9/11.

The Other in Post–9/11 City Fiction

All of the novels depict and elaborate the notion of belonging in the post–9/11 city and address the ambiguity of the confrontation with the post–9/11 Other—the newly emerged enemy prototype, or possibly a construct retrieved from the social subconscious and variety of available fear schemes. It derives from deep sociological fears and is strongly related to the concept of the self.

It is unsurprising that cities provide stages for and enforce these confrontations, as it is the metropolis which structures the wide-ranging social exposure of other inhabitants, i.e., people unlike the self. As Roland Barthes points out already in the 1970s, "the city, essentially and semantically, is the place of our meeting with the other" (Barthes 96). The question about the roots and possible explanations of the emergence of the process of urban "othering" in Western metropolises is central to many of the novels and also to this book.

In the epilogue of his 2009 book *Out of the Blue*, Kristiaan Versluys wonders where post–9/11 fiction will go in the years to come, and suggests that the focus will shift from the "perpetrator-victim dichotomy" characteristic of the first reactions which concentrated on the initial trauma caused by the events of 9/11, to a "triangulating discourse in which the confrontation with the Other is the central concern" (Versluys 183). My book focuses on this very confrontation within an urban space which initiates, supports, and celebrates encounters with the post–9/11 Other.

Outlook

Writing and rewriting the post–9/11 metropolis, as this book shows, is an ongoing and possibly unending process. Different texts written after September 11 form a city corpus that stretches far beyond the temporal frame of 2001 and the present. Being highly intertextual and constantly mixing different levels of fictionality with reality, post–9/11 fiction not only contributes to shaping the contemporary metropolis, but also contextualizes the already existing city literature within the altered circumstances. Characters and places "written" before are granted a new meaning when incorporated into the textual body of the post–9/11 city.

This study could be extended to other texts and genres and, as the post–9/11 city is a global space, could also embrace its other facets and incorporate additional, not only Western metropolises. The unanswered question that remains to be traced in future studies, is how further post–9/11 fiction will contribute to the future shape of a given geographically localizable place and, on a meta-level, of the global city. The latter combines all the individual metropolitan settings into one universal global and ephemeral urban body which will always carry traces of 9/11, but which at some point may have a different name.

The analysis could be expanded to include many more novels; Jonathan Lethem's *Chronic City*, Jonathan Franzen's *Freedom*, Masha Hamilton's *31 Hours*, or *Bleeding Edge* by Thomas Pynchon, published in 2013, to mention just a few. Reaching beyond the genre of the novel, the study could be extended to include drama from both sides of the Atlantic and discuss the creation of places within cities, in for instance Neil LaBute's *The Mercy Seat*, Craig Wright's *Recent Tragic Events* or David Hare's *Stuff Happens*. One could also address films and television series that remap post–9/11 urban space and confront the emergence of the ambiguous Other, for instance in *Homeland*, *District 9* or *London River*.

The city as a space of constant transformation remains unpredictable terrain, the reflection, seismograph and co-creator of which is fiction.

Chapter Notes

Introduction

1. There are a number of philosophical, sociological and anthropological approaches dealing with the meaning of the destruction of the Twin Towers for the city of New York (e.g., Sorkin and Zhukin, Wigley) and there are extensive publications about fictional responses to 9/11 (Banita, Däwes, Gray, Versluys), but there is no study that focuses on the motif of writing the city after 9/11, in other words on the genre which I call post–9/11 city novel. To my knowledge there is also no study that would provide a transatlantic approach in looking at these two metropolises on both sides of the Atlantic as represented in post–9/11 fiction. For a thorough overview of publications about post–9/11 fiction see Birgit Däwes's *Ground Zero Fiction* (37–56).

2. The most prominent example mentioned in this context by scholars working on city fiction is John Dos Passos's *Manhattan Transfer* (1925): Blanche Gelfant defines it as an example of a "synoptic study," a subgenre within the city novel, next to "portrait" and "ecological" studies (Gelfant 14). In *ConspiraCity New York* Antje Dallmann analyzes the text thoroughly in the context of the history of the genre and in relation to other modern and contemporary city novels (72–86).

3. Charlotte Temple is the main character of Susanna Rowson's bestseller *Charlotte, A Tale of Truth* published in the U.S. in 1794. In the novel Charlotte dies in New York City where she is also buried.

4. Term coined by Saskia Sassen in her study *The Global City: New York, London, Tokyo* (Princeton: Princeton University Press, 1992).

5. Birgit Däwes defines the genre of "Ground Zero fiction" by setting a framework of three criteria: the spatial and/or temporal setting, the thematic and/or symbolic relevance of the attacks (implicitly or explicitly represented in the plot), and the characters' involvement with and/or perception of the event, the event being 9/11 (Däwes *Ground Zero Fiction*).

6. Whereas the action of novels and films responding to 7/7 is mostly set in small British towns, see pp. 27–28.

7. According to Michael Roth, in the European understanding when we "frame an object as a ruin, we reclaim that object from its fall into decay and oblivion and often for some kind of cultural attention and care that, in a sense, elevates its value" (*Irresistible Decay* 1).

8. For a chronological account of imagining the city's destruction inscribed into American culture see Max Page's book *The City's End: Two Centuries of Fantasies, Fears, and Premonitions of New York's Destruction* (2008).

9. Seltzer talks about the fascination with serial killings and brutality as a part of America's 20th century culture in which "addictive violence has become a collective spectacle" (253).

10. Page's main claim is to say that each era in New York City's modern history has produced its own apocalyptic imagery that reflected contemporary fears, political and social problems. Imagining the city's end has always been a part of the city's presence. The 21st century's main destruction "motif" is, according to him, global terrorism and climate changes.

11. Philippe Petit's fascination with the projects of the towers seen in a French newspaper could serve as an example here (Marsh, *Man on Wire*).

12. Art Spiegelman in an interview with Claudia Dreifus, *New York Times*, August 7, 2004.

13. Burrows points out to the history of the area of Lower Manhattan since 1625 when it became the trading post of the Dutch West India Company, and to its strategic position

that has always served representational purposes.

14. Richard Sennett in his book *Flesh and Stone* argues that urban spaces take form from the way people experience their own bodies. According to him, cities can be seen as based on living organisms and have developed together with their needs.

15. In his comic *In the Shadow of No Towers*, Art Spiegelman recalls his father's description of the smell of gas chambers in Auschwitz-Birkenau and compares it to the smell of Lower Manhattan on September 11 linking experiencing the terrorist attack to the Holocaust.

16.. The air and settled surface dust samples were, among others, tested for asbestos and synthetic vitreous fibers (SVF). The "border" of exposure is marked by 59th Street—samples tested north from it did not show presence of any toxic substances (New York City Department of Health and Mental Hygiene, *Final Report of the Public Health Investigation* 6).

17. The collection of photographs taken in the hangar was published in 2011 by National Geographic under the title *Memory Remains: 9/11 Artifacts at Hangar 17*.

18. The phenomenon of the right to ownership over a particular space within the city that the families of the dead claim is powerfully reflected in e.g. Amy Waldman's novel *The Submission*.

19. Däwes also points out that in terms of literary techniques Ground Zero fiction is not an innovative or original genre: it continues trends of representation that were well under way at the end of the 20th century.

20. Another example of an attempt at bringing the Other home is the figure of Nicholas Brody in the Showtime series *Homeland* who has been "turned" while fighting for the U.S. Marines in Iraq.

Chapter I

1. Equal, meaning that they are all equally important for the narration, or as Birgit Däwes puts it, "they elude any imposing master narrative" (Däwes *Ground Zero Fiction* 381). For the purpose of coherence and in order to remain focused on the central concept of the city, I concentrate here mainly on two of the narrative voices: Oskar Schell's and his grandfather Thomas Schell, Sr.'s.

2. Kristiaan Versluys in his study of this novel provides a detailed analysis of the relationship between Oskar's grandparents in a subchapter "Constriction," pp. 83–87, in *Out of the Blue*.

3. Oskar's character combines two modern flâneur motifs: he is a child, which according to Baudelaire is the crucial element of every flâneur that allows him to see the world in the "state of newness" (*The Painter of Modern Life* 8), and also he puts on a "mask" when he leaves the apartment in order to become someone else. Walter Benjamin talks about masks, only through which the phantasmagoric dimension of walking becomes visible and possible, and which distinguish flâneurs from one another (*Passagen-Werk* 534).

4. The motif of spontaneous reciprocal responsibility emerging after the attacks is important in post–9/11 fiction and appears among others in Lynne Sharon Schwartz's *The Writing on the Wall*, in which the main character on the afternoon of September 11 checks on her neighbors and hugs with some of them although they hardly know each other.

5. The sequence of controversial photos taken by Richard Drew of Associated Press showing a man falling down head first with one of his legs bent up disappeared from the U.S. media shortly after the attacks.

6. The debate on the meaning of places and spaces is in its foundation interdisciplinary and embraces several centuries of philosophy, geography, social sciences and linguistics. For an overview of the concepts of place and space or "Ort" and "Raum" in the German academia, see e.g., Antje Dallman's *ConspiraCity New York*, Henri Lefebvre's *The Production of Space*, Phil Hubbard's *Key Thinkers on Space and Place*, Edward Soja's *Postmodern Geographies* or Tim Cresswell's *In Place—Out of Place*.

7. Thomas Schell has only once read a letter from his father. Afterwards he has decided to go to Dresden to meet him. The expectations are so high that the confrontation is very difficult for both of them and takes place only once.

Chapter II

1. Hopkins claims that "psychoanalysis is mainly concerned with the relations between past and present phantasies and desires, but takes these to be mediated by mappings which can be regarded as cognitive and metaphorical" (Hopkins 16).

2. Setting the plot in more than one city

on more than one continent gives the possibility of transatlantic referencing and comparisons, and offers an access to transnational memory and experiences. This can be observed in, e.g., Joseph O'Neill's *Netherland* (New York and London), Don DeLillo's *Falling Man* (New York and Hamburg), Mohsin Hamid's *The Reluctant Fundamentalist* (New York and Lahore), J.S. Foer's *Extremely Loud and Incredibly Close* (New York and Dresden), Salman Rushdie's *Shalimar the Clown* (Los Angeles and an imaginary town in the Kashmir region) and others.

3. The term *ground zero* has been metaphorically used before 9/11 in the American context to refer to the Oklahoma City Bombing. For more on the shifting meaning of the term and the way it comes to signify in connection with a specific space, see Sturken's *Tourists of History* (2007).

4. For instance Hans in O'Neill's *Netherland*, Oskar in Foer's *Extremely Loud and Incredibly Close*, Keith in DeLillo's *Falling Man*, Renata in Lynne Schwartz's *The Writing on the Wall*, the three main characters in Naqvi's *Home Boy*.

Chapter III

1. Deriving from poetry and inspired by drama, most commonly exemplified on the 19th century poems of Robert Browning, according to Alan Sinfield dramatic monologue can be traced through the Victorian period up to more contemporary poets, for instance Robert Lowell. It can be also observed in other genres; it features only one speaker and a silent auditor whose presence is crucial as it provides a second though mute/speechless perspective. "On the one hand we have a powerful impression, through his [the speaker's] own mind, of the kind of person the speaker is. On the other, we feel the pressure of an alternative way of viewing these matters and perhaps of an external force which threatens to qualify or even nullify the efforts of the speaker" (Sinfield 34).

2. In his essay *In the Ruins of The Future*, published in 2001, Don DeLillo calls for counter-narratives that would provide a collectively shaped response to the one "written"/ "produced" by the terrorists and imposed on the U.S. and the Western world on September 11. The counter-narratives are forms of responding to the terror and could be any kind of active reaction. Examples DeLillo gives

stretch from posters of the missing people and all the stories they tell, to narratives of survival, to jumps from the burning towers as, according to him they expressed a choice and resistance. Counter-narratives are "stories of heroism and encounters with dread. There are stories that carry around their edges the luminous ring of coincidence, fate, or premonition. They take us beyond the hard numbers of dead and missing and give us a glimpse of elevated being" (DeLillo *In the Ruins of the Future* 34).

3. Where in fact New Jersey appears in post–9/11 novels and does contribute to the collective storytelling. E.g., the already mentioned "Terrorist" by John Updike, or "Shine, Coconut Moon" by Neesha Meminger whose main protagonist Samar lives in Linton, New Jersey, and is subjected to post–9/11 "othering" which certainly did stretch over the Hudson and reached New Jersey.

4. A discourse that dominated the U.S. media around 2005. The MDC in Brooklyn has been called the local Abu Ghraib in, e.g., "Democracy Now" on March 1, 2005, http://www.democracynow.org//shows/2005/3/1/ or in Larry Cohler-Esses's article published in the *New York Daily News* on February 20, 2005, http://www.nydailynews.com/archives/news/brooklyn-abu-ghraib-terror-suspects-allege-lock-up-article-1.589596. Both accessed on February 6, 2016.

5. "Poetry in Motion" is a project launched by MTA, the New York public transportation system, in 1992. It features posters with poems in the subway carriages and stations and poems printed on metro cards, details can be found on http://web.mta.info/mta/aft/poetry.

Chapter IV

1. Here I am tracing this motif semantically and not chronologically. Amy Waldman's novel was published eight years after Ali's *Brick Lane* (*The Submission* 2011, *Brick Lane* 2003) The expression "New York dust" comes from Ali's novel and is discussed in more details in Part Two of the book.

Chapter VI

1. Sebastian Groes calls this experiment a "kind of translation" (*The Making of London* 245) intended to symbolize Hasina's illiteracy in Bengali but which comes across as superficial. Sukhdev Sandhu's review "Come Hungry,

Leave Edgy" published in 2003 in the *London Review of Books* calls it an "odd decision, given that Nazneen speaks Bengali at home and that, on the page, the tragic correspondence looks banal and comic."

2. More precisely, I am referring here to Savitch's article "An Anatomy of Urban Terror: Lessons from Jerusalem and Elsewhere" published in *Urban Studies Journal* 42.3 (2005).

3. Second Release Headline Analysis 1.

4. Foer's novel ends with a vision of turning back time pictured with a flap-book of a man falling back up to the building instead of falling down.

5. The 2011 Census identifies 2.5 occupants per an average household size in Tower Hamlets and marks no change in comparison to the 2001 Census. 19.6 percent of all households in TH are shared by more than one family, a figure significantly higher than for London and for England (only 7.4 percent in the latter case).

Chapter VII

1. Sebastian Groes in his chapter "Ian McEwan and the Modernist Consciousness of the City in *Saturday*" provides a very thorough list of all the intertextual references that appear in the novel and that represent different cultural and artistic fields, languages, origins and epochs, from Sophocles to Cézanne (Groes 102). The exact influences of Virginia Woolf's *Mrs. Dalloway* and the work of Matthew Arnold as traced by Groes are precisely described in the mentioned chapter.

Chapter VIII

1. Parts of this chapter were published as an article in *The Journal of American Culture* under the title "Cricket as a Cure: Post–911 Urban Trauma and Displacement in Joseph O'Neill's Novel 'Netherland,'" *The Journal of American Culture* 36, no. 3 (2013): 230–239. Print.

2. Leaves of Grass 1891–1892.

3. Appadurai stresses the importance of cricket being a social and cultural tool used to promote new standards of public behavior. He defines its values as "sportsmanship, a sense of fair play, control over expression of sentiments, loyalty to the team" (91–92).

4. Baudelaire calls this quality "modernity" arguing that every master has his own one (12–13).

5. Jeffrey Hill claims that "cricket, the English game, somehow seemed to be at odds with Americans' sense of themselves as 'modern'" and mentions publicistic references to cricket as a slow and somewhat "unmanly" game when compared to the more aggressive baseball ("Queering the Pitch" 182).

6. As opposed to "soft cultural forms," which come with "a set of links between value, meaning and embodied practice difficult to break or transform," i.e., cricket as a hard cultural form changes the people that are socialized into it more than they can change the game in order to adapt it to their lives before cricket (Appadurai 90).

Bibliography

Abdel-Shehid, Gamal. *Who Da Man? Black Masculinities and Sporting Cultures.* Toronto: Canadian Scholars' Press, 2005. Print.

Alexander, Claire. "Making Bengali Brick Lane: Claiming and Contesting Space in East London." *The British Journal of Sociology* 62.2 (2011): 201–20. Print.

Ali, Monica. *Brick Lane.* London: Black Swan, 2004. Print.

Alter, Robert. *Imagined Cities: Urban Experience and the Language of the Novel.* New Haven: Yale University Press, 2005. Print.

Amis, Martin. "The Last Days of Muhammad Atta." *The New Yorker* April 24, 2006: 152–61. Print.

_____. *The Second Plane: September 11: Terror and Boredom.* New York: Vintage International, 2009. Print.

Appadurai, Arjun. *Modernity at Large: Cultural Dimensions of Globalization.* Minneapolis: University of Minnesota Press, 1996. Print.

Baer, Ulrich. *110 Stories: New York Writes After September 11.* New York: New York University Press, 2002. Print.

Balaev, Michelle. "Trends in Literary Trauma Theory." *Mosaic (Winnipeg)* 41.2 (2008): 149–166. Print.

Banita, Georgiana. *Plotting Justice: Narrative Ethics and Literary Culture After 9/11.* Lincoln: University of Nebraska Press, 2012. Print.

Barthes, Roland. "Semiology and the Urban." *The City and the Sign: An Introduction to Urban Semiotics.* Ed. Mark Gottdiener and Alexandros P. Lagopoulos. New York: Columbia University Press, 1986. 87–98. Print.

Bateman, Anthony, and Jeffrey Hill, eds. *The Cambridge Companion to Cricket.* Cambridge: Cambridge University Press, 2011. Print.

Baudelaire, Charles. *The Painter of Modern Life and Other Essays.* London: Phaidon Press, 1995. Print.

Baudrillard, Jean. *The Spirit of Terrorism and Requiem for the Twin Towers.* New York: Verso, 2002. Print.

Bauman, Zygmunt. "From Pilgrim to Tourist." *Questions of Cultural Identity.* Ed. Paul Du Gay and Stuart Hall. London: Sage, 1996. 18–36. Print.

Beigbeder, Frédéric. *Windows on the World.* Berlin: Ullstein, 2005. Print.

Benjamin, Walter. *Gesammelte Schriften: Das Passagen-Werk.* Ed. Rolf Tiedemann. Frankfurt am Main: Suhrkamp, 1982. Print.

_____. "On the Concept of History." *Gesammelte Schriften: Das Passagen-Werk.* Ed. Rolf Tiedemann. Frankfurt am Main: Suhrkamp, 1982. Print.

Berman, Marshall. "When Bad Buildings Happen to Good People." *After the World Trade Center: Rethinking New York City.* Ed. Michael Sorkin and Sharon Zukin. New York: Routledge, 2002. 1–12. Print.

Blomkamp, Neill, dir. *District 9.* TriStar Pictures, 2009.

Borradori, Giovanna, Jacques Derrida, and Jurgen Habermas. *Philosophy in a Time of Terror: Dialogues with Jurgen Habermas and Jacques Derrida.* Chicago: University of Chicago Press, 2003. Print.

Bouchareb, Rachid, dir. *London River.* 3B Productions, 2009. Film.

Burrows, Edwin G. "Manhattan at War." *After the World Trade Center: Rethinking New York City.* Ed. Michael Sorkin and Sharon Zukin. New York: Routledge, 2002. 23–32. Print.

Bush, George W. *Address to a Joint Session of Congress and the American People on September 20, 2001.* 2001. Web. 2 Dec. 2011. http://georgewbush-whitehouse.archives.gov/news/releases/2001/09/20010911-16.html.

194 Bibliography

_____. *Statement by the President in His Address to the Nation.* 2001. Web. 2 Dec. 2011.

Butler, Judith. *Precarious Life: The Powers of Mourning and Violence.* London: Verso, 2004. Print.

Calvino, Italo. *Invisible Cities.* New York: Harvest Books, 1974. Print.

Certeau, Michel de. *The Practice of Everyday Life.* Berkeley: University of California Press, 1988. Print.

Chen, Xiangming, Anthony M. Orum, and Krista E. Paulsen. *Introduction to Cities: How Place and Space Shape Human Experience.* Hoboken, NJ: Wiley-Blackwell, 2013. Print.

Cleave, Chris. *Incendiary.* London: Hodder & Stoughton, 2009. Print.

Cohler-Esses, Larry. "'Brooklyn's Abu Ghraib' Terror suspects allege lock-up was...." *New York Daily News* 20 Feb. 2005. Web. 14 Dec. 2013. http://www.nydailynews.com/archives/news/brooklyn-abu-ghraib-terror-suspects-allege-lock-up-article-1.589596#ixzz2moXAGYiV.

Cole, Teju. *Open City.* London: Faber and Faber, 2011. Print.

Corner, James. *Lifescape—Fresh Kills Parkland: Information Material of the New York's Department of Parks & Recreation.* 2005. Web. 13 Dec. 2013. http://www.nextroom.at/data/media/med_binary/original/1121022434.pdf.

Cresswell, Tim. *In Place—Out of Place: Geography, Ideology, and Transgression.* Minneapolis: University of Minnesota Press, 1996. Print.

_____. *Place: A Short Introduction.* Malden: Blackwell, 2004. Print.

Crowe, Cameron, dir. *Vanilla Sky.* Paramount Pictures, 2001. Film.

Dallmann, Antje. *ConspiraCity New York: Großstadtbetrachtung zwischen Paranoia und Selbstermächtigung.* Heidelberg: Universitätsverlag Winter, 2009. Print. American Studies: A Monographic Series 176.

Däwes, Birgit. "Celluloid Recoveries: Cinematic Transformations of Ground Zero." *Transnational American Memories.* Ed. Udo J. Hebel. Berlin: De Gruyter, 2009. 285–309. Print.

_____. *Ground Zero Fiction: History, Memory, and Representation in the American 9/11 Novel.* Heidelberg: Universitätsverlag Winter, 2011. Print.

DeLillo, Don. *Falling Man.* London: Picador, 2011. Print.

_____. "In the Ruins of the Future: Reflections on Terror and Loss in the Shadow of September." *Harper's Magazine* December 2001: 33–40. Print.

DeRosa, Aaron. "September 11 and Cold War Nostalgia." *Portraying 9/11: Essays on Representations in Comics, Literature, Film and Theatre.* Ed. Veronique Bragard, Christophe Dony, and Warren Rosenberg. Jefferson: McFarland, 2011. 58–73. Print.

Deny, Martina. *Lost in the Postmodern Metropolis: Studien zu (Des-)Orientierung und Identitätskonstruktion im zeitgenössischen Londonroman.* Frankfurt am Main: Lang, 2009. Print. Anglo-Amerikanische Studien 37.

Dodds, George, Robert Tavernor, and Joseph Rykwert, eds. *Body and Building: Essays on the Changing Relation of Body and Architecture.* Cambridge: MIT Press, 2002. Print.

Dreifus, Claudia. "A Comic-Book Response to 9/11 and Its Aftermath—Interview with Art Spiegelman." *New York Times* 7 Aug. 2004. Web.

Eisinger, Peter. "The American City in the Age of Terror: A Preliminary Assessment of the Effects of September 11." *Urban Affairs Review* 40.1 (2004): 115–30. Print.

_____. "Business as Usual: New York City After 9/11." *International Journal of Urban and Regional Research* 31.4 (2007): 875–79. Print.

Endler, Tobias. *After 9/11: Leading Political Thinkers Abort the Word, the U.S. and Themselves.* Opladen: Barbara Budrich, 2011. Print.

Foer, Jonathan Safran. *Extremely Loud & Incredibly Close.* Boston: Houghton Mifflin, 2005. Print.

Franzen, Jonathan. *Freedom.* New York: Farrar, Straus and Giroux, 2010. Print.

Freud, Sigmund. "On Beginning the Treatment (Further Recommendations on the Technique of Psychoanalysis)." *The Standard Edition of the Complete Psychological Works of Sigmund Freud: Early Psycho-Analytic Publications,* 12, 1911–1913, *Case History of Schreber, Papers on Technique and Other Works.* Ed. Sigmund Freud, et al. London: Vintage, 2001. 121–44. Print.

Gelfant, Blanche H. *The American City Novel: Theodore Dreiser, Thomas Wolfe, Sherwood Anderson, Edith Wharton, John dos Passos, James T. Farrell, Nelson Algren, Betty Smith, Leonard Bishop, Willard Motley, and Others,* 2d ed. Norman: University of Oklahoma Press, 1970. Print.

Golimowska, Karolina. "Cricket as a Cure: Post–9/11 Urban Trauma and Displacement in Joseph O'Neill's Novel 'Netherland.'" *The Journal of American Culture* 36.3 (2013): 230–39. Print.

Goodman, Amy. "Brooklyn's Abu Ghraib: Detainees in Post 9/11 Sweep Allege Abuse in New York Detention Center." *Democracy Now—A Daily Independent Global News Hour* 1 Mar. 2005. Television.

Grass, Günter. *The Tin Drum*. 1959. London: Vintage, 2005. Print.

Gray, Richard. *After the Fall. American Literature Since 9/11*. Hoboken, NJ: Wiley-Blackwell, 2011. Print.

_____. "Open Doors, Closed Minds: American Prose Writing at a Time of Crisis." *American Literary History* 21.1 (2008): 128–51. Print.

Greenberg, Judith. "Wounded New York." *Trauma at Home: After 9/11*. Ed. Judith Greenberg. Lincoln: University of Nebraska Press, 2003. 21–35. Print.

Groes, Sebastian. "Ian McEwan and the Modernist Consciousness of the City in 'Saturday.'" *Ian McEwan*. Ed. Sebastian Groes. London: Continuum, 2009. 99–114. Print. Contemporary Critical Perspectives.

_____. *The Making of London: London in Contemporary Literature*. Houndmills: Palgrave Macmillan, 2011. Print.

Hall, Stuart, ed. *Representation: Cultural Representations and Signifying Practices*. London: Sage, 2003. Print.

Hamid, Moshin. *The Reluctant Fundamentalist*. London: Penguin, 2007. Print.

Hamilton, Ed. *Legends of the Chelsea Hotel: Living with Artists and Outlaws in New York's Rebel Mecca*. New York: Thunder's Mouth Press, 2007. Print.

Hamilton, Masha. *31 Hours*. Denver: Unbridled Books, 2009. Print.

Hare, David. *Stuff Happens*. London: Faber and Faber, 2004. Print.

Hartnell, Anna. "Moving through America: Race, Place and Resistance in Mohsin Hamid's 'The Reluctant Fundamentalist.'" *Journal of Postcolonial Writing* 46, no. 3–4 (July/September 2010): 336–48. Print.

Head, Dominic. *Britain and Beyond*. Chicester: Wiley-Blackwell, 2008. Print. Blackwell Manifestos.

_____. *Ian McEwan*. Manchester: Manchester University Press, 2007. Print. Contemporary British Novelists.

Hebel, Udo J., ed. *Transnational American*

Memories. Berlin: De Gruyter, 2009. Print.

Hill, Jeffrey. "The American Dream of Chuck Ramkisoon: Cricket in Joseph O'Neill's 'Netherland.'" *Journal of Sport History* 37, no. 2 (2010): 219–324. Print.

_____. "Queering the Pitch: Joseph O'Neill's 'Netherland' and the Cricket Novel." *Sport in Society* 15, no. 2 (2012): 181–93. Print.

Homeland. Season 1. Perf. Damian Lewis and Claire Danes. Fox 21, 2011. Television.

Hopkins, Jim. "Psychoanalysis, Metaphor and Mind." *The Analytic Freud: Philosophy and Psychoanalysis*. Ed. Michael P. Levine. London: Routledge, 2000. 11–35. Print.

Hornung, Alfred. "Terrorist Violence and Transnational Memory: Jonathan Safran Foer and Don DeLillo." *Transnational American Memories*. Ed. Udo J. Hebel. Berlin: De Gruyter, 2009. 171–83. Print.

Hubbard, Phil, and Rob Kitchin, eds. *Key Thinkers on Space and Place*, 2d ed. Los Angeles: Sage, 2011. Print.

Husain, Ed. *The Islamist: Why I Joined Radical Islam in Britain, What I Saw Inside and Why I Left*. London: Penguin, 2007. Print.

Hutcheon, Linda. *A Poetics of Postmodernism: History, Theory, Fiction*. London: Routledge, 1988. Print.

Jacobs, Jane. *The Death and Life of Great American Cities*. Harmondsworth: Penguin, 1964. Print.

James, Cyril L. R. *Beyond a Boundary*. London: Yellow Jersey Press, 2005. Print.

Johnson, Steven. *Emergence: The Connected Lives of Ants, Brains, Cities, and Software*. New York: Scribner, 2001. Print.

Joyce, James. *Ulysses*. Ware: Wordsworth Classics, 2010. Print.

Kalfus, Ken. *A Disorder Peculiar to the Country*. London: Simon & Schuster, 2006. Print.

Kamboj, Kirti. "'The Reluctant Fundamentalist': The Assimilation Narrative Goes International." *Hyphen Magazine*. Web. 24 May 2011. http://www.hyphenmagazine.com/print/3140.

Keeble, Arin. *The 9/11 Novel: Trauma, Politics and Identity*. Jefferson: McFarland, 2014. Print.

Kennedy, Liam. "The Ruins of New York Urban Decline and Representation." *Postmodern New York City: Transfiguring Spaces—Raum-Transformationen*. Ed. Günter H. Lenz. 35–51. Heidelberg: Winter, 2003. Print. Anglistische Forschungen 320.

Kilian, Eveline. "Exploring London. Walking the City—(Re-)Writing the City." *Making of Modern Tourism: The Cultural History of the British Experience 1600–2000.* Ed. Hartmut Berghoff. Basingstoke: Palgrave, 2002. 267–83. Print.

Klotz, Volker. *Die Erzählte Stadt.* Munich: Carl Hanser Verlag, 1969. Print.

Kral, Françoise. "Shaky Ground and New Territorialities in *Brick Lane* by Monica Ali and *The Nameshake* by Jhumpa Lahiri." *Journal of Postcolonial Writing* 43.1 (2007): 65–76. Print.

Krause, Timothy. "Covering 9/11: The New Yorker, Trauma Kitsch, and Popular Memory." *Portraying 9/11: Essays on Representations in Comics, Literature, Film and Theatre.* Ed. Veronique Bragard, Christophe Dony, and Warren Rosenberg. Jefferson: McFarland, 2011. Print.

Kristeva, Julia. *Strangers to Ourselves:* New York: Columbia University Press, 1994. Print.

LaBute, Neil. *The Mercy Seat: A Play.* New York: Faber and Faber, 2003. Print.

Lefebvre, Henri. *The Production of Space.* Malden: Blackwell, 2011. Print.

Lefebvre, Henri, Eleonore Kofman, and Elizabeth Lebas. *Writings on Cities.* Cambridge: Blackwell, 1996. Print.

Lenz, Günter H., Friedrich Ulfers, and Antje Dallmann, eds. *Toward a New Metropolitanism: Reconstituting Public Culture, Urban Citizenship, and the Multicultural Imaginary in New York and Berlin.* Heidelberg: Winter, 2006. Print. American Studies 142.

Lenz, Günter H., ed. *Postmodern New York City: Transfiguring Spaces—Raum-Transformationen.* Heidelberg: Winter, 2003. Print. Anglistische Forschungen 320.

Lethem, Jonathan. *Chronic City.* New York: Doubleday, 2009. Print.

Lindner, Christoph. "New York Undead: Globalization, Landscape Urbanism, and the Afterlife of the Twin Towers." *The Journal of American Culture* 31, no. 3 (2008): 302–14. Print.

Lindner, Rolf. "The Imaginary of the City." *Toward a New Metropolitanism: Reconstituting Public Culture, Urban Citizenship, and the Multicultural Imaginary in New York and Berlin.* Ed. Günter H. Lenz, Friedrich Ulfers, and Antje Dallmann. Heidelberg: Winter, 2006. 209–15. Print. American Studies 142.

Llewellyn, David. *Eleven.* Bridgend: Seren, 2006. Print.

Löw, Martina. *Soziologie der Städte.* Frankfurt am Main: Suhrkamp, 2010. Print. Suhrkamp Taschenbuch Wissenschaft 1976.

Malkani, Gautam. *Londonstani.* London: Penguin, 2006. Print.

Marsh, James, dir. *Man on Wire.* 2008. Film.

McEwan, Ian. *Saturday.* London: Vintage, 2005. Print.

McInerney, Jay. *The Good Life.* New York: Knopf, 2006. Print.

Melnick, Jeffrey P. *9/11 Culture: America Under Construction.* Malden: Wiley-Blackwell, 2009. Print.

Meminger, Neesha. *Shine, Coconut Moon.* New York: Margaret K. McElderry Books, 2010. Print.

Moore, Michael, dir. *Fahrenheit 9/11.* Fellowship Adventure Group, 2004. Film.

Morris, Christopher, dir. *Four Lions.* Film4, 2010. Film.

Naqvi, H.M. *Home Boy.* New York: Shaye Areheart Books, 2009. Print.

Neiger, Motti. *On Media Memory: Collective Memory in a New Media Age.* Houndmills: Palgrave Macmillan, 2011. Print.

New York City Department of Health and Mental Hygiene and U.S. Department of Health and Human Services, *Final Report of the Public Health Investigation to Assess Potential Exposures to Airborne and Settled Surface Dust in Residential Areas of Lower Manhattan,* September 2002. Print. Courtesy Melvin Singer of the World Trade Center Environmental Assessment Working Group.

O'Neill, Joseph. *Netherland.* London: Fourth Estate, 2008. Print.

Oxford University Press, ed. *Oxford English Dictionary Online.* September 2013. Web. 3 Dec. 2013. http://www.oed.com.

Page, Max. *The City's End: Two Centuries of Fantasies, Fears, and Premonitions of New York's Destruction.* New Haven: Yale University Press, 2008. Print.

Park, Robert E., E. W. Burgess, and Roderick D. McKenzie. *The City.* Chicago: University of Chicago Press, 1984. Print.

Phillips, Melanie. *Londonistan.* Jackson: Encounter Books, 2006. Print.

Pile, Steve. *Real Cities: Modernity, Space, and the Phantasmagorias of City Life.* Thousand Oaks: Sage, 2005. Print.

Puar, Jasbir K. *Terrorist Assemblages: Homonationalism in Queer Times.* Durham: Duke University Press, 2007. Print. Next Wave.

Pynchon, Thomas. *Bleeding Edge.* New York: Penguin, 2013. Print.

Rancière, Jacques, and Steven Corcoran, trans. *Dissensus: On Politics and Aesthetics*. London: Continuum, 2011. Print.

Roth, Michael S. *Irresistible Decay: Ruins Reclaimed*. Los Angeles: Getty Research, 1997. Print. Bibliographies & Dossiers.

Rothberg, Michael. "A Failure of the Imagination: Diagnosing the Post–9/11 Novel. A Response to Richard Gray." *American Literary History* 21.1 (2009): 152–58. Print.

Rowson, Susanna. *Charlotte Temple*. New York: Oxford University Press, 1986. Print.

Rushdie, Salman. *The Satanic Verses*. 1988. London: Vintage, 1998. Print.

_____. *Shalimar the Clown*. New York: Random House, 2005. Print.

Sahota, Sunjeev. *Ours Are the Streets*. London: Pan Macmillan, 2011. Print.

Said, Edward W. *Orientalism*. New York: Vintage, 2008. Print.

Sandhu, Sukhdev. "Come Hungry, Leave Edgy." *London Review of Books* 25.19 (2003): 10–13. Print.

Sassen, Saskia. *The Global City: New York, London, Tokyo*. Princeton: Princeton University Press, 2001. Print.

Savitch, H. V. "An Anatomy of Urban Terror: Lessons from Jerusalem and Elsewhere." *Urban Studies Journal* 42.3 (2005): 361–95. Print.

Schillings, Sonja, and Boris Vormann. "The Vanishing Poor: Frontier Narratives in New York City's Gentrification and Security Debate." *Critical Planning—Journal of the UCLA Urban Planning Department* 20 (2013): 144–67. Print.

Schwartz, Lynne S. *The Writing on the Wall*. New York: Counterpoint, 2005. Print.

Seltzer, Mark. *Serial Killers: Death and Life in America's Wound Culture*. New York: Routledge, 1998. Print.

Sennett, Richard. *Flesh and Stone: The Body and the City in Western Civilization*. New York: Norton, 1994. Print.

_____. "The Foreigner." *Body and Building: Essays on the Changing Relation of Body and Architecture*. Ed. George Dodds, Robert Tavernor, and Joseph Rykwert. Cambridge: MIT Press, 2002. 190–210. Print.

Silva, Kumarini. "Brown: From Identity to Identification." *Cultural Studies* 24.2 (2010): 167–82. Print.

Simmel, Georg. *The Metropolis and Mental Life*. 1903. *German History in Documents and Images* 5: *Wilhelmine Germany and the First World War*, 1890–1918. Web.

_____. "The Stranger." *On Individuality and Social Forms: Selected Writings*. Ed. Georg Simmel. Chicago: University of Chicago Press, 1971. 143–50. Print.

_____, ed. *On Individuality and Social Forms: Selected Writings*. Chicago: University of Chicago Press, 1971. Print.

Sinclair, Iain. *Lights Out for the Territory: 9 Excursions in the Secret History of London*. London: Granta, 1997.

_____. *London Orbital*. London: Penguin, 2003. Print.

Sinfield, Alan. *Dramatic Monologue*. London: Barnes & Noble Books, 1977. Print. The Critical Idiom 36.

Smith, Zadie. "Two Paths for the Novel." *New York Times* 20 Nov. 2008. Web. 15 Dec. 2013. http://www.nybooks.com/articles/archives/2008/nov/20/two-paths-for-the-novel/

Soja, Edward W. *Postmodern Geographies: The Reassertion of Space in Critical Social Theory*. London: Verso, 1994. Print.

Sorkin, Michael, and Sharon Zukin, eds. *After the World Trade Center: Rethinking New York City*. New York: Routledge, 2002. Print.

Spiegelman, Art. *In the Shadow of No Towers*. New York: Pantheon Books, 2004. Print.

Steen, Rob. "Writing the Modern Game." *The Cambridge Companion to Cricket*. Ed. Anthony Bateman and Jeffrey Hill. Cambridge: Cambridge University Press, 2011. 238–53. Print.

Stone, Oliver, dir. *World Trade Center*. Paramount Pictures, 2006. Film.

Sturken, Marita. *Tourists of History: Memory, Kitsch, and Consumerism from Oklahoma City to Ground Zero*. Durham: Duke University Press, 2007. Print.

Tocqueville, Alexis de. *Democracy in America*, 2 vols. New York: Vintage, 1963. Print.

Torres, Francesc, and Jerry Adler. *Memory Remains: 9/11 Artifacts at Hangar 17*. National Geographic Society, 2011. Print.

Tower Hamlets Census 2011 Second Release—Headline Analysis. 2013. Web. http://www.towerhamlets.gov.uk/lgnl/council_and_democracy/census_information.aspx. 13 Aug. 2013. Web.

Updike, John. *Terrorist*. New York: Alfred A. Knopf, 2006. Print.

Uytterschout, Sien. "An Extremely Loud Tin Drum: A Comparative Study of Jonathan Safran Foer's Extremely Loud and Incredibly Close and Günter Grass's The Tin

Drum." *Comparative Literature Studies* 47, no. 2 (2010): 185–99. Print.

Versluys, Kristiaan. *Out of the Blue: September 11 and the Novel.* New York: Columbia University Press, 2009. Print.

Virilio, Paul, and Chris Turner. *Ground Zero.* London: Verso, 2002. Print.

Wagg, Stephen. "Cricket and International Politics." *The Cambridge Companion to Cricket.* Ed. Anthony Bateman and Jeffrey Hill. Cambridge: Cambridge University Press, 2011. 254–70. Print.

Waldman, Amy. *The Submission.* London: Random House, 2011. Print.

Whitman, Walt. *Leaves of Grass.* New York: Vintage /Library of America, 1992. Print.

Wigley, Mark. "Insecurity by Design." *Bewitched, Bothered and Bewildered: Spatial Emotion in Contemporary Art and Architecture.* Geneva: JRP/Ringier; Łaźnia Centre for Contemporary Art, 2003. 45–57. Print.

Wirth-Nesher, Hana. *City Codes: Reading the Modern Urban Novel.* Cambridge: Cambridge University Press, 1996. Print.

Woolf, Virginia. *Mrs. Dalloway.* Ware: Wordsworth Editions, 1996. Print.

Wright, Craig. *Recent Tragic Events.* New York: Dramatists Play Service, 2004. Print.

Žižek, Slavoj. *Welcome to the Desert of the Real! Five Essays on 11 September and Related Dates.* London: Verso, 2002. Print.

Zukin, Sharon. "Our World Trade Center." *After the World Trade Center: Rethinking New York City.* Ed. Michael Sorkin and Sharon Zukin. New York: Routledge, 2002. 13–22. Print.

Index

Abu Ghraib 93
Ali, Monica 13, 24, 30, 85, 95, 104, 122–124, 127; see also Brick Lane
American Dream 78, 113, 168, 173, 175
Amis, Martin 30
Angel of History 67, 33
Appadurai, Arjun 168, 169, 177
Arnold, Matthew 153n1, 163
arranged marriage 34, 122, 136, 146, 150
Atta, Muhammad 30
authenticity 140

Baer, Ulrich 15, 17
Balaev, Michelle 128, 133
Barthes, Roland 58, 129, 152, 182, 186
Baudelaire, Charles 6, 12, 42n3, 56, 173, 184
Baudrillard, Jean 18, 22, 65
Bauman, Zygmunt 138, 149
Beigbeder, Frédéric 49
Benjamin, Walter 12, 33, 42, 42n3, 67, 184
Bethnal Green 127, 131
bin Laden, Osama 34, 117, 123, 131–135
Blair, Tony 136, 153, 155, 161, 179, 184
Blix, Hans 154, 162
Borradori, Giovanna 117, 118
Brick Lane 1, 31, 34, 35, 70, 135–152, 183–187; see also Ali, Monica
Brick Lane 34, 110, 117, 135–151
Brooklyn 14, 17, 32, 64, 88, 93, 95, 102, 104, 110, 111, 137, 139, 172, 184, 186
Brussels 6, 30, 56, 62–64, 67, 68, 81
Buckingham Palace 111, 149
Bush, George W. 1, 93, 103, 161, 179
Butler, Judith 26, 30, 31

Central Park 17, 40, 45, 64, 76, 86, 90, 105
Chelsea Hotel 169, 170, 174, 177
city novel 5–10, 22, 32, 62, 68, 90, 113
Cleave, Chris 23, 24, 105, 117–119, 146, 153, 160, 185; see also Incendiary
Cole, Teju 6, 7, 11, 12, 26, 30, 33, 42, 48, 49, 85, 86
collective trauma 40, 43

colonial gaze 72, 128, 140
Connecticut 93
cricket 35, 79, 165–169, 175–184
Critchley, Simon 128

de Certeau, Michel 12, 17, 22, 48–50, 57
DeLillo, Don: Falling Man 11, 14, 19, 20, 22, 26, 30–32, 62n2, 68n4, 72, 106, 157, 162, 166, 171; In the Ruins of the Future 25, 89n2
dementia 154, 156–157
Derrida, Jacques 117
de Tocqueville, Alexis 118
disaster fantasies 19, 34, 109, 124, 186
Dostoyevsky, Fyodor 139
dramatic monologue 26, 71, 73, 123
Dresden 26, 39, 41, 44, 51, 53, 62
Drew, Richard 47n5

Ellis Island 61
Empire State Building 20, 48–50, 64, 77, 174, 175, 181
epistolary narrative 39, 122
Extremely Loud and Incredibly Close 39–54, 57, 58, 68n4, 76, 135n4, 171, 173, 181, 184; see also Foer, Jonathan Safran

Fahrenheit 911 92
falling man 46, 47n5
flâneur 6, 7, 33, 42, 50, 54, 56, 64, 88, 119, 166, 172, 173, 177, 183, 184
Foer, Jonathan Safran 11, 13, 14, 18, 20, 22, 26, 31, 32; see also Extremely Loud and Incredibly Close
Four Lions 20, 27
Franzen, Jonathan 187
Freud, Sigmund 15, 55, 56, 128

Gazeta Wyborcza 1
gentrification 7, 89, 122, 127, 128, 139–141
global city 10, 18, 57, 187
globalization 80
Godzilla 109
Godzilla Apartments 19, 20

Grass, Günter 41
Great Fire of London 119, 123, 125, 135
Great Gatsby (as a figure prototype) 78, 93,
    175
Greenberg, Judith 13
Ground Zero 12, 13, 18, 25–28, 56, 65, 98,
    169

Hamid, Mohsin 96–98, 108, 110, 123–126,
    142, 166, 176, 184, 186; see also The
    Reluctant Fundamentalist
Hamilton, Masha 20, 30–31, 94, 112, 162,
    171, 187
Hare, David 92, 100, 187
Heathrow Airport 154
historiographic metafiction 10, 73
Holocaust 23n15, 107, 171
Home Boy 11, 13, 22, 29, 31–34, 68n4, 85–
    97, 70, 77–79; see also Naqvi, Husain M.
Hornung, Alfred 41, 47, 171
Hudson (river) 60, 87–90, 105, 172
humor 15, 31, 100, 118, 124–126, 128, 129,
    133, 144
Husain, Ed 27
Hutcheon, Linda 10

immigration 57, 109, 150, 165
Incendiary 5, 13, 17, 20, 26, 31, 34, 122–135;
    see also Cleave, Chris
IRA 31, 162, 171
Iraq war 1, 153–155, 158, 159, 161

Jacobs, Jane 17, 128, 129
James, Cyril L.R. 175–178
Jersey City 88–89
JFK Airport 18, 25
Joyce, James 153

Kabul 99, 108, 113
Kalfus, Ken 13, 166
Karachi 71, 79, 85, 88, 91, 95, 96, 176
Kensington (Little Dhaka) 32, 102, 110, 111,
    129, 137, 139
King Kong 109
Klotz, Volker 5, 10
Kristeva, Julia 30
Kwaśniewski, Aleksander 1

LaBute, Neil 13, 187
Lahore 32, 33, 71–77, 79, 82–85, 142
Lethem, Jonathan 187
Levinas, Emmanuel 29, 164
Little Dhaka see Kensington
Little Pakistan 32, 88, 95
London Eye 1811
London River 28, 187

Malkani, Guatam 15
McCann, Column 21
McEwan, Ian 34, 117, 119, 123, 125, 183,
    185; see also Saturday
McInerney, Jay 166
meta-fiction 101, 102
Moore, Michael 92
Mrs. Dalloway 153, 154

Naqvi, Husain M. 136, 166, 176, 184, 186;
    see also Home Boy
national security 107, 119, 133
Netherland 70, 78, 81, 83, 157, 160, 165–
    181; see also O'Neill, Joseph
neurosurgery 58, 119, 156–159, 160, 164
New Amsterdam 67, 169, 172
New Jersey 58, 89, 90
9/11 Memorial 2, 19, 25, 28, 33, 98, 99

Oklahoma City bombing 27, 65n3
One WTC 2, 25
O'Neill, Joseph 12, 13, 14, 18, 22, 23, 32, 35,
    48, 62n2, 68n4; see also Netherland
Open City 55–69, 70, 81, 111, 119, 148, 173,
    184; see also Cole, Teju
Other 11, 13, 15, 16, 24, 28–35, 70–97
    136–140, 186–187

Page, Max 2, 20, 133
Park, Robert Ezra 130
Pearl Harbor 92
Petit, Philippe 21, 21n11
Phillips, Melanie 15, 27
Poetry in Motion (project) 94, 94n5
postmodernity 138
Prospect Park 104
psychoanalysis 55, 56n1
Pynchon, Thomas 13, 182, 187

Queens 1, 14, 18, 53, 58, 64, 95, 103, 166,
    172, 178, 184
quest 20, 28, 32, 42–46, 57, 76,

Rancière, Jacques 30, 89
read-walking 105
Red Army Faction (RAF) 22, 31
The Reluctant Fundamentalist 12, 20, 31–33,
    58, 62n2, 70–85, 93, 95; see also Hamid,
    Mohsin
Rushdie, Salman 15, 27, 62n2

Sahota, Sunjeev 23, 27, 30
Saturday 13, 23, 24, 31, 58, 153–164; see also
    McEwan, Ian
Schwartz, Lynne Sharon 13, 22, 43n4, 68n4
securitization 7, 67, 119, 137

Sennett, Richard 12, 17, 23*n*14, 24, 43, 70, 118, 119, 129
7/7 1, 10, 11, 13, 15, 23, 24, 27, 28, 129, 162, 180
Simmel, Georg 6, 31, 46, 133
Sinclair, Iain 12, 131
skyline 14, 18, 20–22, 28, 48, 92, 105, 111, 121, 186
Soja, Edward 9, 12, 52*n*6
Spiegelman, Art 22, 23, 171
squash 160
Staten Island 18, 53, 103, 166, 172, 175, 181
Stone, Oliver 92
Stuff Happens 92, 100, 187
The Submission 98–113, 129, 131, 137, 139, 142, 183, 184; *see also* Waldman, Amy

Thatcher, Margaret 136
Times Square 91, 173–174, 186
Torres, Francesco 25
Tower Hamlets 1, 34, 35, 111, 122, 123, 127, 135–150, 153
trauma 39–45, 126, 130, 133
Tribeca 78, 92, 169, 173

Union Jack 143
Updike, John 30, 89, 89*n*3
urban ruin 15, 18, 113
urban terror 18, 124, 133, 160, 163

Vanilla Sky 92
Virilio, Paul 21

Waldman, Amy 12, 14, 19–21, 29, 31–33, 81, 152; *see also The Submission*
Warsaw 1, 155
West End 122, 132, 153, 164
Whitechapel 139
Whitman, Walt 166
Wigley, Mark 5*n*1, 15, 20, 21
Windows on the World 49
Wirth-Nesher, Hana 6, 9, 14, 87
Woolf, Virginia 153, 154
Wright, Craig 187
WTC (film) 92

Žižek, Slavoj 19, 117

www.ingramcontent.com/pod-product-compliance
Lightning Source LLC
Chambersburg PA
CBHW031133270326
41929CB00011B/1606